Reading Paul within Judaism

Other volumes in this series:

Reading Romans within Judaism: Collected Essays of Mark D. Nanos, Vol. 2

Reading Galatians within Judaism: Collected Essays of Mark D. Nanos, Vol. 3

Reading Corinthians and Philippians within Judaism: Collected Essays of Mark D. Nanos, Vol. 4

Reading Paul within Judaism

Collected Essays of Mark D. Nanos, Vol. 1

MARK D. NANOS

CASCADE Books • Eugene, Oregon

READING PAUL WITHIN JUDAISM
Collected Essays of Mark D. Nanos, vol. 1

Copyright © 2017 Mark D. Nanos. All rights reserved. Except for brief quotations in critical publications or reviews, no part of this book may be reproduced in any manner without prior written permission from the publisher. Write: Permissions, Wipf and Stock Publishers, 199 W. 8th Ave., Suite 3, Eugene, OR 97401.

Cascade Books
An Imprint of Wipf and Stock Publishers
199 W. 8th Ave., Suite 3
Eugene, OR 97401

www.wipfandstock.com

PAPERBACK ISBN: 978-1-5326-1755-3
HARDCOVER ISBN: 978-1-4982-4231-8
EBOOK ISBN: 978-1-4982-4230-1

Cataloguing-in-Publication data:

Names: Nanos, Mark D., 1954–

Title: Reading Paul within Judaism : collected essays of Mark D. Nanos, vol. 1 / Mark D. Nanos.

Description: Eugene, OR: Cascade Books, 2017 | Includes bibliographical references and index.

Identifiers: ISBN 978-1-5326-1755-3 (paperback) | ISBN 978-1-4982-4231-8 (hardcover) | ISBN 978-1-4982-4230-1 (ebook)

Subjects: LCSH: Paul, the Apostle, Saint—Relations with Jews | Paul, the Apostle, Saint | Judaism—Relations—Christianity | Jews in the New Testament | Judaism (Christian theology)

Classification: BS2506.3 N36 2017 (print) | BS2506.3 (ebook)

Manufactured in the U.S.A.   09/29/17

For Ty

Contents

Preface | ix
Permissions | xxv

PART I: **A New Approach to the Apostle: Paul as a Torah-observant Jew**

1 Paul *and* Judaism: Why Not *Paul's Judaism*? | 3

PART II: **Exploring the Implications for Exegesis and Christian-Jewish Relations**

2 How Inter-Christian Approaches to Paul's Rhetoric Can Perpetuate Negative Valuations of Jewishness—Although Proposing to Avoid That Outcome | 63

3 The Myth of the "Law-Free" Paul Standing between Christians and Jews | 77

4 Paul and the Jewish Tradition: The Ideology of the *Shema* | 108

5 Paul's Non-Jews Do Not Become "Jews," But Do They Become "Jewish"? Reading Romans 2:25–29 within Judaism, alongside Josephus | 127

6 Reading Paul in a Jewish Way: "Oh be joyful all you peoples, with God's people" (Rom 15:10): Who Are the People? | 155

PART III: **A Jewish Contribution to Pope Benedict XVI's Celebration of the Year of St. Paul**

7 Paul and Judaism (*Codex Pauli*) | 173

Index of Ancient Documents | 179

Preface

BEFORE READING PAUL, WE have presuppositions about what we will read—whether shaped by years of study or from hearsay—that range from the messages we expect to encounter in his texts to what we will expect them to mean. Likewise, we have presuppositions before reading secondary texts, such as this one, that offer a perspective on reading Paul. To the degree that we are interested in reading to develop a more probable historical interpretation of Paul, such as these studies are interested in achieving, our presuppositions extend to what we suppose that the author presupposed about his audience, and what the audience presupposed about the author and what he would be seeking to communicate. What we presuppose about each of these and similar matters will shape if not predetermine entirely what we look for, how we do so, and what we conclude that we have found, or found wanting.

Similar observations can be made about the dynamics of *before reading* before reading anyone or any textual artifact, and before reading anyone else's treatment about reading anyone or anything. Literary critics who specialize in such matters, such as Peter J. Rabinowitz, make it clear that this is simply the way reading works. This reading dynamic, and the problem of circularity that it embodies, apply all the more before reading a figure or about a figure or event that has shaped the culture in which we live, directly or indirectly, one known to us independent of whether we have yet read secondary texts about the figure or event, or, in this case, the actual texts written by a figure as influential as Paul. Before reading Paul, or re-reading Paul, we know things—or presuppose that we do.

To hope to achieve probability for a perspective about the historical Paul and his relationship to Jews and Judaism, we must attempt to be aware of what we presuppose about the texts and carefully craft what to ask of them, how we ask it, and how to pursue and recognize the most probable answers. To do this, we must fashion and test multiple hypotheses; otherwise, there is a good chance that we will only reinforce the impression of what we think we already know. One involves the pursuit of historical knowledge; the other, the practice of ideological propaganda.

The very fact that we know beforehand that Paul's texts are in the Bible, in the (Christian) New Testament thereof, like the very fact that he is called "the Apostle" and "St.," that he was "converted" or "called" from Judaism to Christianity "on the Damascus road" and thereafter became "the missionary to the gentiles" who "founded gentile churches" to which he sent the letters we now seek to understand, and so many other things that we may be aware of before we read his texts or any secondary texts proposing to explain him or them, ineluctably shape our expectations of what we are going to read—and how we are likely going to understand and value what we read. Almost certainly, to date, we expect a book or essay discussing Paul's texts directly, or the views others have expressed about him and his texts, whether we know that he never used the word "Christian" and its cognates, or not, to be about reading Paul *within Christianity*. Usually the title, and in the case of a book, usually a cover featuring illustrations of the Christian saint and author of the Christian epistles, supplement this common expectation. This expectation also, naturally, shapes and is shaped by the presupposition that Paul's letters were originally to be read as they have been most often since, as the instructions of a *Christian* apostle to *Christians*, and that they were expected to be such before they were written or read.

Prior to reading this book, the very idea expressed in the title—reading Paul *within Judaism*—or the proposal, anyway, that the book will do so, obviously challenges the prevailing presuppositions for how to read Paul. To the degree that one recognizes that the cover illustration celebrates suffering for love of Torah, rather than rejection of Torah, this impression will be stronger, but perhaps also more puzzling. The presuppositions involved in such a proposal will almost certainly strike some as excitingly new and interesting and others as alarmingly weird and off-putting, almost certainly misinformed if not uninformed, intentionally provocative and untrustworthy, to name but two extreme sets of possibilities.

For those who greet the idea positively, it may suggest a reading to commence wholeheartedly and with the expectation of learning something valuable, perhaps as a welcome challenge to the readings of Paul with which he has been familiar but not satisfied, or of which he disapproved, or maybe a perspective that will supplement ideas already to some degree embraced, perhaps one that will help him to overcome the objections or limitations he has encountered. For those who immediately react to the idea negatively, the very suggestion could seem silly if not outrageous, an unwelcome challenge to the understanding of the apostle and his teachings that the potential reader has long embraced and that continues to inform and shape her worldview and way of trying to live. The apostle's letters and the interpretive traditions to which the reader subscribes have guided her according to essentially "Christian" (a word traditionally understood in binary contrast to "Jewish")—and for many "divinely inspired"—instructions, interpreted by divinely inspired leaders (including "saints") and institutions (including one's "church" or "seminary") to mean what she presently understands them to mean. Why should anyone have to bother with such nonsense if not also heretical presentations of this heritage, much less answer to arguments posed from such a ridiculous premise and to unfamiliar if not also unattractive conclusions? Is it not self-evidently mistaken and easily enough corrected by simply reading Paul, and the scholarship on Paul, even just citing a few obvious texts that demonstrate that such a proposal is simply uninformed, to say the least?

The former reader might take up the task enthusiastically, open to or hopeful of being persuaded, and end up wanting to read more from this perspective, and return to reading Paul's texts in this welcome new way. The latter will likely approach reading this book, if at all, not so much to learn something new or open to being persuaded, but to find fault from the first word, perhaps finding plenty to dissuade her from reading on, although maybe finding a tidbit here or there to be used against the reading proposed, or even to use somewhere in support of an element of the reading to which she is committed. There are, of course, many other expectations and reactions that might better define any given reader's interests before, during, and after reading this book, or any other study of Paul in this direction, or opposed to this perspective or to some other one entirely or in part.

Whether you are a reader who identifies in any way with any of the elements articulated for these extreme reactions to the proposal, there is much at stake in the meaning-making involved in reading Paul, or about Paul, and before doing so too. Your own interests can be assessed, in part, by asking yourself, in terms of Paul or of the proposition adumbrated in the title (or in the name of the author Nanos, if you know his work and what it represents), why you are reading Paul and this or any book about Paul, and what you hope to accomplish by doing so; or why you do not want to read any one of these or have not and will not do so, to the degree that is a conscious choice.

Most Christians, Jews too, approach the reading—or, as it may be, the choice not to engage in the reading—of Paul's texts with a very strong impression of the man and what he represents; secondary literature about him too. Christians raised hearing appeals to his texts to guide them in proper Christian thinking and living, whether during the liturgy, appeals to them in sermons and Sunday school lessons, or from friends and family, naturally have certain fixed impressions about the apostle. It is common to encounter expressions of fondness for Paul on any number of topics and for any number of reasons; similarly, it is also common to hear disgust expressed toward the man and what he stood for on matters like women, gays, slavery, or Jews and Judaism, to mention a few of the widely known controversial topics.

Because of the role that appeals to his writings have played in shaping the cultures that still shape our cultures today, directly or indirectly, those who are *not* Christians, or were *not raised* Christian, especially if living among Christians and thus hearing appeals to these texts or reading them for classes or other reasons, will have impressions of Paul too. This remains the case for those in such cultures who do not generally read his texts, and, indeed, even for those within those cultures who have not read Paul but who have formed impressions about Paul from what they have heard or read second hand. These may indeed be strong impressions of disapproval, even hatred toward the figure and repulsion at the very idea of undertaking to read him, or about him, and if persuaded to do so, certainly would not commence the reading with expectations such as they might bring to reading other figures regarded favorably, for example, to gain guidance or inspiration. This traditionally has been the case for Jews, whether having read Paul's texts or (more commonly) not, because of what is ostensibly known about Paul, knowledge that has been fashioned in direct response to hearing about Paul's negative valuation of Jews and things Jewish from common Christian presentations of him and his teachings that celebrate these features as evidence of the superiority of the apostle's new religious movement, Christianity.

When it comes to presenting a historical reading of Paul, because the historian is a person and has been shaped by the same kinds of cultural conditioning as has any other Christian or non-Christian before undertaking the task, or when continuing to do so, the challenges facing a historian are substantial, and in some ways different from the challenges involved to investigate figures and events that are not so confessionally consequential, at least still so during the historian's own time. There are all of the usual challenges involved to investigate any historical figure from a couple of thousand years ago who wrote a few extant letters in a language of his time, a language that is similar to but not exactly the same as that language today, and for many historians, a language different from their own native tongue, among so many other challenges involved in the study of any historical figure or event.

This is not a book about the practice of historiography (or literary theory), so I will not seek to elaborate the elements further. This book, and series of books, seek to practice the discipline of historiography (among other disciplines), and to do so with integrity and respect for what this figure meant, and means, to readers who welcome the challenge to the consensus readings, and to those who do not, not least to those who write from the perspective of those consensus readings (including some who do so to contest any challenges to them considered dangerous enough to warrant a response), who can be expected to bristle at the perspective adumbrated in the title and commence to read primarily to find fault. I am convinced that approaching the task of reading Paul *as a Jew within Judaism, practicing and promoting a Torah-defined Jewish way of life for followers of Christ*, is historically more probable and therefore more authentic, and that it will contribute to positive developments in Christian-Jewish dialogue and thus relations going forward, where it has more often been used to distance and disrespect, if not even to destroy those Christianity has deemed to be "the quintessential other." I am also convinced, and I say this respectfully as an outsider, that it will contribute to a Christian self-understanding that is useful to Christians on its own terms. By removing the habit or perceived need to develop the positive Christian elements in binary contrast to Jewish elements considered inferior, which are often the product of misreading and misrepresentations developed to serve as foils in this way of making meaning, reading Paul within Judaism offers more helpful ways to think about matters like faith and works, rather than faith *versus* works, and similarly to reconfigure other supposed binaries like spirituality and humanness. In short, I suppose that this approach has the additional benefit of helping those who wish to think with the apostle about a host of concerns for how to conduct their own and their group's journey in this world, including how these intersect with the journeys of the others in this world, to which Paul, like Jesus (and Moses and Isaiah), called those who self-identify as Christians (like those who do so as Jews) to live in lovingkindness.

The chapters in this volume, and in the subsequent volumes in this series, explain and explore the thesis that Paul should be read within Judaism, and argue many of the details for particular texts and topics that function as "flashpoints." I hope you will find the research and reflections both warranted and helpful, even if you are not always persuaded to change your mind from what you thought before reading this book. I welcome your feedback. You can reach me by email through the contact tab at my website (www.marknanos.com), which also provides more information about my other publications and activities, and makes available a number of downloadable files.

THE ORGANIZATION OF THIS VOLUME

The chapters are arranged under three headings. The first chapter, "Paul *and* Judaism: Why Not *Paul's Judaism*?," serves as an introduction to the volume under the section title: "A New Approach to the Apostle: Paul as a Torah-observant Jew." The original essay has been slightly revised to bring the arguments and terminology up to date, and to add cross-references to other research that has become available since it was first published. In conversation with the received views on how to read Paul, the arguments introduce many of the specific "flashpoint" texts and topics involved in this undertaking as well as many of the methodological and terminological concerns, and certain hermeneutical implications, usually related to the concerns of a Christian-Jewish relations critic.

The second section, under the heading "Exploring the Implications for Exegesis and Christian-Jewish Relations," consists of five chapters that engage in more detailed investigations of many of these "flashpoint" texts and topics, including sustained interaction with the received traditions for investigating and discussing Paul's relationship to Judaism. Each chapter explores ideas and texts from a historically oriented perspective and offers reflections on the implications, most often in the area of Christian-Jewish relations, because, whether recognized or admitted, whether helpful or harmful, every interpretation of these "flashpoint" texts informs Christian concepts of, ways of talking about, and behavior toward Jews and Judaism.

The third section consists of an essay written for a special publication dedicated to Pope Benedict in honor of the anniversary of the apostle in 2009. The chapter offers a brief introduction to my reading of Paul within Judaism designed for Catholic clergy and scholars; I trust other readers will find it accessible and useful too.

A SHORT HISTORY OF THESE ESSAYS

The development of each of these essays often overlapped with the research, presentation, and revision of the others, both those in this volume and in the subsequent volumes in this series. In some cases, I have explored relevant passages and topics in essay form, to date at least, which is the case for the broader topic of how to read Paul explored in this volume. That is also the case for the research I have undertaken on Paul's letters to the Corinthians and Philippians, which are collected in volume 4 of this series. For Romans and Galatians, I have completed both a number of essays (many of which are collected in volumes 2 and 3 of this series) and monographs (*The*

Mystery of Romans, Fortress, 1996; *The Irony of Galatians*, Fortress, 2002). Although the research and its presentation may overlap along the way, the essays represented in these chapters were each designed to present their cases independent of the others. Here is a brief history of their development.

Part I. A New Approach to the Apostle: Paul as a Torah-observant Jew

Chapter 1 serves as an introduction to the thesis at work in all the essays in this series; namely, that Paul's life and letters make more probable historical sense when interpreted within Judaism, and that, moreover, the implications are promising enough to merit reconsideration by those who might not be otherwise inclined to interpret Paul or Christian origins from a perspective that challenges their own. The essay has been updated to help serve this introductory purpose, but its title, outline, choice of texts and topics, and style, reflect the history of its development for earlier venues.

The essay was first developed as a paper to present in the NT section of the Central States Regional Meeting of the Society of Biblical Literature (SBL) in March of 2004, entitled simply "Paul and Judaism." The title reflects the theme of the two sessions, each paper covering a topic under the heading, "Paul and . . ."; for example, Paul *and* Rhetoric, Paul *and* Women, Paul *and* the Law, and so on. The *and* in the case of *Paul* and *Judaism* typically signals a contrastive "or," like that of "and women" but unlike the case of "and Rhetoric," which signals instead "Paul's Rhetoric." My paper sought to problematize the assumptions buried in the usual role of "and" in this case, and some of the implications that follow from that way of approaching the topics of Paul *and* Judaism. In particular, I wanted to contest the constraints these working assumptions put on the kinds of research questions posed, which evidence is considered and how it is weighted and construed, the methods employed, and the interpretations considered and developed, all of which ultimately determine the conclusions reached. I proposed that we consider removing the conjunction and begin to fashion hypotheses to test that begin from the premise that his letters communicate *Paul's Judaism*. For example, if he was a Torah-observant Jew, and if the non-Jews who were his target audiences were expected to know that he was, and that he was seeking to acculturate them into Judaism, albeit to remain non-Jews, how would they interpret his arguments? I showed that the evidence can sustain each of these propositions and how his audiences might have understood Paul's messages from a perspective crafted around them. I concluded that this is a reasonable alternative for constructing Paul in conversation with traditional and recent constructions of the apostle.

Mark Given collected these paper, supplemented by others to round out a "Paul and" volume, which became available in 2010 as *Paul Unbound: Other Perspectives on the Apostle* (Peabody, MA: Hendrickson, 2010; later transferred to Baker Academic's list, and no longer in print). I adjusted the title of my chapter to adumbrate the perspective for which the paper argued, adding the question "Why not Paul's Judaism?"

Between the presentation of the paper for the regional SBL in 2004, its publication as a chapter in 2010, and now here as chapter 1, I have developed the basic theses and arguments in a variety of ways for a number of different venues. These include the welcome invitation from Wilburn Stancil to offer a public lecture at Rockhurst University in the Autumn of 2004, where I had begun to teach classes. The lecture was entitled, "A Jewish Paul? What Difference Would It Make for Jewish/Christian Relations Today?" I continued to expand this slightly different angle for a discussion by the participants who meet semi-annually as the Christian Scholars Group on Christian-Jewish Relations, sponsored by the Center for Christian-Jewish Learning at Boston College, at their June 4-6, 2005 session. I am grateful for the invitation from the chair, Joseph Tyson, and for the collegial feedback from those who read and discussed the paper. The original (and lengthy) paper, which surveys some of the implications as I saw them in 2005, to which I still hope to return to develop a monograph, is available for download at the web site, <http://www.marknanos.com/Boston-Torah-Obs-5-9-05.pdf>.

I also continued to build on the original paper under the title, "Rethinking the 'Paul and Judaism' Paradigm." I presented this paper at Yale's colloquy for New Testament studies, by the invitation of Dale Martin and John Collins, in March of 2005. One of the surprising but welcome aspects of this experience was learning from some students that the approach I was advocating for was, for them, self-evident; it was the logical course to pursue in Pauline studies, as if the warrant for this perspective need hardly be argued for! (Welcome, promising, but also baffling: need I state that this is not usually the case, or, in fact, that one would not have concluded it was the case that day from the formal discussion period?) In March 2008, I had the opportunity to discuss this paper, following further development, at a graduate research seminar at McMaster University, by the invitation of Anders Runesson; and later at a graduate seminar at University of Toronto, by the invitation of Terry Donaldson. In May of that year I traveled from a seminar on Romans 9-11 in Germany (more about that in vol. 2) to Lund University in Sweden, by the invitation of Magnus Zetterholm, to present this paper as a public lecture. I am grateful to each of them for the opportunities, and to those who discussed the papers in each venue.

In addition to these rather lengthy and detail-oriented research papers, I developed two very short versions of the basic argument for non-specialists, each entitled "Paul and Judaism": one for the *Jewish Annotated New Testament* (Oxford University Press, 2011; pages 551–54); and another for a Catholic audience in *Codex Pauli*, which is available in chapter 7 of this volume, discussed below.

To bring the essay up to date for this collection, I have revisited some of the arguments, added a few details that supplement or in some cases alter positions, adjusted some of the terminology to reflect the way I present these matters today, and updated a number of bibliographical references to account for publications, my own and those of others that have become available since the completion of the original chapter in *Paul Unbound*. As with the other chapters in these volumes, the page numbers to the original publication are provided in brackets ("[00]") for cross-reference, but unlike the others, because of these revisions they do not correspond as precisely.

Part II. Exploring the Implications for Exegesis and Christian-Jewish Relations

The second section brings together five essays that expand upon many of the elements introduced in the first chapter, and other topics and texts too. Each undertakes exegetical investigations and explicitly discusses, to various degrees, specific implications that this paradigmatic shift might offer for discovering more promising ways to consider the role of Paul's voice for Christian-Jewish relations.

Chapter 2 represents a paper presented in November of 2004 for a session of the Early Jewish/Christian Relations Section at the Society of Biblical Literature Annual Meeting in Atlanta, entitled "How Inter-Christian Approaches to Paul's Rhetoric Can Perpetuate Negative Valuations of Jewishness—Although Proposing to Avoid that Outcome." I am grateful to Elizabeth Struthers Malbon for inviting us to collect the papers from this session (which was entitled "Paul as a Site for Jewish-Christian Relations") and submit them to *Biblical Interpretation* for consideration. We added a paper from a related session and two invited responses, which were peer reviewed and published as a special issue in 2005 (vol. 13, no. 3) under the subtitle, "Paul between Jews and Christians." I served as the Guest Editor and wrote an "Introduction." These sessions and the resultant journal volume attest to a collegial awareness arising among ourselves that we represented a perspective or a school of thought, shared sensibilities at least, and several contributed chapters to the 2015 Fortress edited volume explaining this perspective, *Paul within Judaism: Restoring the First-Century Context to the Apostle*, which Magnus Zetterholm and I coedited.

Chapter 3, "The Myth of the 'Law-free' Paul Standing between Christians and Jews," began life as a paper for the Hermeneutics section of the Evangelical Theological Society Annual Meeting, Providence, RI, November 21, 2008, for a session entitled, "New Perspectives on Paul." I am grateful to Michael Bird for inviting me to offer a Jewish guest's perspective. The argument tackles an idea about Paul so deeply engrained that it is repeated as if a "fact" that can be assumed for any construction of the apostle; namely, following his encounter on the road to Damascus, Paul lived and promoted a "Law-free gospel." This "myth" about Paul shapes—and by definition, limits—the options explored for his voice by both Jews and Christians engaged in Christian-Jewish dialogue. I explored the "flashpoint" texts upon which the prevailing view that Paul abandoned Torah-based dietary customs is constructed. The paper examined exegetical alternatives for each text that challenge the consensus conclusions and arguably indicate that Paul conducted his diet according to the prevailing practices of a Torah-observant Jew, and, just as importantly, indicate that the arguments about food in his letters presume that his audiences knew this about him. A revised version of the paper was submitted for peer-review and published in the *Journal for Christian-Jewish Relations*, an e-journal of the Center for Christian-Jewish Learning at Boston College, which initiated a call for papers on Paul in part to accompany the Catholic Church's Jubilee Year dedicated to St. Paul, discussed below for both chapters 4 and 7. I am grateful to the editor, Ruth Langer, for a careful reading and useful suggestions. I dedicated the essay to Krister Stendahl, an important, inspirational figure for those of us engaged in challenging the consensus views, and no doubt for many who still promote them, who passed away that year.

I subsequently completed a related attempt to inform evangelical audiences about this new way to read Paul, again by the welcome invitation of Michael Bird, who was editing a volume for Zondervan, and to whom I am again thankful for the opportunity. My essay addressed some of the same issues in this chapter's argument from a different angle, trying to explain how the traditional and other recent views on Paul relative to Jews and Judaism struck a Jewish reader of the secondary material who did not accept the usual "myths" about Paul as "Law-free," and offered a Paul-within-Judaism perspective. This chapter, entitled "A Jewish View," is available in *Four Views on Paul* (ed. Michael F. Bird; Grand Rapids: Zondervan, 2012, pages 159–93).

Chapter 4 explores a dynamic I believe is central to Paul's theological reasoning. The traditional view holds that Paul insisted that Christ-following non-Jews remain uncircumcised because the role of Torah was finished, superseded and replaced by Christ, and, concomitantly, that Christ-following Jews should also give up this and other Torah-based ritual practices—deductions that reflect a "Paul, not Judaism" set of assumptions about Paul's reasoning. There are many problems with this reasoning, and texts that undermine it. Paul insisted that Christ-following non-Jews remain non-Jews, and thus remain uncircumcised and not "under" Torah, but his arguments—and "the rule" that he says he upholds for all of his assemblies (1 Cor 7:17–20)—logically require that Christ-following Jews remain Jews, and thus, it follows, they remain "under" Torah, and would still, by definition, circumcise their sons. These arguments do not proceed from the premise that Torah was of no consequence, but rather, interestingly, appeal to the logic of God's oneness as confessed in the *Shema' Israel*. I first explored this dynamic in a chapter in my first monograph (*The Mystery of Romans: The Jewish Context of Paul's Letter*. Minneapolis: Fortress, 1996). In fact, this feature of my argument was highlighted at the ceremony in New York in November of 1996 when the book received The National Jewish Book Award for Jewish-Christians Relations.

I expanded the research on Paul's development of the Shema to his other letters in a paper at the Mid-Central States Society of Biblical Literature meeting in St. Louis in March of 1996, shortly after the publication of *Mystery of Romans*, under the title, "Why was Gentile Circumcision so Unacceptable to Paul? The Role of the *Shema* in Paul's Gospel." That paper reflected my discovery, upon turning my attention to the research on Galatians that eventually resulted in publication of *The Irony of Galatians: Paul's Letter in First-Century Context* (Minneapolis: Fortress, 2002), that Paul's reasoning there, and in other letters too, was similarly based on logical inferences from the *Shema*.

I turned to the task of explaining this feature in more detail in response to a welcome invitation from Peter Spitaler in the Autumn of 2008 to present a lecture on "Paul and the Jewish Tradition." The lecture was part of a series of lectures and events that Villanova was offering during 2008/9 in honor of Pope Benedict's declaration of "The Year of St. Paul" (see discussion in chapter 7 below). I am grateful for the opportunity to be a part of this distinguished series, and subsequently, for inclusion of the revised paper in the Festschrift that Peter edited thereafter under the title *Celebrating Paul* (Washington, DC: Catholic Biblical Association of America, 2011). These lectures were also video-recorded; mine can be viewed at https://www.youtube.com/watch?v=5cpJbMsy9MQ.

Chapter 5 began life as a paper for the Society of Biblical Literature Annual Meeting in Baltimore in November, 2013, at which the "Paul and Judaism" Consultation hosted a session to explore the theme, "The Relationship of Paul's Non-Jews to Torah and Judaism." My paper, "Paul's Non-Jews Do Not Become 'Jews,' But Do They Become 'Jewish'?," explored what Paul taught the non-Jews turning to Jesus about their relationship to Torah and a Jewish way of life in comparison to what other Jews upheld for them, especially as related by Josephus. Such a topic involves weighing in on the controversial issue of what Paul and his contemporaries meant to communicate when using the Greek terms that we translate as *Jew* or *Judean* and cognates, such as *Jewish*, *Jewishly*, *Jewishness*, and *Judaism*, with special focus on the relevance of such terms for identification of the non-Jews who were joining Paul's communities. I suggested that although they (must) remain non-Jews, their new identification might be usefully described as jewish*ish*.

The research incorporated a close re-reading of Paul's argument in Romans 2:25–29, a text that has been almost always understood to indicate that Paul considered Jewish identity to be of no consequence for anyone following Jesus, including ethnic Jews, while, at the same time, conversely, to communicate that non-Jews become "true" or "spiritual" Jews, "the circumcised" even, when they become believers in Jesus. Logically, that means the continuation of Jewish identity in fact remains significant to God, although it has been transferred to "Christians," as it were, making it one of those texts where Paul's supersessionistic and replacement theological thinking as traditionally construed remains ostensibly inescapable, even when explicitly disavowed or denied. I discovered, once again, that if the text was approached with a different set of assumptions and sensibilities, there was good reason to question the consensus interpretations and explore alternatives that might offer better historical probability, certainly so if Paul continued to think and behave like a Jew practicing Judaism and expected the recipients of his letters to know this. For interpreters wanting to escape the traditional tropes, this reading offers an exegetical alternative.

In response to the welcome suggestion of Anders Runesson, I submitted a revised version of the paper to the inaugural issue of *The Journal of the Jesus Movement in Its Jewish Setting (JJMJS)* for peer review, and changed the title to reflect that, in addition to the general topics covered, the essay dealt with specific passages from Josephus, and Romans 2:25–29. Following acceptance and publication, I had the opportunity to submit the published version to the New Testament Traditions in the Context of Early Judaism Seminar at the Nordic New Testament Conference at Aarhus University, Denmark, on June 1, 2015, where I could benefit from the discussion of these arguments in a seminar setting of specialists on the matters addressed in the arguments.

Chapter 6 was developed for Kirchentag, the German Evangelical Protestant Church's conference that attracts over 100,000 participants biennially. When initially invited by Silke Lechner and Volker Haarmann to offer a paper at the 2015 gathering in Stuttgart, I was not aware that this is Germany's largest civil society forum and festival of faiths with over 2,000 events. I am very grateful to them and the committees they represented for the wonderful honor and opportunity. I want to thank Volker also for assistance preparing for the occasion, and for being a gracious host during the conference, which was indeed an amazing experience. My assignment was to give a lecture discussing who Paul meant by "the people" in Romans 15:10, where he cited from Deuteronomy to warrant his instructions, and in my case, to weigh in on the matter as a Jewish interpreter of the ("Christian") apostle.

The presentation was translated simultaneously into German, and followed by an ecumenical discussion involving a distinguished panel: Dr. Clare Amos from the World Council of Churches; Rev. Dr. Yohanna Katanacho, a Palestinian Old Testament scholar from Jerusalem; Prof. Dr. Claudia Janssen, a New Testament scholar from Marburg University; and Dr. Volker Haarmann, who oversees Christian-Jewish dialogue in the Rhineland. I offered a new translation and several interpretive deductions that contrast sharply with the way that the passage is usually translated and interpreted, which I am confident that those who invited me expected me to do, and which the panelists as well as several who commented from the audience kindly welcomed. Following the conference, I was again honored to have the lecture selected for inclusion in the conference volume, published in 2016, which allowed for publication of the paper. The chapter herein includes a more complete version of the paper and a few minor adjustments, so that the argument can function clearly independent of the original context and primarily German-speaking audience.

On my way to Stuttgart to present the Kirchentag lecture, I attended the Nordic New Testament Conference at Aarhus University, Denmark, where—in addition to the discussion of the essay in chapter 5 in a seminar, which is noted above—I also offered a main paper entitled, "How to Read Paul in a Jewish Way: A Case Study of Romans 15:10 Citing Deuteronomy 32:43." For this scholarly venue, I focused the paper on the intertextual dynamics of the series of proofs that the lecture at Kirchentag was designed around. I am grateful especially to Kasper Larsen, who invited my paper on behalf of the conference committee, and to Magnus Zetterholm, my host overall for the time in Denmark, and before and after in Sweden, which included a lecture at Lund (on my research on Romans 11, see volume 2), and, not least, a two-day cycling trip along the coasts of these countries, which every cyclist would prize.

Part III. A Jewish Contribution to Pope Benedict XVI's Celebration of the Year of St. Paul

Chapter 7 reproduces a short essay originally written for inclusion in a monumental volume created by the Society of St. Paul to celebrate Pope Benedict XVI's declaration of the Year of St. Paul in 2009, to mark the 2000th anniversary of Paul's birth. In addition to the texts of Paul's letters and many explanatory essays, the volume included contributions from major figures representing Christian denominations from around the world; Catholic, Protestant, Orthodox, and others. It was my special pleasure to write "*a* Jewish" contribution under the heading "Paul and Judaism." I wish to especially thank Daniela D'Andrea, my contact in Rome, for graciously facilitating my participation and communication throughout the project.

This unique volume is unlike any contemporary publication of which I am aware, from its jeweled cover to the illustration and calligraphy based upon the ninth-century Carolingian Bible housed at the Basilica of St. Paul Outside the Walls in Rome. The limited edition (998) was 428 pages long, written primarily in Italian with parallel Greek pages for the letters traditionally attributed to Paul and to his disciples in subsequent centuries. The book is stunning, but so too is the price of 3,500 euros, which, unfortunately, means that most of us will never see this majestic undertaking first hand, even be able to read the contributions. A copy of the printed pages of my essay is downloadable at my web site, which offers the interested reader a glimpse at the beautiful detail of this production: http://www.marknanos.com/CodexPauli-Nanos-Printed%5B1%5D.pdf. A video summary of the project is available for viewing online at: https://www.youtube.com/watch?v=OwwzwUzNHk8.

A WORD ABOUT THE COVER IMAGE

Solitude, oil on canvas, by Marc Chagall (Paris, 1933; Tel Aviv Museum of Art). Painted at the rise of the Nazi period, Chagall's imagery evokes the feeling of being alone, victimized for being a Jew and believing and practicing the sacred traditions of the Jewish people, not least the love of Torah Guidance, from the time of Jeremiah to Chagall's own time. If my reading of

Paul as a figure who loved Torah and Jewish identity and tradition is at all on target, then Paul almost certainly experienced similar sadness, because of Israel's subordination to Rome, and for those within his Christ-following Jewish subgroups suffering marginalization for the chronometrical claims of "the good news." Ironically, this imagery might also capture Paul's lament that the love of Torah has been taken from him and his movement, replaced by the ostensible "Law-free gospel" of *Paulinism*.

EDITORIAL NOTES

The reader will encounter numbers in brackets ("[00]") in the text of each article, which indicate the page numbers in the original publication of the essay.

Other essays included as chapters in this volume are indicated in the bibliographic information listed for them at the end of each chapter. For example "(See chapter x in this volume of collected essays)" or "(See volume x in this series of collected essays)."

ACKNOWLEDGEMENTS

In the case of these essays, which, as just discussed, have been in development for many years, there are many to thank besides those specifically mentioned in the recounting above or in the notes to various chapters. For all who have inspired, facilitated, discussed, or simply given me the opportunity to present my research, I am very grateful; thank you. For this volume, as for the others in this series, I am especially grateful to my wife, Vicky, for her encouragement and editorial assistance. Special thanks also to Robin Parry, my editor at Cascade, for his excellent assistance in bringing this volume and series to the light of day.

This volume *is dedicated to Ty*, my first granddaughter, who came into this world the same week as my first book, *The Mystery of Romans*. Ty is a resolute seeker of wisdom, an inspiration to those who want to see the world become a better place for living in a just, meaning-filled way. It is my sincere hope that this collection of work will make a small yet useful contribution toward the noble goals to which she aspires, for, I do believe—as she can attest, having had to listen to a favorite maxim repeatedly—that *the means are the ends in the making.*

Mark D. Nanos, September 6, 2017

Permissions

The articles are reproduced here with permission.

"Paul and Judaism: Why Not *Paul's Judaism?*" In *Paul Unbound: Other Perspectives on the Apostle*, edited by Mark Given, 117–60. Peabody, MA: Hendrickson, 2009. (Now published by Baker Academic, a division of Baker Publishing Group).

"Paul and the Jewish Tradition: The Ideology of the *Shema*." In *Celebrating Paul. Festschrift in Honor of Jerome Murphy-O'Connor, O.P., and Joseph A. Fitzmyer, S.J.*, edited by Peter Spitaler, 62–80. CBQMS 48. Washington, DC: Catholic Biblical Association of America, 2012.

"Paul's Non-Jews Do Not Become 'Jews,' But Do They Become 'Jewish'? Reading Romans 2:25–29 within Judaism, alongside Josephus." *Journal of the Jesus Movement in Its Jewish Setting* 1.1 (2014) 26–53. (http://www.jjmjs.org/uploads/1/1/9/0/11908749/nanos_pauls_non-jews.pdf).

"Reading Paul in a Jewish way: 'Oh be joyful all you peoples, with God's people' (Rom 15:10): Who are the People? An Ecumenical Discussion." In *Deutschor Evangelisher Kirchentag Stuttgart 2015*, edited by Silke Lechner et al., 436–47. Gütersloh and München: Gütersloher Verlagshaus/Random House Gmbh, 2016.

"How Inter-Christian Approaches to Paul's Rhetoric Can Perpetuate Negative Valuations of Jewishness—Although Proposing to Avoid that Outcome." *Biblical Interpretation* 13.3 (2005) 255–69.

"The Myth of the 'Law-Free' Paul Standing between Christians and Jews." *Studies in Christian-Jewish Relations (SCJR)* 4.1 (2009) 1–21. (Online journal access at https://ejournals.bc.edu/ojs/index.php/scjr/article/view/1511/1364).

"Paul and Judaism." In *Codex Pauli: A Monumental Volume Presented to Pope Benedict XVI in Celebration of the Year of St. Paul*, 54–55. Rome: Società San Paolo, 2009.

PART I

A New Approach to the Apostle

Paul as a Torah-observant Jew

1

Paul *and* Judaism
Why Not *Paul's Judaism*?[1]

[117] WHEN NEW TESTAMENT scholars address the topic of Paul *and* Judaism, the conjunction generally signals an adversative: Paul *or* Judaism; Paul *against* Judaism; Paul *outside of* Judaism; or Paul, *not* Judaism. Traditionally, the emphasis is on the distance between Paul's new religion based upon Jesus Christ *and* Judaism, his *former* religion.[2] The level of continuity or discontinuity assessed differs from interpreter to interpreter, but a shared perception remains assumed, if not argued: the religious life of Paul's communities, Paulinism, and the religious life of Jewish communities, Judaism, including Jewish Christianity, represent two fundamentally different religious systems.[3] One does not hear or read

---

1. This chapter represents a slightly modified version of the original essay published in *Paul Unbound*, reflecting developments in my thinking and terminology, also updating the bibliography; see the Preface for details.

2. E.g., Betz, *Galatians*, 251: "the Galatians have to choose between Paul and Judaism."

3. That there is a geo-ethnic dimension to Jewish identity, hence, Judeanness, is naturally relevant, but the discussion about Paul focuses on the religio-ethnic dimension of the life of the Jewish communities and the various ways that each person or group or subgroup interpreted the scriptures and traditions of their heritage, by which Paul's teachings and life are measured. In English usage, "Jew" and "Jewish" carry ethnic *and* religious meanings, including connotations of birth, while "Judean" emphasizes the geographical element. Judeanness can remain salient when discussing Jews from places other than Judea proper, such as of the Diaspora, or even Galilee, who are nevertheless still described as *Ioudaioi* (Acts 2:5–11), or Israelites, even when the land was not Israel but Judea (1 Macc 7:13; Rom 9:4; Acts 2:22; 4 Macc 18:5). At the same time, the significance of the geo-political (i.e., the land of Israel/Judea) remains salient in

[118] about *Paul's Judaism*,[4] or Pauline Judaism, of Judaism or Jewishness the terms "Jew" and "Judaism" as well, witnessed in the importance of Israel to Jews throughout the world and in contemporary Jewish theology, prayers, and aspirations. Rabbinic literature remained concerned to define proper behavior in the land and temple even when prohibited from living there and the temple was destroyed. Hence, this essay will generally refer to Jews and Jewish and Jewishness or Judaism, unless the geo-ethnic element of Judeanness is perceived to be specifically more salient (note: non-Jews could also live in Judea and thus be Judeans, just as today non-Jews can live in Israel and be Israelis). That there was a religious dimension to Judean/Jewish ethnicity properly named Judaism seems to me evident from relevant sources for discussing Paul's period; it arises in Paul's language in Gal 1:13-14 (discussed below). In the Maccabean literature, Judeans can either leave or return or observe the traditional religious practices of this people in different ways and to different degrees. For example, in 2 Maccabees 6:1-11, there are those in Judea who are described to be prohibited "even from confessing themselves to be *Ioudaioi*," which would make less sense to translate "Judeans" rather than "Jews." In 9:13-17, Antiochus IV Epiphanes is described as willing to become a *Ioudaios*, which most likely means Jew, not Judean, for he was not giving up his role as the Seleucid king. Philo, *On the Special Laws* 1.186, notes the range of observance among Jews, but is not describing their level of Judeanness. Josephus, *Ant.* 20.34-48, relates that Izates, the king of Adiabene, seeks to live a Jewish lifestyle guided by Scripture, apparently independent of participation in a Jewish community or role in ruling Judea or a Judean satellite nation, or even any idea of relocating to Judea. His interests and practices make more sense to classify as Judaism, even after his circumcision, although the geo-ethnic element is relevant, as witnessed by the concern about how his subjects will react, and later, with almsgiving to Judeans and sending his sons for education there. Moreover, note that the teacher advocating circumcision (Eleazar) is described as coming from Galilee, not Judea, so he is not arguably a Judean, although described as a *Ioudaios* (43), while the other one (Ananias) is not described in terms of coming from somewhere but yet as a *Ioudaios* merchant. See Daniel Schwartz, "'Judaean' or 'Jew'?"; Schwartz, *Judeans and Jews* (esp. 91-112, for response to Mason's arguments, upholding the value not only for using *Jew* but also for using *Judaism* and *religion* in the ways I employ them herein); Williams, "The Meaning and Function of *Ioudaios* in Graeco-Roman Inscriptions"; Cohen, *The Beginnings of Jewishness*, 69-139; Goodblatt, *Elements of Ancient Jewish Nationalism*; Jones and Pearce, eds., *Jewish Local Patriotism and Self-Identification in the Graeco-Roman Period*; Runesson, "Inventing Christian Identity"; Nanos, "Paul's Non-Jews Do Not Become 'Jews,' But Do They Become 'Jewish'?"; Nanos, "The Question of Conceptualization." Among those arguing instead for use of Judean throughout, see e.g., Esler, *Conflict and Identity in Romans*, 19-76; Mason, "Jews, Judaeans, Judaizing, Judaism."

4. The term "Judaism" is used herein to refer to "a way of life developed by and for communities of Jews" to discuss Paul and his contexts, although there are those who uphold that the terminology is anachronistic. We could refer instead to "a way of life developed by and for communities of Judeans" and thus to "Judeannism." I find the use of Jew and Judaism and cognates quite useful for sharpening focal points for discussions of Paul's thought, teaching, and way of life, and the foundational ideas and practices of the communities that he founded and to which he wrote letters. It is still the language most often used in New Testament and Pauline studies today, but still primarily to measure the distance of Judaism from Paul's thought, teaching, and way of life, as well as that of his communities. See references in n. 3 above, in the discussion below, and the challenges to the prevailing views in the various essays in Nanos and

as the propositional basis of Paul's way of life, or of the communities he establishes and addresses.

Most interpreters today pronounce that Paul had been a Jew, and also that he remained one (albeit not without equivocation, discussed below). At the same time, very few have or would argue that Paul continued to practice and promote Judaism as an expression of covenant faithfulness after his experience of Jesus Christ. When Paul is upheld to be a Jew it thus signifies a kind of ethnic identity independent of the religious elements [119] of ethnicity related to covenant standing; Paul is treated as a Jew or Judean who does not behave Jewishly. He is the leader if not the founder of a new religious movement, one functioning outside the boundaries of Judaism. Although some other Christ-followers, like James and Peter, may be considered to remain within the circle of Judaism, so-called Jewish Christianity, Paul's "churches" gathered not in "synagogues," but in house-churches of believers in Jesus Christ that were clearly distinguishable from Jewish gathering places or meetings. That they are usually simply called "gentile churches" demonstrates what remains presupposed.[5] These new communities are portrayed to consist primarily of *non*-Jews, with perhaps a few *former* Jews. They are understood to represent a new religious movement that was distinguished from Judaism, namely, Christianity, even when it is acknowledged that the name Christian had not yet been coined.[6]

Zetterholm, eds., *Paul within Judaism*; Boccaccini and Segovia, eds., *Paul the Jew*.

5. E.g., Watson, *Paul, Judaism, and the Gentiles*, argues that Paul's strategic goal was to create "Gentile Christian communities in sharp separation from the Jewish community" (19; *passim*); Esler, *Conflict and Identity in Romans*, 89–97, 120–25, maintains that the policy of creating house churches was by definition a clear differentiation from synagogue gatherings; Barclay, *Jews in the Mediterranean Diaspora*, 386: "In social reality Paul's churches were distinct from the synagogues, and their predominantly Gentile members unattached to the Jewish community"; Segal, *Paul the Convert*, 6–7, argues that Paul represents "a new apocalyptic, Jewish sect," yet writes of him living "in a Hellenistic, gentile *Christian community* as a Jew among gentiles" (emphasis added). I argue that the communities Paul addresses in Rome and Galatia are meeting as *subgroups within* the Jewish communities in *Mystery of Romans*; Nanos, *Irony of Galatians*. See now the development of this matter reframed in terms of associations, in, e.g., Harland, *Dynamics of Identity in the World of the Early Christians*; Harland, *Associations, Synagogues, and Congregations*; Ascough, "Paul, Synagogues, and Associations"; Korner, "*Ekklēsia* as a Jewish Synagogue Term"; Runesson, "The Question of Terminology"; Runesson, "Placing Paul"; Last, *The Pauline Church and the Corinthian Ekklēsia*.

6. Betz, *Galatians*, 179: "Paul draws a line between being a Jew and being a Christian. Of course, this line of demarcation is polemical, but, as Romans shows (Rom 9–11), it was in no way intended to establish a new religion. Yet the establishment of a new religion is in effect what happened. If the validity of the Jewish Torah ends for the Jew when he becomes a Christian, there is no point or basis for Gentiles as well as for Jews to adhere to the Jewish religion. Since those Christians no longer regard

Furthermore, Paul has been traditionally understood to be antagonistic toward Torah-identity and practice. Some propose that he was instead simply "indifferent" (ἀδιάφορος; although Paul's letters do not contain the term).[7] Others grant that he observed Torah to various degrees, but not as an expression of faith, certainly not as covenant fidelity. Either way, Paul believed that the era of [120] Torah had ended, being made obsolete, or fulfilled, or superseded in the work of Christ. He did not regard Jewish covenant identity or behavior to have any "soteriological" significance.[8] To the degree that he observed Torah occasionally, it simply reflected cultural conditioning from which he had not yet been liberated, having been born and raised a Jew.[9] Or it demonstrated the chameleon-like behavioral extremes to which he would go to win other Jews to his convictions. The latter view relies largely upon the prevailing interpretations of 1 Cor 9:19–23, wherein Paul describes becoming all things to all people in order to win them to the gospel of Christ, and specifically, of becoming to Jews and to those under law, like a Jew and like one under law, and alternatively, of becoming lawless or without law as well as weak, to those who are lawless or without law, or weak.

The role of 1 Cor 9:19–23 in Pauline studies provides a useful place to define the topics that generally arise in discussion of Paul and Judaism. Donald Hagner speaks for many when he writes: "Paul regards himself as no longer under the law," since he "obeys it now and then. Paul thus feels free to identify with the Gentiles and not to remain an observant Jew. Incidentally, how remarkable it is that the Jew Paul can speak of himself as an outsider: 'To the Jews I became as a Jew'!" This implies a "break with

---

themselves as pagans, a new religion has *de facto* come into existence." So too Wright, *Paul and the Faithfulness of God*, 359–75, 538–69, 1426–49, *passim*, for an example of denying terminologically what is otherwise clearly being argued by other terminology, and at the same time even using and defending the traditional terms. More helpful are Eisenbaum, *Paul Was Not a Christian*; Runesson, "Inventing Christian Identity"; Runesson, "The Question of Terminology"; Zetterholm, "Paul within Judaism: The State of the Questions"; Scott, *The Real Paul*, for an effort to work out the implications for non-specialists.

7. E.g., Schoeps, *Paul*, 197–200.

8. Hagner, "Paul as a Jewish Believer—According to his Letters," 113.

9. E.g., Dodd, *Epistle to the Romans*, 43; Sanders, *Paul, the Law, and the Jewish People*, 103, 198–99, discusses Paul's struggle to reconcile revelation with "his native convictions"; Hagner, "Paul as a Jewish Believer," 114, observes that while Paul may have continued to behave in some ways like a Jew, it was "by habit, if for no other reason . . . as an expression of his ethnic Jewishness, and as a matter of convenience because of the fact that he moved among Jews so frequently. This conduct no longer had any soteriological significance, however, nor was he under compulsion to obey the commandments. His conduct was now solely under the sway of Christ."

Judaism," and "it is clear, furthermore, that observing or not observing the law is an unimportant issue before God. The position taken by Paul is one of complete expedience: he will or will not observe the law only in relation to its usefulness in the proclamation of the gospel. Before God the issue of obeying the commandments is in the category of *adiaphora*."[10] Heikki Räisänen declares the implications for the traditional consensus [121] view quite clearly: "1 Cor 9.20 f. is absolutely incompatible with the theory of an observant Paul."[11] This view continues to guide interpreters representing the New Perspective on Paul; for example, N. T. Wright insists, in view of this passage, that the idea Paul remained a Torah-observant Jew is not only anachronistic and ignorant, but also that a reasonable person would naturally recognize that "*[b]eing a 'Jew' was no longer Paul's basic identity.*"[12]

This interpretive tradition overwhelmingly upholds the view that Paul subscribed to a policy of mimicking the behavior of non-Jews, on the one hand, and of Jews, including fully Torah-observant Jews, or proselytes, on the other. I write "mimicking" because, while the negative aspect of this behavior that such a term conveys is not generally highlighted, it nevertheless represents what is signified for "becoming like" in the arguments made. *Becoming like* is not interpreted to mean Paul actually becomes the same as or like each, for he is not portrayed to subscribe to the propositional bases of the behavior he appears to adopt. Those whom he mimics presumably behave as they do to express their worldview and convictions. But he is understood to merely imitate the outward behavioral trappings when in the company of each of these different people or groups: it is not internalized, not of the heart. He does not "become" in the true sense, the sense that he wishes for them to "become" Christ-followers by conviction, and to live that way thereafter inwardly as well as outwardly, like himself. Paul merely adjusts his conduct to fit the lifestyle of different people and groups in order to gain the trust of each of them in a gospel that intends for them to believe in something other than what Paul's outward bait and switch behavior has made it seem.[13]

---

10. Hagner, "Paul as a Jewish Believer," 113; see also Fee, *First Epistle to the Corinthians*, 427; Dunn, *Theology of Paul the Apostle*, 577; Hays, *First Corinthians*, 153–54; Segal, *Paul*, 228, 238.

11. Räisänen, *Paul and the Law*, 75 n. 171.

12. Wright, *Paul and the Faithfulness of God*, 1436 (emphasis his!); 1447: "he [Paul] saw the people of the crucified Messiah as having a Messiah-shaped identity which marked them off from Jew and Greek alike"; see 1434–49.

13. For the consensus view, see, e.g., Richardson, "Pauline Inconsistency," 347; Given, *Paul's True Rhetoric*, 105–17; and those noted in the footnotes below.

What is also not often discussed is that such a policy, supposedly calculated to persuade people with entirely different behavioral patterns and cultural premises, would instead over time almost certainly alienate all of them. Surely some Jews would hear rumors of his non-Jewish eating behavior, for example, when with non-Jews, and others would no doubt witness this behavior. The same is true about non-Jews witnessing Jewish behavior when he was among Jews. This would especially be the case within the context of communal gatherings, which many also suppose this passage to address, that is, the winning of Christ-following Jews and non-Jews to a more mature life in Christ.[14] In such settings, where push comes to shove, Paul is understood to forgo Jewish practices.[15] Why? Because he did not subscribe to Jewish behavior as a matter of conviction anyway, so he can hardly be expected to choose Torah, if that would imply to non-Jews that the gospel was in some way yoked to Torah. However [122] conceptualized, Paul's behavior, when interpreted along this traditional line, would eventually be observed by those who found it to be the opposite of what they supposed him to sustain for himself. Hence, the effect would be the opposite of that which he intends. To Jews he would quickly appear to be (become) like a non-Jew, to non-Jews he would quickly appear to be (become) like a Jew.

On this popular reading, Paul is understood to have, for example, eaten like non-Jews when in their company, and like Jews when in theirs. To "gain" them, he *behaved* "like" them. But he did so disingenuously, especially when playing the part of a practicing Jew.[16] For this policy obscured the fact that Jews who valued Torah-observance enough for Paul to adopt this behavior in order to gain their trust, would be, if they accepted his message, commencing on a faith-journey characterized by the renunciation of Torah-faith, yet unbeknownst to them. It follows that if "converted," they too would adopt this chameleon-like expedient behavior thereafter on the same terms, i.e., only to dupe other Jews, creating a spiral of duplicity, a culture wherein misunderstanding and continued "immature" or "weak" notions of the value of Jewish practice among Jewish believers in Christ would be self-perpetuating.

---

14. E.g., Hays, *First Corinthians*, 155.

15. Sanders, *Paul, the Law*, 177–78, 185–87.

16. For most of these interpreters, Paul actually did share the propositional base of non-Jews about food, because he is understood to have eaten like a gentile: his behavior was no longer governed by Torah. Paul only mimicked Jewish behavior when calculated to be useful for propagating the gospel. The traditional definition of "becoming" is less precise than recognized, for it signifies mere imitation of outward behavior for Jewish practices, but embracing of the propositional values for gentile practices.

John Barclay recognizes this logical element in the traditional construction of Paul, but upholds it nevertheless to be the correct interpretation, cleverly comparing Paul's theology with "a Trojan horse which threatens the integrity of those who sought to live according to the law."[17] Many Jewish interpreters, accepting the traditional Christian construction, have observed the duplicity of Paul's strategy, and it has been used to substantiate the arguments of those wishing to expose suspect values at the heart of nascent Christianity.[18] At the same time, [123] many Christian interpreters do not mention the problematic subversion of Paul's integrity this interpretation creates, or explain how they reconcile it with the high moral standing otherwise attributed to Paul's life and teaching.

This interpretive approach is also popular among those who seek to reconcile the Torah-observant Paul presented by Luke in Acts with the Paul of his letters, where he is generally understood to be indifferent to Torah observance, if not actually opposed to it. For them, Paul's adoption of Torah in Acts exemplifies his missionary strategy as expressed in 1 Cor 9:19-23, wherein he supposedly undertakes Torah-observance sometimes in the expedient pursuit of a value championed to be superior, evangelism, regardless of, and generally without discussion of the moral problematic of duplicity: "The undisputable fact that he was raised as a law-observant Jew makes it reasonable to assume that he often observed Jewish customs in his daily life—as long as they did not blur the gospel. For the historical Paul, traditional law-observance was certainly subordinated to the preaching of the gospel and his concern for the salvation of mankind."[19]

Even when Paul is understood to encourage respect for Jewish behavior among Christ-followers, it amounts to little more than patronizing. For example, when Paul urges those who were secure in their faith to respect the sensibilities of the "weak in faith" in Rome, the latter are portrayed to be Jewish believers in Jesus who still "fail to trust God completely and without qualification," that is, they have not freed themselves from Torah-practice as

---

17. Barclay, "'Do We Undermine the Law?'" 308.

18. Jewish critiques of Paul's "opportunist" subversion of Torah to gain converts developed in response to the way this strategy has been portrayed by Christian interpreters, often as if a positive trait, subjecting everything to the highest value of evangelism, are discussed by Fuchs-Kreimer, "The 'Essential Heresy,'" 63-82, and see, Maccoby, *Mythmaker*, 151-57, 166-67; Klinghoffer, *Why the Jews Rejected Jesus*, 106-10. Fuchs-Kreimer also discusses some Jewish scholars who do not read Paul in this way. See also Langton, "The Myth of the 'Traditional View of Paul' and the Role of the Apostle in Modern Jewish-Christian Polemics"; Meißner, *Die Heimholung des Ketzers*.

19. Hvalvik, "Paul as a Jewish Believer," 153; cf. Hagner, "Paul as a Jewish Believer," 113, cited above.

integral to Christ-faith.[20] In Corinth, although Paul is understood to call for the "knowledgeable" to refrain from eating idol food for the sake of those who remain conscious that it is sacred, it is understood to be but a temporary concession, because in the long run Paul is believed to actually share the values of those Christ-followers who would eat idol food as a [124] matter of indifference to Jewish covenant food conventions.[21] On the prevailing interpretation of Phil 3:2–7, Paul counted the value of Jewish identity and behavior to amount to nothing more than "crap" (σκύβαλα).[22]

According to the consensus of Pauline scholars, while Paul may have resisted the logical conclusion that he was no longer a representative of Judaism or a Jew in good standing, but instead an apostate, one who now represented a new religion, that was an assessment hardly shared by others, including those who represented so-called "Jewish Christianity."[23] He may have thought of himself as a "good Jew," but no other practicing Jews would have. To the degree that Judaism continued to be lived in a meaningful way by Christ-followers—as an expression of personal and communal faith and lifestyle, of *kavannah* (*kawwanah* from the root *kwn*; intention)—this was reserved for so-called *Jewish* Christianity, represented by James or Peter. That was a way of interpreting the meaning of life after the resurrection of Jesus Christ that Paul ostensibly opposed because the Mosaic legislation no longer expressed God's purpose for humankind, either because with the work of Christ the Mosaic covenant had successfully completed its purpose, or because it had failed to do so and was rendered thereafter obsolete.

In short, when NT scholars speak of Paul's religious life and values, of Paulinism or *Pauline* Christianity, with its "*Law-free* Gospel," most mean to signify that Paul taught and practiced a *Judaism-free* way of living based on his belief in Jesus Christ.[24]

---

20. Dunn, *Romans 9–16*, 798. This common understanding of Paul's language, e.g., in Rom 14—15, is challenged in Nanos, *Mystery of Romans*, 85–165, 345–47 (88–95, for "Luther's trap," where comments such as this one by Dunn are discussed).

21. E.g., Barrett, ed., *Essays on Paul*, 40–59 ["Things Sacrificed to Idols"]. Challenges to this reading are mounted by Tomson, *Paul and the Jewish Law*; Cheung, *Idol Food in Corinth*; Nanos, "The Polytheist Identity of the 'Weak,' and Paul's Strategy to 'Gain' Them"; Nanos, "Why the 'Weak' in 1 Corinthians 8—10 Were Not Christ-believers."

22. This prevailing view of Paul's polemic is challenged in Nanos, "Paul's Reversal of Jews Calling Gentiles 'Dogs' (Philippians 3:2)"; Nanos, "Paul's Polemic in Philippians 3 as Jewish-Subgroup Vilification"; Nanos, "Out-Howling the Cynics."

23. Barclay, "Paul among Diaspora Jews," for a construction of Paul whose assimilation is understood to leave only himself supposing he is not an apostate. Elliott, "The Question of Politics," 232–43, for a critique of Barclay's methodology for assessing Paul to be an "anomalous Jew."

24. This nomenclature as well as the exegetical bases for using it, especially related to

THE NEW PERSPECTIVE
ON PAUL AND JUDAISM

In recent years, a position recognized as the New Perspective on Paul (NPP) has challenged the traditional characterizations of the Judaism of Paul's time as [125] legalistic and arrogantly self-righteous.[25] Instead, interpreters upholding this view recognize that Judaism was focused on responsible behavior (Torah-observance) undertaken in a spirit of gratitude appropriate to the expression of faith (i.e., loyalty) by those called by a gracious God to a covenantal relationship (covenantal nomism). In other words, these observations reflect the ideals prized by Christians in positive terms usually reserved to describe Christianity, but traditionally denied to Judaism.

Taking Judaism on its own terms is the welcome advance made by its proponents, largely based on the ability of Krister Stendahl's and E. P. Sanders's arguments,[26] and those made by others since, to succeed where those making similar observations had been previously unable to convince Pauline scholars, and Christians in general.[27] This historically more viable and cross-culturally more respectful development, with its new level of sociological and rhetorical sensitivity, has done little, however, to alter the traditional view that Paul, as apostle, did not practice the Judaism of his day. As was observed above for N. T. Wright, another leading voice of the New Perspective, James Dunn, who generally emphasizes that Paul always regarded himself to be a Jew, nevertheless still writes also that Paul did *not* "think of himself as a Jew,"

---

decisions about Paul's arguments dealing with dietary matters, are challenged in Nanos, "The Myth of the 'Law-Free' Paul Standing between Christians and Jews." For a helpful reframing of the concepts and language related to Torah and Law when discussing Paul and other Jews of his time, see Hedner Zetterholm, "The Question of Assumptions"; and more extensively, Hayes, *What's Divine about Divine Law?*

25. The position and coining of the phrase by James Dunn is well summarized in his "The New Perspective on Paul." This development and others impacting contemporary Pauline studies are explained in Zetterholm, *Approaches to Paul*. "The Paul Page" is dedicated to discussion of this topic: http://www.thepaulpage.com/.

26. Stendahl, *Paul among Jews and Gentiles*; Sanders, *Paul and Palestinian Judaism*.

27. See e.g., Schoeps, *The Jewish-Christian Argument*, 40–52, 165, published in German in 1961 (Schoeps, *Israel und Christenheit*, 57–59. Note that the first edition of 1937 contains this same language: *Jüdisch-Christliches Religionsgespräch in 19 Jahrhunderten*, 49–61, 152). Similar observations are in Schoeps, *Paul*, 168–218, 280–93. There were naturally others who anticipated these positive developments, and some examples such as G. F. Moore, W. D. Davies, and S. Sandmel, as well as central protagonists of the traditional negative biases, are discussed by Sanders, *Paul and Palestinian Judaism*, 33–59; see too Heschel, *Abraham Geiger and the Jewish Jesus*; Langton, "The Myth of the 'Traditional View of Paul.'" For the earlier ideas and influence of John Toland, see Jones, ed., *The Rediscovery of Jewish Christianity*; and for that of Johann Tobias Beck, see Gerdmar, *Roots of Theological Anti-Semitism*, 203–12.

emphasizing that he did not observe Torah as a matter of conviction, but also that "insofar as 'Jew' was an ethnic identifier (and insofar as he was an ethnic Jew), Paul wished neither to be known as such nor to identify himself as such. Insofar as 'Jew' denoted a lifestyle, a commitment to the ancestral [126] customs of the Jews, Paul wished neither to exercise such a commitment nor to insist that other Jews be true to their ethnic-religious identity."[28] This trajectory was anticipated in Dunn's initial discussion of the new possibilities for interpreting Paul that he discovered through Sanders's work. Regarding Gal 2:16, Dunn observed that he detected in Paul a "crucial development for the history of Christianity taking place": "the transition from a form of Jewish Messianism to a faith which sooner or later must break away from Judaism to exist in its own terms."[29]

Moreover, most New Perspective interpreters still find fault with Judaism, albeit emphasizing different reasons, or at least with Judaism as Paul (mis)understood it. Paul is portrayed to have transcended Jewish particularism, expressed in nationalism, in specific boundary-marking behavior, such as circumcision, Sabbath, and food conventions (cf. James Dunn; N. T. Wright). Or they find fault with Paul, in that he seems to have misunderstood his "former" religion (E. P. Sanders, and earlier, e.g., H. J. Schoeps), or to have failed to reconcile it with his new "Christian" religion (H. Räisänen), leaving an irreconcilable contradiction in his theology.[30]

---

28. Dunn, "Who Did Paul Think He Was?" 182. On 179, Dunn argues, that "of course Paul did not cease to be a Jew—how could he? Nor did he convert from one religion ('Judaism') to another ('Christianity'), since the term 'Christianity' did not yet exist, and the Nazarene movement was still within the matrix of Second Temple Judaism." He nuances the definition of Jew, emphasizing the religious dimension, and of Judaism, inscrutably from my perspective, to denote for Paul only "the national-religious identity which emerged particularly as a result of the Maccabean crisis and revolt. He meant Judaism identified by its zeal for the law and its willingness to use the sword to prevent the dilution of its national-religious distinctiveness. But that Judaism was only one part (or aspect?) of what we now call Second Temple Judaism" (184). In his conclusions (192), Dunn argues that Paul would not give a straight "No" to his identity as a Jew, as long as it was qualified "to come from within and not from without, and that the trappings of Jewish identity, most explicitly the practice of circumcision and food laws, could be equally taken on or put off without affecting the integrity of that Jewishness either way." But he would give a clear "No" to being "in Judaism": "the term had become too much identified with ethnicity and separation from other nations; and Paul's self-understanding on just these points had been too radically transformed by his conversion . . . for 'Judaism' to continue to define and identify himself or his apostolic work."

29. Dunn, "New Perspective," in *Jesus, Paul*, 198. Similar statements by Wright were indicated earlier (n. 11), and are commonly encountered in publications by proponents of the NPP who otherwise, and often in the same publication, also state emphatically that Paul remained a Jew, and in a few cases even that Paul still respected some level of Jewish practices.

30. Cf. the observations and criticisms of Elliott, *Liberating Paul*, 66–72, 108; Elliott, "The Question of Politics." On the problem of a continued logical negative valuation of

[127] Thus, as several interpreters have noted, what has been named the "New Perspective on *Paul*," arguably represents not so much a new perspective on Paul as a new perspective on *Judaism*. The effort of Christian scholars to make sense of Paul's arguments in new terms has instead often resulted in a new level of confusion about Paul, or better, about the traditional construction of Paul, a construction of Paul that still generally prevails for the proponents of the New Perspective. Especially problematic is how to reconcile the implications that follow from recognizing Judaism to be grace- and faith-based with the role that Paul's voice has traditionally played in the critique of Judaism, as well as the foundations of Christian theology, wherein defining terms like faith and grace and works has always taken place in binary contrast to what they were perceived to represent in Judaism, the misguided religion of the other. But if Judaism is based on grace, then why did Paul find something wrong with it? Or did he? What does this imply about the role of Jesus for Jews?[31] Is not "Pauline" Christianity necessarily something other than Judaism? If not, what kind of Judaism was it, or should it be?

Naturally, not all Pauline interpreters believe that these positive re-evaluations of Judaism are warranted, much less the efforts toward new interpretations of Paul or Christian origins they provoke. Many continue to view both Judaism and Paul through traditional Christian, especially Reformation-ground lenses,[32] or the bifocals shaped by F. C. Baur,[33] [128]

Judaism in recent inter-mural Christian approaches pitting Paul against Jewish Christianity, and thus claiming to avoid the traditional Paul against Judaism judgments, see Nanos, "How Inter-Christian Approaches to Paul's Rhetoric Can Perpetuate Negative Valuations of Jewishness."

31. E.g., although beyond the scope of this essay, many debates now turn around the New Perspective emphasis on reading the language of justification by faith to refer to the inclusion of non-Jews as equals rather than addressing personal salvation of "everyone," as traditionally interpreted, which logically brings up the topic of whether from Paul's perspective Jews also need to believe in Jesus Christ, in particular, to be saved. I have begun to address this topic: Nanos, "Are Jews Outside of the Covenants If Not Confessing Jesus as Messiah?"; Nanos, "'The Gifts and the Calling of God are Irrevocable' (Romans 11:29)."

32. E.g., Hagner, "Paul and Judaism—The Jewish Matrix of Early Christianity"; Kim, *Paul and the New Perspective*; Das, *Paul, the Law, and the Covenant*; Gathercole, *Where is Boasting?*; Carson et al., eds., *Justification and Variegated Nomism, vol. 2, The Paradoxes of Paul*; Westerholm, *Perspectives Old and New on Paul*; Bird, *An Anomalous Jew*. A detailed bibliography of the New Perspective and its critics is available in Bird, *Saving Righteousness of God*, 194–211; Bird, "The New Perspective on Paul: A Bibliographical Essay." For the history of this traditional view, see Gerdmar, *Roots of Theological Anti-Semitism*.

33. Baur, *Paul the Apostle of Jesus Christ*; Paget, "The Definition of the Terms Jewish Christian and Jewish Christianity in the History of Research"; Jackson-McCabe, ed., *Jewish Christianity Reconsidered*; Jones, ed., *Rediscovery of Jewish Christianity*.

through which the superiority of *Pauline* "Christianity" can be clearly seen.³⁴ It is also notable that Jewish interpreters of Paul, who do not generally share the traditional Christian perspectives on Judaism, nevertheless often adopt the traditional interpretations of Paul.³⁵ For the valuations that Christians have championed in this construal of Paul are easily viewed from an oppositional perspective to highlight, interestingly enough, the inferiority of Pauline "Christianity."³⁶

Ironically, the lack of substantial newness in the way Paul is portrayed or understood to relate to what is newly perceived about Judaism is signaled in the research that arguably inaugurated the so-called New Perspective on Paul. In his often-repeated statement, E. P. Sanders cleverly poses [129] the matter in starkly contrasting terms: "*this is what Paul finds wrong in Judaism:*

---

34. In sharp contrast to the critique offered here, which largely revolves around the relative lack of newness in the perspectives on Paul that have been offered, those resisting the New Perspective are critical of its newness, of its departure from traditional and especially Reformation interpretations of Paul as well as of Judaism, however minor the changes proposed may be in the case of Paul. The efforts to undermine the New Perspective are frequently occupied with showing that Judaism is as Christianity has interpreted Judaism to be through the traditional interpretation of Paul's rhetoric, thereby confirming that Paul has been interpreted properly to be offering a very different religious system than that of Judaism.

35. Although some have grouped me among New Perspective interpreters, this category represents Christians who newly discovered that Judaism is not as it has been polemically constructed in Christian tradition, which does not apply in the same way for a Jewish person who did not hold to the traditional Christian views of Judaism in the first place, or of Paul, and thus did not undergo the changes signified by the label "New Perspective." Previous to Sanders, a number of Jews and Christians unsuccessfully sought to inform the Christian tradition that Judaism was and is grace-based, and that acts of righteousness are undertaken in terms of covenant loyalty, and so on; thus, the change of perspective on Judaism is indeed new and welcome. For me, it made it possible to enter the discussion of redefining Paul without also undertaking the task of redefining Judaism along this line first, which, when I first imagined this task in the 1970s, appeared too daunting a course to pursue. When I learned of the New Perspective and its impact in the 1980s, I could then reconsider offering a new interpretation of Paul, although one that is in many ways significantly different from that of the "New Perspective on Paul" proper. Since then, I have certainly been engaged in offering a new perspective on Paul, if not also Judaism, on some points, and along with others, now refer to this as the "Paul within Judaism" perspective, which others sometimes refer to as the "radical new perspective," among other labels.

36. Cf. Langton, "The Myth of the 'Traditional View of Paul,'" which includes a discussion of how my work differs from the main lines the traditional Jewish perspectives on Paul have followed (this essay and others tracing the history of Jewish perceptions of Paul are in Langton, *The Apostle Paul in the Jewish Imagination*). See also Nanos, "A Jewish View"; and see the above discussion of Jewish reactions to the prevailing interpretations of 1 Cor 9:19–23, on which my views are briefly set out below.

it is not Christianity."[37] Sanders defines this problem not as a critique of "the means of being properly religious," but of "the prior fundamentals of Judaism: the election, the covenant and the law; and it is because these are *wrong* that the means appropriate to 'righteousness according to the law' (Torah observance and repentance) are held to be wrong or are not mentioned."[38]

To my knowledge, what has gone largely unrecognized in Sanders's turn of phrase, and in much of the work by New Perspective interpreters, are the traditional assumptions that remain necessary to it. Firstly, Sanders's statement requires the institutional development of Christianity to make sense, however historically unlikely that remains, and regardless of how often the formation of Christianity in Paul's time is otherwise denied.[39] This results in a great deal of confusion in recent discussions about Paul and Judaism. Initial claims that there was no such thing as Christianity are regularly emptied of significance as the arguments proceed. It becomes evident that the interpreter is still working with a perception of Paul and his communities as something *other* than Judaism. This includes the problem of the continued use of nomenclature like Christian and Christianity to refer to him, his teachings, and his communities.[40] [130] Secondly, Sanders's phrase requires the construction of a Paul who finds something wrong *with Judaism*. It is with the pillars of Jewish identity and religious values that Paul finds fault: election, covenant, Torah, and repentance. And he does so from

37. Sanders, *Paul and Palestinian Judaism*, 552 (emphasis his).
38. Ibid., 551–52 (emphasis added).
39. Stowers, *A Rereading of Romans*, 24–25, similarly notes this problem.

40. Dunn regularly notes that Paul was not converted to a new religion and that he precedes what can be properly denoted as Christianity (cf. Dunn, *The Partings of the Ways*, 116–19, 135). Even after the Antioch incident, which Dunn takes to represent a monumental realization of incompatibility, he still conceptualizes the eventual developments to be "as much a parting of the ways *within* the new movement as *between* Christianity and Judaism, or better, as within Judaism" (emphasis his). And he challenges the idea that Paul should be defined only in discontinuity with Judaism, as opposite to it (Dunn, "How New Was Paul's Gospel?" 385). Yet Dunn also writes, "we must be careful about defining Pauline Christianity simply as a kind of Judaism" (385; in the same sentence upon which my prior sentence was based). Note that here we see that it is Christianity that Paul is described as doing (although he refers to denoting Jew and Christian as "anachronistic" for Paul's time on 387), and moreover, he observes that it is not Judaism. How does one square this with the idea that Paul precedes Christianity and did not convert to a new religion, or abandon Judaism? Similar logical problems on these topics are common in New Perspective arguments, just as they remain common in tradition-oriented arguments: after denying that Christianity had begun or that anyone was yet known as a Christian, the conceptualizations expressed in language choices and argumentation do not follow this logic out, or express a viable alternative at work. Hagner, "Paul as a Jewish Believer," 97–120, proceeds similarly, which I critiqued in Nanos, "Have Paul and His Communities Left Judaism for Christianity?"

outside Judaism rather than from on the inside, since the problem lies *in* the prior fundamentals of Judaism.

The problem, as Sanders's Paul sees it, is not with *some* or *other* Judaisms, not with *some* Jewish people[41] or ideas or institutions or practices, not with *some* or *other* Christ-following Jews or Jewish groups,[42] or *their ways* of interpreting the meaning of Jesus Christ—but with and in Judaism per se, which his Paul "*opposed*."[43] Granted, this is not because Judaism was legalistic or based on achieving righteousness by fulfilling commandments rather than by grace, as the traditional views that Sanders criticizes maintained, because he recognized that these were not how Judaism operated. But for Sanders, Paul does not level his critique from *within* Judaism: he is not engaged in prophetic speech based upon an appeal to the noble values [131] of these fundamental Jewish ideals, accusing competing Jewish groups or Judaisms of compromising them. Rather, Paul devalues or challenges the ideals themselves, *and* he does so *from outside* Judaism. In this sense, the New Perspective view of Paul remains similar to traditional approaches, holding variations of the same views as those expressed by many challenging them for ostensibly compromising traditional notions held to be fundamental to certain Christian truths.

Sanders does mention the limitation of referring to "Paul and Judaism" in a way that fails to suggest something other than "Paul and *the rest* of Judaism," but concludes that "the traditional terminology would seem to be justified by his being engaged in a mission which *went beyond the bounds of*

---

41. Gaston, *Paul and the Torah*, 140, makes a similar observation: "this is what Paul finds wrong with other Jews: that they did not share his revelation in Damascus."

42. I prefer not to use the terms *Christian* and *Christianity* except where it is necessary to the discussion, and refer to, e.g., Christ-followers and Christ-following Jewish coalitions in an effort to avoid perpetuating this problem. I hope my readers will be encouraged to do so too, although I recognize that the change of terminology can be taxing, creating cumbersome language—and that these choices are still not perfect. Likewise, I try to minimize the use of "gentile(s)" to label the non-Jew(s), because it obscures the implied "*not*-ness" of the Hebrew and Greek terms for the non-Jew (and non-Israelite) other, a way of conceptualizing the world present in Paul's choice of language and thus with some relevance to the historical interpretive task. In this same direction, it would be clearer, although even more taxing, to refer to "a member of the nations (or 'peoples') other than Israel" when ἔθνος is translated, and for the plural, "nations" or "peoples" and thus "members (or 'peoples') of the other nations," i.e., other than *the* nation (or 'people') Israel.

43. Sanders, *Paul, the Law*, 156 (emphasis his). Posing the question in a slightly different way, Boyarin, *A Radical Jew*, 52, observes: "What was *wrong* with Jewish culture in Paul's eyes that necessitated a radical reform? And what in the culture provided the grounds for making that critique? The culture itself was in tension with itself, characterized both by narrow ethnocentrism and universalist monotheism."

Judaism."⁴⁴ For Sanders, Paul's problem remains *with* or *in* Judaism as a system that does not offer salvation in Jesus Christ. But does it not do so? Is it not precisely *within* Judaism where Paul as well as all of the other Jewish and Judean believers in Jesus Christ understood themselves to find him? Did not Paul persecute (i.e., seek to discipline) a group *within* Judaism for failing to exemplify Jewish values according to *his* Jewish group's terms, and then later, was it not instead this persecuted group's values that he upheld to be the most representative *of Judaism*—Judaism as it should and will be when the end of the ages has arrived, having now—from his group's perspective, conceptualized in specifically Jewish communal terms—already dawned? Is it not *Judaism's* ideals as represented in Judaism's Scriptures to which he appeals in order that his addressees will "hear Torah" aright (Gal 4:21), that is, according to Paul's interpretation? Was he not disciplined *as a Jew* by his fellow Jews because his activities were deemed by them, and him, to be undertaken *within* Judaism?

Interestingly, Sanders argues as much when discussing Paul's thirty-nine lashings five times as evidence that Paul remained within the orbit of synagogue authority, for receipt of this disciplinary action logically implies Paul's continued presence in synagogues.⁴⁵ This fact involves voluntarily yielding to the jurisdiction of local Jewish authorities who would not be able to wield such authority over *former* Jews, those who have chosen to leave the community and the practice of Judaism. Reaching across Jewish communal lines to discipline those outside the community would run afoul of prevailing Roman conventions.

COMPARING VIEWS OF JUDAISM FOR *NON-JEWS (GENTILES)* VERSUS FOR *EVERYONE*

[132] I do not wish to downplay the many innovative developments in Pauline scholarship, as a result of which many advances in the study of Paul as well as Judaism have been made (for which I am deeply grateful), and certainly not the contribution of Sanders or Dunn or any of the other scholars whom my discussion engages, and from whom I have learned much. At the same time, I would like to focus attention on a few issues that seem to

---

44. Sanders, *Paul and Palestinian Judaism*, 1 (emphasis added).

45. Sanders, *Paul, the Law*, 192, interestingly enough, in this later work (although without engaging the earlier contrary viewpoint he expressed), writes of Paul as still attending synagogue, that is, as Jewish in socially measurable terms, and argues that Paul and all of the parties, including his non-Jewish addressees as well as those who opposed Paul's work, understood the "Christian movement" they were involved in to be within "the bounds of Judaism. *Punishment implies inclusion*" (emphasis his).

remain unaddressed or, better, confusing in a way that obstructs the gains that might be made in the direction of re-reading Paul within the framework of the Judaism (or Judaisms) of his time. My aim is to prod the Pauline interpretive community to paradigmatic change. To begin this process, let us look a little closer at what Sanders wrote.

Sanders compared "how *one* gains righteousness" in Paul's religious system to that of so-called Palestinian Judaism.[46] He found that the Paul he constructed did not share many of the values of the Jewish systems to which Sanders compared him. Besides approaching Paul as outside Judaism, this is a decisive move that continues to reverberate not only in the work of those who constitute the New Perspective and its variations, but in the work of those who oppose it too, in that he seeks to measure how *one* gains righteousness in these two systems.

That approach poses the topic in universal terms: for *every*one. However, this formulation does not exemplify how either Paul or the other Jewish groups approached social reality, which for them consisted of Jews and non-Jews, who were understood to stand in a different relationship to God and to each other from birth (cf. Gal 2:15; 1 Cor 7:17–24; Rom 3:29–30).[47] The question requires a more precise formulation: How does [133] *one not born Jewish* gain equal standing among *the righteous ones* (i.e., among those who call themselves Israelites, Jews, children of Abraham, people of God)?

Sanders's attempt to compare the rabbis to Paul in soteriological terms is problematic for several reasons. The construal is predicated on later Christian ways of framing that which is to be discovered and compared; namely, focused upon salvation, as if that was the self-evident concern of the rabbis in the same way that it was of later Christians. At the same time, that was a reasonable way to approach the topic, because Sanders sought to inform Christians that the rabbis were not teaching a works-righteous approach to salvation in the way that Christians had attributed that to them. Even so, to pose the matter in the universal terms of "when a man . . ." subverts the potential for the comparison. The rabbis were seldom asking about the

---

46. Sanders, *Paul and Palestinian Judaism*, 12 (emphasis added).

47. For recent discussions of the problems with the way Paul's voice has been understood in universalizing terms, often with Jewish particularism as its foil, and offering more positive terms for understanding Paul's relationship with Judaism, see e.g., Runesson, "Particularistic Judaism and Universalistic Christianity?"; Ehrensperger, *That We May Be Mutually Encouraged*; Ehrensperger, "The Question(s) of Gender"; Buell and Johnson Hodge, "The Politics of Interpretation"; Eisenbaum, "Paul, Polemics, and the Problem of Essentialism"; Campbell, "Perceptions of Compatibility between Christianity and Judaism in Pauline Interpretation"; Campbell, *Paul and the Creation of Christian Identity*; Johnson Hodge, *If Sons, Then Heirs*; Johnson Hodge, "Apostle to the Gentiles"; Tucker, *You Belong to Christ*; Lee, *Paul and the Politics of Difference*.

rescue of those from the nations, and Paul was almost always writing about just that particular categorical case.[48] The question, to the degree that male circumcision is central to the discussion, should be either, "when a *Jewish* man," or in this case, since it is to be compared to the "when a non-Jewish man" context of Paul's rhetoric, "how does a *non-Jewish* man gain standing among the righteous ones." Naturally, apart from circumcision, the implications apply to women as well as men.[49]

When Sanders does look specifically at the question of the inclusion of *non-Jews* as righteous ones, both in this age and in the age to come, he readily admits that unlike the literature addressing the members of the covenant from which he develops the notion of covenantal nomism, "the Gentiles are dealt with only sporadically, . . . and different Rabbis had different opinions about their destiny."[50] Recognition of this fact should profoundly alter the interpretive landscape for comparing Paul and Judaism.[51] That move is further accentuated if one attends to Second Temple Jewish literature rather than the rabbis.[52]

Consider Josephus's account of the two very different opinions about how the non-Jewish King Izates should proceed in the present age to worship God and express pious adherence to a Jewish (Judean) way of life, either by becoming circumcised or not. Contrary opinions were espoused by two different Jewish informants, Ananias and Eleazer, and, interestingly enough, within a Diaspora setting during Paul's period (*Ant.* 20.17–96). Upon his arrival, Eleazer, a Jew from Galilee (and apparently a Pharisee), was quick to inform Izates that if he wished to respect the Torah that he was reading for guidance, he should do what was commanded therein (although this is not self-evidently the case for a non-Israelite/non-Jew, and ironically may represent universalizing to "a Jewish man" universal!); namely, undertake circumcision. Previous to this, Ananias, a Jew identified as a merchant who was already present at the king's court and who had responded to Izates's similar deduction that he had to undertake circumcision to become a Jew "completely," not only emphatically opposed the circumcision of Izates, he proposed that Izates's resolve to practice a Jewish way of life completely apart from ethnic conversion represented a way of worshiping God that was more highly valued than circumcision, given his present situation

---

48. Sanders, *Paul and Palestinian Judaism*, 75.

49. Although I have not dealt with gender issues in this essay, for a helpful reconsideration of this matter from a similar perspective, see Ehrensperger, "The Question(s) of Gender."

50. Sanders, *Paul and Palestinian Judaism*, 207.

51. Cf. Gaston, *Paul and the Torah*, 23.

52. See Donaldson, *Judaism and the Gentiles*.

(20.38–42). I have not noticed any secondary source argue that Ananias's teaching against the circumcision of Izates represents a religious viewpoint arising from outside of Judaism or from a "former" Jew, one who no longer observed Torah, or that Eleazer's teaching was outside the bounds of Judaism either, even though Torah does not state that non-Jews should become circumcised if wishing to be instructed by Torah. Rather, the conceptualizations are stretched to encompass the breadth of Jewish [134] views that just such an incident makes necessary.[53] Josephus and his interpreters treat both Ananias and Eleazer as Jews who espoused different points of view on the role of circumcision for conversion, as well as on how God should be properly worshipped by a non-Jew. Both drew their interpretations from Jewish Scripture and tradition, and both did so to address the case of this particular non-Jew, who happened to also be the king of a non-Jewish nation. Both found something wrong with the solution proposed by the other. In other words, it is the interpreter's definitions of Judaism that are challenged by this case: one must find a way to explain this example *within* the boundaries of Judaism rather than suppose that one or the other participant stood *outside* of it, or found something wrong *with* or *in* Judaism itself.

Unfortunately, to date the distinction between a proposition discussing righteous standing with God for Jews and one discussing the topic for non-Jews continues to be obscured by the manner in which the issues are posed. Since this is a subject about which Paul specifically writes and around which a variety of Jewish views can be expected to emerge, delineating this distinction should be central to all such "Paul and Judaism" debates.

THE ROLE OF ETHNIC DISTINCTION IN PAUL'S ARGUMENTATION

If Paul's rhetoric does not collapse the ethnic boundary defining Jew and non-Jew, then why do interpreters not maintain that difference when seeking to compare Paul and other Jewish voices on any given issue? Thus, we do not read of "Paul against Torah-observance *for non-Jews* (as if they were under Torah on the same terms as are Jews)," but of "Paul against Torah-observance," implying, "Paul against Torah-observance *for all humankind*." The normal shorthand for calling up this paradigmatic

53. As a case in point, the note to this comment in the Loeb volume (Josephus, *Ant.* 20), edited and translated by Louis Feldman (p. 22 n. a), discusses (although rejects) a possible rabbinic parallel (no less!) wherein Rabbi Joshua argues in Yebam. 46a that circumcision was not required for a convert, just baptism, according to Bamberger and Klausner. A logical reason for this teaching by a Jew and within Judaism is offered: the policy of caution and the exception for circumstances where life would be endangered.

understanding of that for which Paul stands is "Paul's *Law-free* gospel." That phrase is so common as to seem unremarkable, beyond requiring defense. But should that be the case?

If we were to limit comparisons to those within the realm of Paul's rhetorical (i.e., argumentative) concerns, that is, to the matter of righteous standing for *non-Jews*, we would find that other Jewish sources also do [135] not believe that non-Jews are obliged to observe Torah on the same terms as Jews.[54] We would find differences emerge around the question of the standing of non-Jewish people within the community of the people of God *in the present age*. That would be different still than a discussion about the age to come, because according to some Jewish voices the righteous non-Jew can gain equal or even higher standing then (Isa 66:18–20; Zeph 3:9; Zech 2:15; Tobit 13:11; 14:5–6; cf. t. Sanhedrin 13.2; b. Megilla 13a). Are such views to be classified as "Law-free"? Or are they qualified as related specifically to

---

54. See Donaldson, *Paul and the Gentiles*, 60–74, for discussion of various expectations for non-Jews, including a natural-law non-Jew who turns from idolatry but is not identified with circumcision and other special laws for Israelites, e.g., observing dietary customs; righteous gentiles; and eschatological pilgrimage scenarios. Examples include Josephus, *Ant.* 20.41 (34–48); Philo, *QE* 2.2; *Moses* 2.4; *Abraham* 3–6, 60–61; *Virtues* 102, 181–82, 212–19; *Spec. Laws* 1.51; 2.42–48; 4.178; Jos. Asen.; t. Sanh. 13.2. Cf. Fredriksen, "Judaism, the Circumcision of Gentiles, and Apocalyptic Hope"; Wyschogrod, *Abraham's Promise*, 162–63, 190–95.

At the same time, as the case for Ananias, one of the teachers of Izates, exemplifies—in contrast to the other teacher, Eleazer, who upholds that unless he is circumcised the Torah will not benefit him—there are Jews who upheld that members of the nations are called to Torah apart from becoming Jews (*Ant.* 20.34–48). Even the outrage expressed by Eleazer arguably demonstrates that he views Izates breaking the very laws he reads in Scripture, if he remains uncircumcised, although Izates is at this point a non-Jew reader. Both cases, however, may demonstrate that Izates is not simply a non-Jew, but of a special category, a non-Jew who seeks to worship the God of the Jews, and thus, that he is obliged to a different level of Torah adherence. See Nanos, "The Question of Conceptualization." The view that gentiles are in some way obligated to Torah observance is also expressed in a few rabbinic texts, although a minority view; e.g., Mek. R. Yis. [Bahodesh 1], on Exod 19:2; Sipra to Lev 18:1–5; Hirshman, "Rabbinic Universalism in the Second and Third Centuries," and aspects of this notion are implicit in the very idea of the Apostolic Decree of Acts 15, and the Noahide Commandments (t. 'Abod. Zar. 8.4). Zetterholm, "Paul and the Missing Messiah," applies the tension between these views to an interpretation of Paul, with Paul taking the side of those who uphold that Torah belongs only to Israel; hence, non-Jews in Christ are taught not to seek to observe it as if Jews, in contrast to other Christ-following Jews who are teaching non-Jews in Christ to observe Torah, because gentiles too are under obligation to Torah. See also Thiessen, *Contesting Conversion*, for Jews and groups who oppose the very notion of converting non-Jews into Jews for various reasons, which differentiates them from the rival Jews and Jewish groups that Paul's rhetoric suggests that he opposed, who apparently promoted proselyte conversion for the non-Jews he addressed in Galatia, for example; also Thiessen, *Paul and the Gentile Problem*.

non-Jews, those not by definition under Torah on the same terms as Jews, and thus, not to be universalized to "everyone"?

[136] Moreover, Paul's argument is *time* specific—*chronometrical*, a term coined to differentiate what was at dispute in a way that will hopefully avoid the usual problem of essentializing of the issues.[55] We do well to approach the topic without assuming a priori that other Jews and groups were against the very notion of non-Jews being included among the people of God *when the age to come arrives*, including them remaining non-Jews. What more likely set apart Paul's position was the claim that the awaited age *had arrived* in the midst of the present age. Because Paul's Jewish coalition claims that the end of the ages has *already* dawned, it follows that the re-identification of non-Jews takes place *now*, on the *awaited-age* terms. That proposition is unique to the Christ-following Jewish groups.[56] It revolves around a different answer to the question, "What time *is* it now?" which dictates a different answer to the follow-up question, "What policies and behavioral norms are *appropriate* now?" The answers for Paul's groups are based on a different conviction about the meaning of Jesus Christ, and in particular, about the claim that God has already raised him from the grave. It is on *this* matter, on what is appropriate *chronometrically* regarding non-Jews turning to Judaism's God, that we can more accurately seek to compare Paul's Judaism with other Judaisms.

We thus encounter a familiar difference arising between Jewish groups, one that turns around eschatological convictions. The issue is not *whether*

---

55. "Chronometrical" is intended to offer a concise way to communicate the idea that Paul's gospel proposition and the conflicts it often engendered revolved around a time-oriented claim that the end of the ages had begun in the midst of the present age. While other Jews might agree in principle with the idea that a day might come when members from the rest of the nations will join alongside Israel in worship of the One God (and behave according to the standards of righteousness and justice and mercy laid out in Torah even if not technically under Torah since not becoming Jews/Israel), nevertheless these Jews might still dispute the claim that it has arrived (even the claim that it had merely begun/dawned). This might help undermine the notion that this kind of theological position or change of behavior is somehow essentially not Jewish but uniquely "Christian," as well as superior, and representative of the end of Judaism, or its replacement, and so on. Rather, the issue was whether this kind of time-based claim and associated behavioral changes were appropriate "now." In a similar direction, although not using the term chronometrical, see Fredriksen, "The Question of Worship," esp. 185–89.

56. Depending on how one reads Acts and Paul, it is a propositional truth shared by the other apostles of this movement; cf. Nanos, "Intruding 'Spies' and 'Pseudo-brethren'"; Nanos, "What Was at Stake in Peter's 'Eating with Gentiles' at Antioch?" Exceptions that appear to prove the rule among other Jewish groups include the Izates story, just discussed, and may be implied in Philo's criticism of some Jews in Alexandria (*Migration* 92).

the Torah obtains, but *how* it functions in the present age for non-Jews, in contrast to Jews. Differences of opinion are contested between these groups over where humankind is *presently* standing on God's timeline, and thus, about what kind of behavior is appropriate *today*, and more importantly, in the case of Christ-following groups, over what to do *now* about the identity of the non-Jews who have turned to Christ. That is why Paul was so opposed to these non-Jews undertaking to become Jews, to become members of Israel, to become circumcised—because if the age to come has arrived, then they join alongside of Israel to worship the One God of all humankind, as expected on *that day* (see below for discussion of how Paul draws from the *Shema* to make this case).[57] It was because of different answers to these kinds of questions from the ones offered by those who controlled the Jerusalem Temple that the Dead Sea Scrolls community of the Righteous Teacher apparently withdrew from the temple worship of its time.[58] It was because of a different and controversial answer to the question of what God was doing among the nations that the Christ-following Jewish groups suffered for upholding that non-Jews were full and equal members of the righteous ones apart from proselyte conversion. Neither group opposed Torah-observance, but they disagreed with the way that other Jewish groups interpreted how Torah was to be observed, given the *present* circumstances.[59]

[137] Here is a simple suggestion. To be more faithful to the contextual usage of Paul's language, the interpreter of Paul's rhetoric should add, "for *non-Jews*" as well as "*followers of* (or: *believers in*) *Jesus Christ*" to the end of virtually every sentence in his letters about these matters, certainly so when he is specifically addressing non-Jews within them.[60] As historical critics,

---

57. See Nanos, *Mystery of Romans*, 179–92; Nanos, "Paul and the Jewish Tradition"; and the discussion below of Paul's development of the *Shema*.

58. Cf. Ps 37:33; 4QMMT C 25–32; 4QpPs^a 1–10 iv 7–9; 1 QpHab 8:10–13; 11:2–8; 1 Macc 10:21.

59. Cf. Dunn, "Echoes of Intra-Jewish Polemic in Paul's Letter to the Galatians," 467. It is interesting to note the subtle shifts in Dunn's language that betray the way that Jewish groups other than Christ-following ones, such as those exemplified by the Dead Sea Scroll community's conflicts with other Jewish groups, are portrayed. Theirs revolve around different views of how *to properly interpret* Torah on the matter at hand ("the *correct* and only *legitimate* enactment of what the Torah laid down at these points"), but when the dispute is within groups of Christ-following Jews or between them and other Jewish groups, the terms change to *how much* Torah *applies* ("the *extent* and *detail* of Torah obligation"; emphases added). If Paul was practicing his faith in Christ within Judaism, however, we would expect him to argue that his position exemplifies the ideals of Torah in contrast to other interpretations no less than do the writers of the Dead Sea Scrolls, or the authors of any other Jewish literature of his time.

60. This is a major topic in contemporary Pauline studies. Many interpreters now highlight that in his letters—including the most important ones bearing on these topics,

why not keep the specificity of the case before us? A question like "Why did Paul oppose circumcision?" misses the point. It implies that he opposed it in principle for *all* Christ-followers, and thus for Jews as well as for non-Jews. It leads to hermeneutical applications of supposed universal values for *everyone*. Admittedly cumbersome, one should ask instead, "Why did Paul oppose the circumcision of (adult male)[61] *non-Jew followers of Jesus Christ*?" Then theological propositions that appeal to Paul's language have a better chance of reflecting Paul's contextual perspective, and likewise each hermeneutical application can better reflect the tension between what he meant and what it might mean for the later interpreter.[62]

There is no reason to believe that Paul opposed circumcision of children born to Jewish parents, and good reason to suppose that he did not.[63]

---

like Galatians and Romans—Paul's rhetoric targets the encoded or implied audience as non-Jew Christ-followers. I maintain not only that Paul is targeting non-Jews, but that they are within Jewish synagogue subgroup assemblies (*Mystery of Romans*, esp. 75–84, and *Irony of Galatians*, esp. 75–85). Some suppose that the presence of Jews in these assemblies means that Paul must be directly addressing both Jews and non-Jews. Others maintain that this means there were only non-Jews in the assemblies addressed. In my view, however, targeting non-Jews meant neither that there were no Jews present in the assemblies, nor that, if both were present that he had to target both. Paul was setting these non-Jews straight at least in part for the benefit of the Jews present in these subgroups (as well as for those of the larger Jewish communities impacted by the behavior of these subgroups). The idea that Paul designed his rhetoric (in Romans and Galatians, for example) to target the non-Jews also does not mean he did not consider, while creating them, how it would be read or heard by the Jews present, or even by those simply impacted by it, whether directly or indirectly, including by way of rumors heard or explanations offered for any changes observed in the behavior of these non-Jews.

61. For at least some discussions, this adds another useful element of specificity.

62. Cf. Stendahl, *Paul among Jews and Gentiles*, 35–36, 74–75, 125, for the programmatic call to never ask merely "What does it mean?" without adding "... to whom?"; Stendahl, "Biblical Theology, Contemporary."

63. Many suppose that in Rom 2:25–29, Paul dismisses the role of bodily circumcision for Jews. But this language as well as that in chapter 3 represent diatribe, and the questions that follow immediately in 3:1 indicate that Paul is here writing to non-Jews about how Jews should behave in view of their circumcision, with circumcised hearts as well as bodies. If they do not, they fail to represent the real meaning of the circumcision of their bodies. The point is not that non-Jews become Jews, as if they somehow gain the real objective for which Jews are circumcised. And they do not become "true" or "spiritual" Jews; they remain non-Jews. Only Jews are circumcised in order to indicate in their bodies the dedication to God of their whole person, to living according to the precepts God has given for right living, and not merely to teaching them to others. Only they can become in that sense "true" or "spiritual" Jews. That identity is particular to Jews, to those of the nation Israel, whose dedication to the One God includes circumcised bodies as well as it should involve circumcised hearts, unlike non-Jews, non-Israelites, which the addressees remain. Their non-Jewish hearts, however, can be "like" the circumcised hearts of Jews (the circumcised) directed toward God, and

And there is no reason to suppose that he opposed circumcision of [138] non-Jews who were not Christ-followers. At many points the logic of his position suggests that Jewish believers in Christ, including Paul, observed his instruction to remain in the state in which they were called, keeping the commandments of God (1 Cor 7:17–24), which, for a Jewish person, involved guarding the whole Torah, by Paul's own admission (Gal 2:15; 5:3; 6:13; discussion below). And it makes sense to suppose that Paul, like the Christ-following Jews described by James in Acts 21, would be zealous in his observation of halakhic behavior, and take the steps necessary to demonstrate this fact and dispel any rumors that he did not do so. The Luke that Paul presents, who undertakes a Nazarite vow in the temple, which involved a burnt offering (Acts 21:19–26), appears to signify a later interpreter presenting Paul similarly on this matter.

If Paul does not observe Torah, he leaves himself open to the easiest objection to his proposition that Jesus is the Christ that the very Jews he seeks to convince would be expected to level, an objection which has been repeated ever since the construction of Paul and Paulinism as Torah-free was invented.[64] If Paul did not himself represent the highest ideals of the Judaism that maintained the hope of just such a day, how could he expect to convince Jews, much less non-Jews, of the propositional claim that the awaited restoration of Israel and of the rest of the nations (of creation itself) had begun with the resurrection of Jesus?

Pursuing clarification of Paul's teaching and the implications for Jews is not the same task as investigating the meaning of Paul's rhetoric for *non-Jews*, the members of the nations other than Israel whom he directly addresses.[65] For example, note that in Gal 5:11, Paul does not argue that he is persecuted for failure to observe Torah, for failing [139] to keep a Jewish diet or Sabbath or uphold circumcision for Jews, but specifically for the policy of not teaching non-Jewish Christ-followers to become proselytes, that is, to

---

living right, not merely professing the precepts of right living (Rom 12:1–2); see Nanos, "Paul's Non-Jews Do Not Become 'Jews,' But Do They Become 'Jewish'?"

64. Cf. Davies, *Paul and Rabbinic Judaism*, 73–74.

65. Boyarin, *A Radical Jew*, 17, evaluates Paul's critique of Judaism as dissatisfaction with Jewish difference: "the quintessentially 'different' people for Paul were Jews and women." Leaving aside the topic of women, as a "Jew from birth" (Gal 2:14), which Paul claimed to be, the "different" should be expected to be non-Jews, and indeed Paul's rhetoric addresses how non-Jews, who are different from Jews/Israelites, now fit into God's universal plan for humanity (the rest of the nations) by way of Israel's service and Messiah. I think Boyarin's point is correct, however, with regard to the constructed Paul of traditional Paulinism, which has been populated by non-Jew Christians for whom the Jew is the different other. But should that be expected to be Paul's vantage point?

become circumcised. Note that his letters do not concern themselves with answering other charges.

Many point to the implications of 1 Cor 9:19–23 to undermine the proposition of a Torah-observant Paul, as discussed above, but I understand Paul to be expressing *a rhetorical strategy*, not a change of halakhic behavior.[66] As noted, the consensus interpretation understands Paul's "becoming like" the different parties to signify "mimicking" each, not actually becoming like them in the sense of sharing their convictional bases for the behavior. Instead, he merely imitates their cultural conventions temporarily in order to seek to gain them to an entirely different set of convictions that will, if accepted, lead them to abandon the continued practice of those conventions thereafter—even though he appeared to them to practice these conventions while holding to the convictions he proposed. That represents a deceptive strategy, pretending to share propositional values in order to persuade others away from those values by way of *behavioral adaptability*. But I propose that Paul's appeal to a policy of "becoming like" signifies his *rhetorical adaptability*, a tactic of "arguing from the premises" of each different interest group to bring them to conclusions about the gospel that they might not have otherwise considered relevant for themselves.[67]

When seeking to win Jews to the message of good in Christ, Paul argues from Jewish premises; that is easy enough for him to do, because he shares them. He argues from Law-based premises when among those "under Law," a phrase that can be variously understood. When Paul mentions causing himself to become like the "lawless" or "sinner" (ἄνομος), often translated "without Law," it is no more likely that he means he abandons

---

66. For full discussion, see Nanos, "Paul's Relationship to Torah in Light of His Strategy 'to Become Everything to Everyone' (1 Corinthians 9:19–23)"; Nanos, "Was Paul a 'Liar' for the Gospel?"

67. Understanding Paul to signify rhetorical conduct to various degrees (although not proposing that Paul maintained Torah-observant behavior, or that he specifically is communicating that he appealed to their various argumentative premises), see Chadwick, "'All Things to All Men' (1 Cor. IX.22)"; Chadwick, "St. Paul and Philo of Alexandria," 297–98; Longenecker, *Paul, Apostle of Liberty*, 244; Glad, *Paul and Philodemus*, esp. 1, 240, 273, 327; Johnson Hodge, "If Sons, Then Heirs," 124–25. Mitchell, "Pauline Accommodation and 'Condescension' (συγκατάβασις)," 197–214, traces some language in the church fathers, esp. Chrysostom and Origin, that points in this direction, although for them this included changing conduct too. Fee grants that Paul *may* have accommodated the content of the message for different audiences but concludes that 1 Cor 9:19–23 itself is about conduct, not content (*First Epistle to the Corinthians*, 428 n. 36; and 432–33). Given holds that Paul's modus operandi was to accommodate rhetorically in both content and conduct (e.g., *Paul's True Rhetoric*, 36–37 and 97), but his discussion of 1 Cor 9:19–23 focuses almost exclusively on conduct and reflects the consensus interpretation (103–15). See additional discussion below.

halakhic behavior or acts like a sinner than it is that Jesus behaved [140] like a prostitute or tax-collector to relate to them.⁶⁸ Paul is a self-confessed slave to righteous living. Communicating the message of Christ to sinners does not entail behaving sinfully in order to do so, but quite the contrary: it behooves one seeking to influence them to the message of good in Christ, to membership among the righteous ones of God, and to righteous lifestyles, to behave righteously as a matter of conviction, and *at all times among everyone*.

Paul is not here admitting to compromising Jewish behavioral practices when among non-Jews, but explaining how he relates the message of Christ to them on their own terms. In the midst of his discourse throughout chapters 8–10, wherein he explains why the Christ-followers in Corinth cannot eat idol food, Paul relates his strategy toward non-Christ-followers in 9:19-23. Just as he explains to the "knowledgeable" in Corinth why they must respect the sensibilities of the "weak" or "impaired" (ἀσθενής), and not eat according to their theoretical "rights," his argument nevertheless aims to convince them not to exercise those rights.⁶⁹ They cannot eat at the table of the Lord and the table of daemons; they cannot eat food that they know to be idol food, whether from the market, or at someone's home.

Although Paul solicits the support of Scriptural precedent, he does not proceed as he would if a Jew asked him about eating idol food. He does not simply cite Torah against eating idol food to make this case; at least not initially. Rather, he argues from their own worldview as Christ-following non-Jews. He begins his argument in terms of their own premises, but he drives them to a very different conclusion than they have otherwise arrived at on their own: they must flee from anything that can be understood to represent idolatry.⁷⁰

Paul does not act like the knowledgeable, but he *argues* in a way that they might. In that sense he "causes himself to become like" the knowledgeable, to convince them to become like himself, one who regards idol

---

68. See also Rudolph, *A Jew to the Jews*.

69. For full discussion, see Nanos, "Why the 'Weak' in 1 Corinthians 8–10 Were Not Christ-believers"; Nanos, "The Polytheist Identity"; see also Land, "'We Put No Stumbling Block in Anyone's Path.'"

70. Apparently Paul did not anticipate that former polytheists would reason that since they no longer believed idols represented gods, that there was no reason to abstain from eating food that was being or had been offered to them, regarding it to be profane, perhaps even that doing so with indifference demonstrated the strength of their new convictions. Although Jews had long ago declared that idols did not represent real gods, this nevertheless was accompanied by the very different conclusion that anything associated with idolatry is by definition out of bounds, and that eating idol food would instead show their lack of conviction; see Nanos, "The Polytheist Identity."

[141] food as anathema.[71] This approach is exemplified in Acts 17:16–34, where Luke portrays Paul appealing to a statue (idol) to the Unknown God in order to make his case to polytheists, even though Paul did not believe that such statues should be made. In stark contrast to the rhetorical behavior described in verses 1–3 when Paul came into a synagogue and began from the shared premises of the Scripture and the reign of the One God to convince Jews about Jesus as Messiah, his behavior among the non-Jew philosophers in Athens is described in terms of rhetorically adapting to non-Jew philosophers. He "became like" a polytheist to make his point to polytheists, but in no way did he become a polytheist or practice idolatry to do so. Luke's Paul appeals to the logic of their own premises to seek to bring them to a very different conclusion than they have drawn. In the case of seeking to persuade non-Jews of the message of good in Jesus Christ, Paul must sacrifice his "right" to assert the perspective of Jewish Scriptures and traditions about the revelation of the One God as if self-evident.[72] Such

---

71. Pace Given, *Paul's True Rhetoric*, 105–17. Although I appreciate the argument against interpretations that seek to protect Paul's integrity, on 111, after he concludes that Paul's "becoming like" signifies eating or otherwise behaving like each of the groups (in concert with the prevailing views), nevertheless, Given's interpretation does not represent "the realm of being" rather than "that of seeming" anymore than do the viewpoints he criticizes (Glad in particular). For Given imagines only the behavior of mimicking: not subscribing to the philosophical basis of the various behaviors, not *being* like them, but merely *seeming* to be like them. On 112, Given uses "appearing as" synonymously with "becoming like." At the same time, I do not think that Given's reading need be far from the one I propose, if dropping *acting* like but keeping *speaking* like, for on 117 he concludes that Paul shapes his "insinuative rhetorical strategy similar to that imagined by Luke with respect to Jews and Gentiles."

72. Although on this interpretation Paul is still involved in a persuasive enterprise, and thus does not necessarily actually believe in the premises that he adopts as the basis for initiating arguments, but merely seeks to manipulate the listener by beginning from their own premises, such rhetorical behavior does not require the compromise of integrity that the traditional interpretation of his change of behavioral conduct necessitates. Philosophical and religious arguments between people and groups approaching a topic with different points of view are understood by each to proceed by way of the tactic of beginning from the opposition's presuppositions and premises in order to undermine their conclusions, and lead them to one's own. There was a lively debate stretching back to Antisthenes about whether Odysseus should be interpreted along this line, as exemplifying a *polytrope*, one who adapted his figures of speech to his various audiences, such as the Stoics and Cynics sought to do, rather than as an unethical chameleon who changed his behavior in a way that compromised his moral character. The details are discussed in Nanos, "Paul's Relationship to Torah in Light of His Strategy 'to Become Everything to Everyone' (1 Corinthians 9:19–23)." See Stanford, *The Ulysses Theme*, 90–101; Caizzi, ed., *Antisthenis Fragmenta*, 24–28, 43–44. For application to Paul, although not to the same conclusion I am drawing, see Malherbe, *Paul and the Popular Philosophers*, 91–119; Glad, *Paul and Philodemus*, 21–22, 26, 28–29, 251, 272–73. For an in-depth comparative analysis of Paul's rhetorical style, especially in conversation

rhetorical adaptability was to be expected of a philosopher attempting to win adherents, just as it would be, *mutatis mutandis*, of a Jew seeking to win his fellow Jews to new claims about the meaning of current events precisely by appealing to Scripture.

PAUL'S JUDAISM

Let us look at how Paul used the term Ἰουδαϊσμός (Judaism/a Jewish way [of living]) to see if my proposition can be sustained in that context. Paul uses this [142] terminology only two times, and both cases are in Gal 1:13–14. He writes that his addressees have heard of "my former behavior in Judaism" (τὴν ἐμὴν ἀναστροφήν ποτε ἐν τῷ Ἰουδαϊσμῷ) in verse 13, which could be translated as, "my former behavior in the Jewish way of living," or "my former practice of Judaism/of the Jewish way of living."[73] The clause appears in the midst of a sentence describing a certain feature of his former way of living Jewishly with which his addressees are presumed to be familiar. That way of living involved specifically that he "was persecuting [ἐδίωκον]" the Jewish subgroup communities of believers in Jesus Christ with the intent of "destroying/ruining [ἐπόρθουν]" them, to which we will return. In further describing that time, Paul writes in verse 14 that back then he "was advancing in Judaism (or: the Jewish way of living) [according to his former behavior therein] beyond many of my contemporaries in my ethnic group" (προέκοπτον ἐν τῷ Ἰουδαϊσμῷ ὑπὲρ πολλοὺς συνηλικιώτας ἐν τῷ γένει μου), that is, "I was being a much greater zealot (or: much more jealous) [than they were] for the traditions of my fathers" (περισσοτέρως ζηλωτὴς ὑπάρχων τῶν πατρικῶν μου παραδόσεων). Note that Paul writes of his relationship to the *traditions* in personal as well as comparative terms, as "of *my* fathers," and not simply "of *the* fathers." Does Paul betray here that his identity continues to be bound up with the particular interpretive tradition that he still considers himself to represent, albeit in some way that no longer enjoys the approval or at least admiration that he formerly received from them? If so, then is what is "former" his harmful behavior toward the Christ-followers, and also that he was so much more zealous about that, rather than his practice of Pharisaic Judaism, which continues, whatever differences might obtain, to define his way of practicing a Jewish way of life?

Interpreters traditionally have understood Paul to be describing himself as presently no longer living in Judaism. Leaving aside the traditional

---

with the styles of Epictetus and Philodemus, see Robertson, *Paul's Letters and Contemporary Greco-Roman Literature.*

73. See ns. 3 and 4 for my use of *Judaism* and related terms.

problem of conceptualizing and naming this as Paul's *conversion* rather than, as is now widely recognized, his *calling*.[74] Paul's phrasing here continues to lead interpreters to portray Paul in terms of a binary contrast between being a Jew and practicing Judaism versus being a Christian and practicing Christianity, whatever terms might be used. But the language Paul uses here arguably describes *a certain way of living* in Judaism that no longer characterizes *the way he lives* in Judaism *now*. That is not to deny some change in social relations, which Paul signals. We might advance the discourse by thinking in terms of familial relationships that a person has simultaneously, but that can and do change. One may be born a son, a brother too, and later become a husband, and a father too. It makes little sense to imagine that the new roles eliminate the other identifications and relationships. At any given time one or the other can be more salient, more important, more estranged, and so on, but they do not usually represent either/or options in the way that Paul's change of convictions and affiliations has been conceptualized, and, for that matter, similar decisions by other Jews of his time to move between or within other Jewish groups or Judaisms.[75]

Paul's former way of living involved a more zealous approach than his fellow subgroup members apparently pursued to protecting "the traditions of my fathers," a catch-phrase almost certainly denoting Pharisaic Judaism.[76] It may be the case, although it is not certain, that the specific area in which his zeal for the traditions of the fathers was demonstrated to be greater than his peers was in his taking action against what he considered to be a threat posed by the Christ-following Jewish subgroups. This could imply that he has moved within Pharisaism from a group of Pharisees that approved of his zeal to seek to destroy these groups of Christ-followers to a group of Pharisees[77] (or a coalition of groups [143] that included Pharisees)

74. Since at least Stendahl, *Paul among Jews and Gentiles*, 7–23, made the case, Paul's phrasing has been understood to echo the language in Isaiah and Jeremiah's direct callings by God to particular service in spite of the resistance they encounter thereafter from their peers (Isa 49:1; Jer 1:5, 7).

75. Paul's language is analogous to a Christian speaking of their *former way of living as a Christian*, when remaining a Christian, but of a different kind. This language is then used to represent, e.g., moving between denominations, or faith traditions such as from Catholic to Protestant or vice versa, or between subgroups of a denomination, such as to or from Charismatic or some other subgroup identity within a larger denominational body, or to a different set of responsibilities, or to different convictions about or degrees of commitment to certain matters, and so on—*within Christianity*.

76. Josephus, *Ant.* 13.297, 408; 17.41; cf. Baumgarten, "The Pharisaic Paradosis." Paul refers to himself explicitly as a Pharisee in another context where he also mentions his zeal to persecute the Christ-followers (Phil 3:5–6).

77. According to Acts 15:5, there were Christ-followers who belonged to the sect of the Pharisees, and Paul is portrayed as affiliated with Pharisaism in his proclamations

that now expressed the aspirations of them. It might also suggest that these groups, whether Pharisaic per se or not, were understood to fall under a Pharisaic orbit of authority.

We should revisit whether it was "persecution" as usually envisaged in terms of physical violence and the like to which Paul was referring. His choice of terms could indicate discursive behavior. The rhetorical behavior could be in a legal sense of "accusing" or "prosecuting" or a more general sense of "arguing" or "declaiming."[78] In Pharisaic terms, to which Paul is

---

of Christ (23:6; 26:5). In Phil 3:5-6, this claim arguably aligns with the self-identity he still asserts to express that although advantageous in Jewish communal comparative terms, it does not make him better than those Christ-followers who cannot make the same claims to comparable status, which for them is not the problem of not being a Pharisee among Jews, but of not being a Jew at all. His self-deprecation appears to target cases where the non-Jews may be suffering marginality in Jewish communal terms for not having become proselytes, and thus to be paying for failure to substantiate their claims to full membership on the prevailing terms (Phil 3:3-11, esp. v. 5; Nanos, "Paul's Reversal"; "Paul's Polemic in Philippians 3"; "Out-Howling the Cynics"; cf. Gal 6:12-15; Nanos, *Irony of Galatians*, 226-33).

78. The use of "persecute" and cognates is problematic for several reasons, and we should consider using different language here. Persecution can connote anything from violence to innuendo, and it is generally a term used by the "victim" to express that what they are suffering is illegitimate. From the perspective of the one accused of persecuting, this behavior will more than likely be perceived and described in more positive terms, as just or deserved, representing "discipline," "punishment," "protecting interests," and so on. Paul is here, from hindsight, describing former behavior that he now judges to have been seriously wrong.

On a lexical level, the term translated "persecuted" is a form of διώκω, which usually refers "to pursuing," "chasing" or "chasing away," not necessarily to physical violence as usually envisaged (see LSJ entry; cf. the suggestive insight by Wendt, *At the Temple Gates*, 158 n. 43, who pursued different implications, but inspired me to return to my argument regarding the Pharisaic element in Paul's language to consider these additional implications). It can refer to "pursuing an argument" when used with regard to people. It could also indicate "to prosecute" or "to accuse" in a legal context, and still largely falls within the realm of verbal rather than physical activity per se (of course these can overlap, to be expected if, e.g., rights to assemble to uphold a certain policy are lost in a legal dispute). Perhaps the Christ-followers understood themselves to fall under the jurisdiction of Paul's particular Pharisaic group's authority in some way, which would not preclude that of the temple (cf. Acts 9:1-2), but might be more complicated in inter-group political terms than Acts 9 is usually read to indicate. Acts 23 and 26, also present the disputes about and with these Jewish groups in terms of legal, political, discursive dynamics, now against Paul, and Paul also speaks of his later situation in Gal 5:11, with διώκω, where it also could indicate being accused or prosecuted if not simply pursued in argument over his policy of not circumcising these non-Jews, and again, could indicate an intra-Pharisaic-type dispute, now from the other, and minority, position on the matter. Note that unlike the lists that include physical punishments in 2 Cor 11:23-33 (where διώκω does not appear), in Gal 1:13, 23, and 5:11, Paul does not disclose the nature of the διώκω, but it has to do with disputes over propositional claims, i.e., "proclaiming the faith," 1:23; not "still preaching circumcision," 5:11.

appealing, he could be indicating that he tried to *discredit* these groups through *argumentation* (perhaps through "precise" [i.e., Pharisaic] textual interpretation) and thereby to "ruin" or "destroy" them. That could involve undermining their confidence and reputation or even seeking to legally deny to them the conditions that made it possible for them to continue to assemble as groups. If so, and this would apply as well to the traditional sense of persecution, he sought to bring them into compliance if not conformity to his own present group's point of view, and if not membership then at least recognition of its authority on the matters in dispute.

However translated, it appears to be the case that Paul is making a comparative point, that he has moved from his particular Pharisaic group's appeal to the traditions of the fathers as the ultimate authority for interpreting the matter at issue to Christ-following Judaism's conviction that the ultimate authority on this matter derives from the revelation of Christ. It is less clear, but possible, that Paul now saw himself representing the subgroups of Christ-followers who still subscribed to Pharisaic principles, *mutatis mutandis*.[79] Whatever the case, Paul is not denying that he behaves Jewishly, that he practices Judaism or a Jewish way of life. We should seek to understand his arguments as expressions of Paul's Judaism following this change of conviction about the well-being of the followers of Christ. In his time, believing that Jesus was the Messiah and affiliating with other Jews who shared that conviction involved making a choice between different groups of Jews, but the choices then were *within* Judaism, they did not signify leaving the practice of a Jewish way of life.

Paul claims to have had a revelation that his peers have not experienced,[80] and I understand this to be the background for his dissociat-

---

The word ὑπερβολή, usually translated "violently," is used to express that he did so with "excess" (*LSJ*), which would not suggest a translation denoting physical violence if διώκω was not understood to indicate that. The normal sense of rhetorical behavior that is comparatively in "excess" or "immoderate" or even "hyperbolic" with respect to the matter at hand aligns with his claim in v. 14 to be *more zealous* than his peers within his own Pharisaic group (a group whose interpretive reputation is characterized to be "*precise* [ἀκριβής] about the ancestral traditions" [Josephus, *Ant.* 20.43; cf. *J.W.* 1.110; Acts 26:5], and quarreling over proper behavior based on their special interpretations is a trope throughout the Gospels).

The term translated "to destroy" is πορθέω, which here could connote "to ruin" in the discursive or legal ways (however intensely, even savagely) suggested by this reading of διώκω (*LSJ*).

79. Cf. Segal, *Paul the Convert*.

80. Elliott, "The Question of Politics," 217–22, in discussion with the work of Alan Segal and Paula Fredriksen, interprets Paul's vision as evidence of his apocalyptic as well as Pharisaic contexts, one in which it would be natural to have such visions of the resurrection of the righteous and of heavenly figures as divine agents, and to draw

ing statement that his good-news message and authority as an apostle (ambassador, envoy) are "not from human agency or agents, but from God" (Gal 1:1). In contrast to the prevailing views, I think it likely that his references to "humans" and the "flesh and blood" from whom he does not gain approval or seek advice (Gal 1:1, 10–12, 16), are not to the other apostles who knew Jesus personally, but to the specific group of Pharisees he had represented, from whom he had won great approval until he changed course following that revelation (1:13-16). Although he also expresses relative independence from the other apostles for many years, he makes this point to argue for their ultimate unanimity on the matters at hand, even though arrived at independently (1:17—2:10).[81] Hence, Paul is not indicating that he formerly lived in Judaism but no longer does so, but that he has changed the way he lives *within* Judaism, his social location relative to his former group and its approval, probably the particular Judaism to which he owes allegiance, that is, his former Pharisaic subgroup if not Pharisaism per se.[82] Behaving so as

---

ethical and political conclusions from the experience.

81. Wendt, *At the Temple Gates*, 146–89, argues that Paul was a "freelance expert."

82. The reference to the "flesh and blood" with whom he does not confer has traditionally been understood to refer to the apostles who knew Jesus in a human sense that Paul did not share, but that is unlikely in my view; rather, Paul believes they all work from shared grace and revelation (cf. 2:2, 7–8; 1 Cor 15:5–8). Although he arrived at his understanding without consulting the Jerusalem apostles, when he did go to them later, he admits he was seeking their approval (Gal 2:1–2). Thus, rather than a redundant reference to flesh and blood and the other apostles, I suggest they are two different parties he did not immediately consult: neither his former group of Pharisees, nor his new group leaders, the apostles in Jerusalem. In the first case, Paul is referring to not having conferred with the leaders of his Pharisaic group. Flesh and blood may refer to the traditions handed down among the Pharisees that are attributed to the fathers and constitute their own special group rulings, or perhaps may imply that the rabbinic policy of the rule of the majority of sages was characteristic of his Pharisaic group already. If the first option, he did not subject his new convictions to their deliberation; if the second, he did not return and thereby violated these Pharisees' policy of not contesting the views of the elders, which his new conviction would be expected to challenge (cf. Josephus, *Ant.* 18.12). Paul is indicating that he did not immediately seek to win formal approval of this revelation and call to bring this message to the nations from the Pharisaic group among whom he had previously held high esteem. For the Galatians, the likely rhetorical purpose is to relate to them in their own circumstances: if they follow Paul's teaching and resist proselyte conversion, they will need to stand alone against the opinions of the local Jewish communal leaders too. Paul understands this, having stood alone for this truth claim. But it is also the position of the other apostles to which he calls them, even if he initially arrived at this understanding independently. He seeks to relate his experiences to the vulnerability of his Galatian audience: he wants them to know that he understands what it is to stand alone and be marginalized for the gospel's proposition, just as his Galatian audience is now experiencing. It is what all Christ-following group leaders uphold (cf. Nanos, "Intruding 'Spies'"; Nanos, "What Was at Stake?"; Nanos, *Irony of Galatians*; Nanos, "How could Paul Accuse Peter of

[144] to gain the approval of those peers no longer characterizes the way he *is living in Judaism*—Jesus-Christ-based Judaism, perhaps even Jesus-Christ-based Pharisaic Judaism—*now*.[83]

Paul does not specify what the Christ-following Jewish groups were doing that he deemed to be so threatening, thus one must develop a proposition to make sense of Paul's earlier life and change of course. Interpreters have generally understood Paul's opposition to be to a lax attitude toward Torah observance, perhaps even outright renunciation—proto-Paulinism, you might say.[84] The issues of the letter, and the topic of his calling as described in 1:16, to proclaim God's son to the nations, suggest that Paul objected specifically to the policy of regarding non-Jews who believed in Jesus Christ to be full members having equal status with Jews (especially with proselytes) without having become Jews, of the claim to be children of Abraham apart from the traditional convention of proselyte conversion to gain that standing.[85] That policy is [145] the one for which he claims to be "persecuted" later (probably better: *hassled, argued with, accused*, maybe even *prosecuted*),[86] namely, for not "still" preaching circumcision of non-Jews (Gal 5:11). While Paul championed this change of policy for Christ-following Jewish subgroups, he probably did not initiate it. Rather, since before the dramatic revelation of Christ in him and the call to bring this message to the nations, he had been the most vicious opponent of this policy. This policy of including non-Jews as full members was a propositional truth for Christ-based groups that likely predated his change of course. If so, what probably motivated Paul's zealous response was not a failure by Jewish members of the Christ groups to observe Torah per se. They were likely observing, for example, Sabbath and dietary customs, and circum-

---

'living *ethné*-ishly' in Antioch (Gal 2:11–21)?" On the rabbinic policy of majority rule, see Bab. Meṣ 59b; on the topic of interpretive authority and the role of revelation during this period, see Ben Sira 24; 39.1–8; 1QS 5; 8; Nickelsburg, "Revealed Wisdom as a Criterion for Inclusion and Exclusion"; Schwartz, *Judeans and Jews*, 21–47.

83. Goodman, "A Note on Josephus, the Pharisees and Ancestral Tradition," makes an interesting case for recognizing that the Pharisees were not characterized only by distinctive theological ideas such as resurrection, but that they upheld proper behavior according to ancestral customs that were not necessarily Pharisaic. If so, this would fit well with the issue at hand in Paul's opposition to the traditional convention for non-Jews to gain membership via proselyte conversion. It is not just Pharisaic tradition that is being challenged, but general Jewish tradition, which the Pharisees uphold more zealously than other interest groups (from Paul's point of view).

84. Traditional views and an interesting proposal are described by Fredriksen, "Judaism, the Circumcision of Gentiles, and Apocalyptic Hope," 248–55.

85. The topic of Nanos, *Irony of Galatians*.

86. The above discussion of the nuances of the word διώκω as well as concepts related to "persecution" apply here as well; see n. 78.

cising their sons. At issue, based on an alternative interpretation of Torah, was a change of policy for defining the inclusion of non-Jews as full and equal members *now*. For the Christ-following Jewish groups, inclusion was based on the chronometrical claim that God has in Christ initiated the age to come kingdom already, and thus members from the rest of the nations are (and should be) participating alongside of Israel in the worship of the One God in the ways to be expected when that day arrived.

Unlike the conventions in place in other Jewish groups of the time of which we are aware, the non-Jews in these Jewish groups were being identified not simply as *guests*, however welcome and celebrated. They were instead being treated as *members* in full standing, on the same terms as proselytes, as children of Abraham, and yet at the same time not having become proselytes, so they are not members of Israel but representatives of the other nations bearing witness to the chronometrical proposition that the end of the ages had dawned in Christ.[87] They were celebrating a kind of messianic banquet expected in the age to come, but doing so already in the midst of the present evil age.[88]

It seems likely that what Paul and his fellow group members objected to were rumors of insurrectionist agendas among some Jewish groups proclaiming the seditious message that there was already a ruler anointed to rule Israel and the nations rather than Caesar. This was made manifest by the new way Jews and non-Jews were interacting within these groups as if the awaited banquet of all nations [146] worshiping together as equals under God's reign had begun. Jews and non-Jews were eating together as equal members of the righteous ones, as brothers and sisters in the family of Abraham. Such a stance threatened to undermine the way that the political exigencies of compliance with Roman rule were understood to be

---

87. I am suggesting here an alternative that Fredriksen, "Judaism, the Circumcision of Gentiles, and Apocalyptic Hope," does not discuss, although a variation of one she dismisses (251) on the grounds that it was not objectionable for Jewish groups to include gentiles. The difference is that she is dealing with a proposition that these gentiles remained merely *guests*, while I am proposing that the gentiles in these groups were being identified and treated as *full members* in a way that other Jewish groups reserved for proselytes. At the same time, I do not believe that they were being classified by Paul as proselytes (*contra* Donaldson, *Paul and the Gentiles*). Rather, it was important to Paul's proposition that they remain representatives of the other nations, but in membership standing on a par with proselytes, indeed, with natural-born Jews as well, so that the "new creation" community consisted of members of Israel *and* the rest of the nations with one voice worshipping the One God of all humankind (cf. Rom 3:29–30; 10:12; 15:5–13; Gal 3:28; cf. Nanos, *Mystery of Romans*, 179–92; Nanos, "Paul and the Jewish Tradition").

88. See Nanos, "Reading the Antioch Incident (Gal 2:11–21) as a Subversive Banquet Narrative."

best expressed by Paul's Pharisaic group, and other Jewish interest groups to which they answered, such as the temple authorities, who did the bidding of the Roman regime.[89] Hence, as their representative seeking to sustain the ostensible gains of maintaining the status quo, he had sought "to destroy" the Jesus-as-Christ/Lord confessing groups.

Paul refers to a specific way of living Jewishly, *within* Judaism, that is, among those Jews who looked to the traditions of the fathers for authority. Based upon his arguments throughout Galatians, and especially the dissociating of his authority as directly from God and not human agencies and agents, I believe that Paul seeks to remind the addressees that what he taught them ran against the prevailing views of Jewish groups that looked to "the traditions of the fathers" on the matter at hand, the place of proselyte conversion for non-Jew believers in Jesus as Christ. In the present age, those who protect this convention among Jewish groups may have the authority to compel compliance, but the non-Jew addressees are to resist that authority and to suffer any consequences required, awaiting God's vindication of their righteous standing according to the chronometrical gospel message he had proclaimed (5:5). Paul argues that he too suffers for this policy, but he does not alter his course to gain relief by relaxing it (5:11). Now they are to join him in suffering for challenging the prevailing conventions, looking to the suffering of the one in whom they have believed (3:1; 4:12; 6:14).[90] "Do [they] not hear Torah" rightly (4:21)—that is, with Paul?[91]

Although Paul believes it should be otherwise, he does not *yet* expect Jewish authorities who do not share his faith in Jesus to legitimate his way of incorporating non-Jews according to the revelation of Christ. He [147] tells this story to serve as an example to his non-Jewish addressees; they should not expect approval of their identity claims by the Jewish authorities either—at least, not yet.[92] Instead, they must resist pressure to comply with or

---

89. Cf. Nanos, "Intruding 'Spies,'" 59-97; Goodman, *Ruling Class of Judaea*.

90. Cf. Mitternacht, "Foolish Galatians?"

91. Note that Paul does not write "Do not hear Torah," as if Torah was no longer the authority on the matter at hand, i.e., as if its role for Christ-followers was finished (which undermines the usual interpretations of Paul's statement earlier, in 3:23-25, when taken to mean that the role of Torah is finished with the coming of Christ).

92. Paul's hostile rhetoric betrays that he believes those influencing his addressees should instead accept the truth claims of his proclamation of the gospel (cf. Gal 1:6-9; 3:1; 4:17-18; 5:7-12; 6:12-13; cf. Nanos, *Irony of Galatians*, 226-33), and that they will, when the course of his two-step ministry of proclaiming Christ to the representatives of Israel in each location, followed by decisively turning to the nations also ("the fullness of the nations begins"), has reached its climax, when the rest of those of Israel will reconsider, for he is convinced that "all Israel will be saved (i.e., 'protected')" (Rom 11, as explained in Nanos, *Mystery of Romans*, 239-88; Nanos, "'The Gifts and the Calling

conform to prevailing conventions to gain undisputed standing among the righteous ones: they must "out of faithfulness to the Spirit wait for the hope of righteousness" (Gal 5:5). This intra-group disapproval extends not only to Paul, however independent his ministry among the non-Jews has been, but to the other apostles of this coalition too, who stand up for the same principle truth of the message Paul delivered to the Galatian addressees, albeit sometimes a bit too tentatively for Paul's taste (cf. 2:1–21).[93]

In Christ-following-based Judaism, non-Jews do not become proselytes after becoming believers in Jesus Christ, for doing so would undermine the propositional truth upon which their faith is based, namely, that with the resurrection of Jesus Christ the end of the ages has dawned. Incorporating non-Jews into the people of God in the present age as proselytes according to the traditions of the fathers is no longer halakhically warranted. That is not because Paul or the non-Jewish addressees are no longer a part of Judaism, but because they are members of a particular Judaism, or alternatively, of a Jewish coalition that understands itself playing the role of the remnant representing the interests and eventual destiny of the whole cloth, of every Jewish group and way of living Jewishly. In other words, regardless of how triumphalistic it may be, these Christ-following Jews—and non-Jews!—are to live *on behalf of* Judaism and every Jewish person, not against them (Rom 9–11; esp. 11:11–36).[94] During the present, anomalous period, in which the age to come has begun but not been revealed in full, many Jews are suffering vicariously on behalf of the non-Jews to whom Paul writes, but they are also being "kept safe," protected by God, which should guide the concerns of these non-Jews to behave righteously and generously toward them.[95]

In this service, Christ-following Jews like Paul do not reject Torah, but develop halakhot that articulate the appropriate way to observe Torah now, in view of the revelation of Christ that the representatives of the nations are not to become Israelites, but to join with Israelites in a new community [148] adumbrating the restoration of all humankind.[96] Otherwise,

---

of God are Irrevocable' [Romans 11:29]").

93. Nanos, "What Was at Stake?"; Nanos, "Intruding 'Spies.'"

94. Nanos, "'Broken Branches.'"

95. Nanos, "'Callused,' Not 'Hardened'"; Nanos, "'The Gifts and the Calling of God are Irrevocable' (Romans 11:29)."

96. When Sanders writes, "He [Paul] seems to have 'held together' his native view that the law is one and given by God and his new conviction that Gentiles and Jews stand on equal footing, which requires the deletion of some of the law, by asserting them both without theoretical explanation" (*Paul, the Law, and the Jewish People*, 103), because of the inscrutability of 1 Cor 7:19 in Sanders's system, his view overlooks the option I am trying to articulate here. From the oneness of the particular Lord of Israel and the universal God of all the rest of the nations, one can claim equal footing for

Paul's question in Romans 3:29, "Or is God of the Jews only, and not also of members of the other nations?" could not be answered to affirm the inclusion of anyone but Jews. However, Paul's answer was: "Yes, God is the one God of the members of the other nations also." According to Paul's logic, the alternative would have been to argue instead that God is only the God of Israel, that anyone from the other nations wanting to become part of God's people must become Jewish proselytes, as was the case for the present age before the death and resurrection of Jesus Christ changed what was chronometrically appropriate, within Judaism, to age-to-come terms.

To put this another way, Paul understands the Oneness of God in view of the faith of/in Christ to warrant a change of perspective on the way to incorporate non-Jewish people into the righteous ones, into the family of Abraham, without joining the family of Jacob/Israel. That change, Paul argued, is according to the teaching of Torah, according to the declaration of God's Oneness, according to the expectations of the prophets.[97] To maintain otherwise is to experience "stumbling" instead of enjoying Israel's special privilege (alongside Paul) of bringing light to all of the nations when that day has come (Rom 11:13–36).[98] It is Israel that has been entrusted with the words of God for the nations; it is thus Israel that Paul claims to represent as an ambassador to the nations (3:2; 10:14—11:12).

Israelites and members of the other nations without requiring "the deletion of some of the law." By regarding the Torah to be particular to Israel, to Jewish observance, the need arises for halakhic developments to incorporate non-Jews as equals within this subgroup/coalition. Likewise, when Sanders states that circumcision, Sabbath observance, and dietary restrictions, although clear to Paul as prescribed in Scripture, "are not binding on those in Christ" (103), he again does not make the distinction that I uphold, that is, that they are binding on the Jew in Christ, but not on the non-Jew. Moreover, making halakhic decisions for Jews who live in view of faith in Christ that may require some deviation from prevailing conventions being upheld by other Jewish groups is not the same thing as deleting laws. The making of halakhah is a dynamic enterprise, which Sanders knows well.

97. Cf. Lapide, "The Rabbi From Tarsus," 48–49.

98. Paul seeks to provoke his fellow Jews to jealousy "of his *ministry*" (v. 13), not because non-Jews are being included per se, but because they are not participating in this awaited task (i.e., "ministry") of bringing light to the nations too (Rom 3:2; 10:14–17; cf. Nanos, *The Mystery of Romans*, 247–51; Nanos, "The Jewish Context," 300–304). The assessment of those Jews who have not yet joined Paul in his faith in Christ as stumbling, but not fallen, bespeak the position of one who views himself and his coalition to be upholding the righteous standing of Israel in the sense of the remnant preserving the certain destiny of the whole cloth. The issue for Jews, unlike for non-Jews, is not getting-in, *contra* Sanders, but staying in, now by way of response to Christ. Even the culpability for failing to yet make that decision is mitigated by the admission that God is involved in a complicated scheme to include the nations that will eventually include the restoration of all Israel, for which some of Israel is vicariously suffering presently, while some of Israel is engaged in bringing about the eventual complete restoration.

[149] It is interesting to note that Rashi, who writes around halfway between Paul's time and our own, finds in the repetition of God's name in the *Shema* the anticipation of a day not unlike that which Paul argues to have arrived:

> The LORD who is our God now, but not (yet) the God of the (other) nations, is destined to be the One LORD, as it is said, "For then will I give to the people a pure language, that they may all call upon the name of the LORD, to serve Him with one consent" (Zeph 3:9). And (likewise) it is said, "And the LORD shall be King over all the earth; on that day shall the LORD be One and His name One" (Zech 14:9).[99]

This logic helps us to understand how all of the parties present in Antioch when Paul confronted Peter could be eating according to prevailing Jewish diets, but not arranged at the table according to prevailing conventions that discriminated seating or food distribution or in other ways that demonstrated relative status based upon identity as Jew or non-Jew (Gal 2:11-14).[100] Jews (if males) in this subgroup had been circumcised as infants (i.e., they had *erga nomou*), yet still sought the same righteous status before God as did the non-Jews who did so without having become circumcised (without *erga nomou*), because these Jews were convinced that Jesus was the Messiah promised by a faithful God.[101] Non-Jews were not under Torah; they were nevertheless obliged to observe the appropriate *halakhah* for this association as equals to take place. That is an idealistic notion within the constraints of the present age, when discrimination ineluctably

---

99. Translation from Lamm, *The Shema*, 31. See too Sipre on Deut 6:4 (Piska 31), "But Israel said to the Holy One, blessed be He: out of all these gods we have chosen only you, as it is said: 'The LORD is my portion, says my soul'" (from Gaston, *Paul and the Torah*, 200 n. 27, citing D. Hoffmann, ed., *Midrasch Tannaim zum Deuteronomium* [Berlin, 1908/9; reprint Jerusalem, n.p., 1984], 190-91). Cf. Nanos, *Mystery of Romans*, 179-92; Nanos, "Paul and the Jewish Tradition."

100. Nanos, "What Was at Stake?"; Nanos, "How could Paul Accuse Peter of 'living *ethné*-ishly' in Antioch (Gal 2:11-21)?"; Nanos, "Reading the Antioch Incident (Gal 2:11-21) as a Subversive Banquet Narrative."

101. Too often the tenure of Paul's argument in Gal 2:16-17 is undermined by failure to account for the fact that he does not put the *erga nomou* (that still distinguishes the Jews from the non-Jews in Christ) into contrast with *pistis*; Paul argues for "this *and* that" ("except through ['unless accompanied (by)'] Jesus Christ's faithfulness [ἐὰν μὴ διὰ πίστεως Ἰησοῦ Χριστοῦ] . . . even we"); see Nanos, "How Could Paul Accuse Peter of 'living *ethné*-ishly' in Antioch (Gal 2:11-21)?," esp. 215-21. Paul's arguments throughout Gal. 2 provide good examples for how eschewing the use of *Christian, Christianity, church*, and similar anachronistic terms is helpful if trying to understand his language in historical context.

accompanies difference.[102] But Paul believed the age to come had dawned, changing the terms, so that discrimination was to be eliminated by way of living according to the Spirit, that is, according to the age-to-come way of life that the Spirit made [150] possible within this community, if they will dedicate themselves to walking in the Spirit. Hence, Paul can write of equality of Jew and non-Jew in Christ, and of keeping the commandments of God as paramount, without negating any of Torah. Within this community, the ethnic or national difference between Jew/Israelite and non-Jew/member of the nations, and therefore their different relationships to the Torah, remain, but the present-age *discrimination* inherently concomitant with such distinctions should not.

For Paul, it is fundamental to the truth of the gospel that *difference remains*, that social boundaries are acknowledged, but that *discrimination should not*, in this age as in the age to come. It is an age that, according to the gospel, has dawned in Christ, and should thus be made evident in the body of those who are committed to that trust when they meet and live together in community. Everyone is to live in a way respecting the different other, in love as the perfect expression of the commandments of God, of Torah for Jews, and the Law of Christ for Jews and non-Jews too. Figuring out how to make this work constitutes establishing halakhah for Paul, not its elimination.[103] And the difficult reality of exemplifying this chronometrical challenge in the present evil age is realized in Paul's constant appeal to live in "faith working through love," which is defined by Torah, but energized by the work of God in them through the Holy Spirit. They can thereby embody the life of the age to come, and not that of human conventions that instead legitimate discrimination where difference is found, amplified, for example, by the creation of norms by which to measure each other hierarchically. In Christ's body, they are to be equals in rank, but otherwise different, which extends even to the ways that God's Spirit is manifest in their lives, including how their different gifts and ministries are manifest. Like a body, they all represent different parts, but contribute those parts to the health of the whole (Rom 12; 1 Cor 12–14). Otherwise, the whole would be but one part. As there is a place for non-Jews in that body, so too there is a place for Jews, *a fortiori*, and thus for Torah; logically, on the "irrevocable" covenantal terms Paul upholds (Rom 11:28–29), how could it be otherwise?

---

102. Cf. Hogg and Abrams, *Social Identifications*.
103. *Contra* Sanders, *Paul, the Law*, 144.

CONTEXTUALIZING PAUL'S TORAH OBSERVANCE AND RHETORIC FOR NON-JEWS

To evaluate Paul's rhetoric we must decide or otherwise assume what his audience knows about him, often firsthand. Paul's interpreters have proceeded on the basis that his addressees know him to live a Torah-free life. However, the opposite hypothesis should be tested. If Paul writes from [151] within Judaism, if, for example, he is Torah-observant, then his polemical language would carry very different implications for those it addressed. To name a few important indicators, I understand him to eat according to prevailing halakhic conventions for Diaspora Jews in each location he visits;[104] to respect the ideals of temple worship in the ways that religiously observant Diaspora Jews would, such as attempting to travel to Jerusalem in time to celebrate Shavuot/Pentecost, which marks the receipt of Torah by Moses and is calculated from the dating of Passover (Lev 23:15-16), suggesting that his addressees were expected to know when Jewish festivals were celebrated as well as their continued importance to Paul and to others in their coalition (1 Cor 16:8; cf. 5:7-8);[105] to make a collection for those in Jerusalem suffering economic hardship for upholding the policy of non-Jew inclusion apart from proselyte conversion (Rom 15:25-31; Gal 2:7-10). These attitudes and actions would be compatible with Luke's account in Acts 21 that Paul took a Nazarite vow (which involved a burnt offering) in the temple in order to confirm that he lived and taught according to Torah, in the face of rumors that he did not, whether this actually took place or not.

Consider Gal 5:3, where Paul seeks to undermine the addressees' confidence that they have proper motives for assessing the social advantages proselyte conversion appears to offer, at the same time putting in doubt

---

104. Certain texts that have been traditionally understood to suggest that Paul opposed a Jewish diet for himself, and by implication, for other Jewish believers in Christ, imply instead that Paul observed Jewish dietary customs, and was understood by his non-Jewish addressees to do so. See my arguments related to Rom 14, in Nanos, *Mystery of Romans*, esp. chs 3 and 4; related to the Antioch Incident, in Nanos, "What Was at Stake?" and "How Could Paul Accuse Peter of 'living *ethné*-ishly' in Antioch (Gal 2:11-21)"; related to idol food at Corinth, in Nanos, "The Polytheist Identity"; and overall in "The Myth of the 'Law-free' Paul."

105. The implications extend to Paul's metaphorical references: Wassen, "Do You Have to Be Pure in a Metaphorical Temple?" Paul's treatment of these non-Jews in temple holiness terminology is also relevant here; see Fredriksen, "Judaizing the Nations," esp. 244-49; Johnson Hodge, "The Question of Identity," esp. 164-67.

I understand the calendar Paul opposes in Gal 4:10 to be a polytheistic calendar, one that does not contain the distinctive mark of the Jewish calendar, "weeks," by which Paul's groups should mark time (Nanos, *Irony of Galatians*, 267-68; Martin, "Pagan and Judeo-Christian Time-Keeping Schemes in Gal. 4:10 and Col. 2:16."

the motives of those influencing them, implying that they have not made a full disclosure of the obligations concomitant with the re-identification that they are promoting. Paul argues that if these non-Jewish Christ-followers are circumcised they will be responsible to "observe the whole Torah." This has been understood to mean that Paul is against Torah observance, that he sees it as a burden to be avoided. But if Paul is Torah-observant, and known to be such by the Christ-following non-Jews to whom he writes, it would signal a very different meaning. His warning is delivered to expose and undermine a lack of integrity in the rival message that his recipients are apparently too distracted by the benefits promised to detect. (The message and motives of those Paul vilifies cannot be known, and should be approached with suspicion; after all, Paul's polemic aimed to influence in response to rival influencers he suspected were appealing enough that they might win over his addressees to their course of action rather than his.) That message ostensibly promoted the good to be gained by undertaking proselyte conversion, providing a method to overcome the marginality that non-Jews claiming full standing as righteous ones apart from such conversion might suffer in both the larger (but still minority) Jewish and overarching pagan communities in which they live, communities that do not share their conviction about the meaning of Christ. Paul's rhetorical approach was calculated to subvert its proponents' [152] projected neglect to disclose that this step involves more than an identity solution, it also necessarily involves the obligations of Torah-identity. The tone of ironic rebuke here and throughout the letter seeks to expose the naïveté of these non-Jews, much as does the ironic rebuke of a parent aimed at a teenager for failure to calculate the long-term cost of the short-term aims they seek to gain by satisfying peer pressure.[106]

To carry weight, this rhetoric bespeaks knowledge of Paul as a Torah-protector, since he is a Jewish person by birth, one who has, in keeping with his teaching, remained in that circumcised state in which he was called (1 Cor 7:17–24; 2 Cor 11:22; Phil 3:4–7).[107] Otherwise, his non-Jewish audience would be expected to reply that they simply want what Paul has achieved, the advantage of traditionally accepted social identity for those claiming to be full members within these Jewish groups, without the obligation to observe the Torah. Consistent with this observation, Paul instructs his non-Jew addressees to remain in their ethnic status as non-Jews, although, importantly, in a way that represents righteousness according to Jewish norms for defining human behavior (further evidence of his

---

106. The topic of Nanos, *Irony of Galatians*; Mitternacht, *Forum fur Sprachlose*.
107. See Tucker, "Remain in Your Calling."

continued perspective from within Judaism). Even the love to which they are called to work out their faith is an articulation of the Torah: note, not by love working through faith, but by "faith" or "faithfulness working through love" (Gal 5:6, 13-14).[108] In doing so, they represent the nations turning from idolatry to worship Israel's Lord as the One God of all humankind (cf. Rom 3:29-31; 6:15-23; 13:8-14; 15:15-16; 1 Cor 10; 1 Thess 1:9).

One may wonder then, why does Paul employ rhetoric that seemingly qualifies the advantages of being a Jew and having Torah? It is not hard to understand this development if Paul's non-Jew target addressees are suffering [153] status-uncertainty and disadvantage because they have accepted the chronometrical proposition that they have become equal members of Abraham's family from the other nations without becoming equal members of Israel via proselyte conversion. These non-Jews have discovered the *bad news* social *consequences* in the *present* age for believing and acting according to the *good news proposition* of the dawning of the age *to come*. Paul and those whose teaching has brought about this painful identity dissonance and social disadvantage need to qualify their own advantage as Israelites, Jews who have the privilege of the promises, of covenant, of Torah and temple, etc. (cf. Rom 9:4-5; Gal 2:15; Phil 3:4-6). That was just what was at stake in the Antioch Incident (Gal 2:11-14), mentioned earlier. The problem, Paul tells Peter, is not that the conviction of these Jews about Jesus as Messiah and resultant faithfulness to the gospel has brought them down to the standing of non-Jews, but the proposition that the non-Jews have been brought up to equal standing before God with Jews: these non-Jew are now members of the righteous ones also (2:15-21). From this follows the need to qualify their relative advantages, and by implication, the relative advantages of those Jews who do not accept this re-identification proposition apart from proselyte conversion. Hence, as noted earlier, in Romans Paul asks whether God is the God of Jews only. Of course not, he answers, because God is One (Rom 3:29-30). Note that Paul's argument for the place

108. This is but one of many indications throughout Galatians that Paul is not challenging a rival proposition upholding Torah-observance for his addressees, or proposing a sharp distinction between faith or faithfulness and works of righteousness, for then he would have presumably been more careful to write "love working through faith" here, and to avoid the many other instructions about striving to undertake to behave righteously, or else not be counted among those who are of the kingdom of God (5:21). This implication is even present when Paul warns them that adopting proselyte conversion involves the obligation to observe the whole Torah (5:3), for his warning implies that the rival message is not properly emphasizing (if even teaching) Torah-observance, but rather focusing on the benefits to be gained by proselyte conversion. Paul thus seeks to undermine that approach as being based on a half-truth to serve the interests of the influencers. These and other elements pointing in this direction are discussed at length in Nanos, *Irony of Galatians*.

of non-Jews depends upon the prior assumption of the place of the Jews as God's own. The continued place of Jews, which he goes so far as to call an "advantage" still (3:1–2), is not what is being contested, but instead forms the logical basis for extending the concern of that same one and only Creator God of all humankind to facilitating in Christ the inclusion of members of the other nations *also*.

That these comments are not to be taken apart from their rhetorical function as arguments for relative equality among Jews and non-Jews in Christ is logically demonstrated in Paul's many negative answers to the questions he poses in the midst of these arguments: "May it never be" that there is no "advantage" to "being a Jew" and "circumcised," he pronounces in Rom 3:1, because "the Jews are entrusted with the oracles of God" (v. 2), the special prophetic privilege of bringing God's word to the rest of the nations (cf. Rom 10–11). "May it never be" that we "overthrow the Torah by this faith," he thunders at the end of that chapter's argument (3:31). Moreover, what many overlook are his many positive statements about the Torah that should make the traditional portrait of Paul nonsensical, but that have usually been ignored, downplayed, or reasoned away.[109] For Paul not only writes that what matters is the "keeping of the commandments of God" (1 Cor 7:19), but also that "the Torah is holy, and the commandment is holy and just and good" (7:12); he even argues [154] that "the Torah is spiritual" (v. 14)! How many dissertations, monographs, or even essays have been written on these un-Pauline like declarations; indeed, how many sermons have ever been delivered on them?

Paul's rhetoric is rhetorical.[110] When it is isolated from its argumentative context for non-Jews within the first century, from Jewish communal and conceptual concerns, and made into universal-whatever-the-context-truths for every person, for all times, interpretations run a high risk of missing entirely what the historical Paul and his Judaism represented to his audiences, the good news along with the bad. If we approach Paul with the hypothesis that he was a figure within Judaism, indeed, propagating a particular Jewish community-forming viewpoint to Diaspora Jews and non-Jews around the Mediterranean coast, and one whom his addressees know to observe Torah as a matter of faith, many different possibilities for interpreting his language to be *representing Judaism* emerge. So too do many new possibilities for how we interpret and interact in our own time, not least, for my concerns, the potential for better Christian-Jewish relations.

---

109. Gaston, *Paul and the Torah*, and Gager, *Reinventing Paul*, have criticized this tendency similarly.

110. Cf. Thurén, *Derhetorizing Paul*.

We can begin to read his letters as expressions of Judaism pre-Christianity, however deviant that form of Judaism was and came to be regarded by the other Jewish groups that survived. Paul's arguments read very differently if we keep in focus that the issue for his targeted non-Jew addressees was their relative identity and behavior within Judaism—among groups and subgroups of Jews who were practicing Jewish ways of life. Because they have not become Jews themselves—regardless of how jewish*ish* they may be learning to think and behave—the idea of claiming acceptance as full members rather than as simply guests within the Jewish community is going to be contested by other Jews and Jewish groups, and by their non-Jew families and neighbors. That is why the issues of identity focus on whether or not it is appropriate for them to undertake proselyte conversion (the *erga nomou* that turns a non-Jew into a Jew).[111] The reason that Paul denies this option to his addressees need not be confused with Torah-observance for Jews, [155] or with some kind of fault along the lines usually proposed, whether works-righteousness, or nationalism, or exclusivism, and so on.[112]

---

111. *Erga nomou*, usually translated "works of law," functions in Paul's arguments as a synonym for "circumcision." Circumcision is also used as a metonym in Paul's arguments to signify the role of what came to be called proselyte conversion, the process by which non-Jews undertake the *rites* (hence, acts or works) by which, according to the traditional interpretation of the Torah, they can become children of Abraham's covenant on the same standing with (male) Jews from birth, who are circumcised as children. In my view, then, *erga nomou* is Paul's way of referring to the process by which, in the Jewish communities that Paul's addressees are in anyway, non-Jews can become Jews in addition to becoming faithful to God in Christ; hence, a better translation would be "*rites of a (or: the) convention [of circumcision]*" or "*rites of a (or: the) convention [for becoming a Jew]*"). In all but one case (Gal 2:16)—where in order to argue that Christ-following non-Jews have equal standing before God (and thus, before each other) to highlight that even though Peter and he have *erga nomou* (having been circumcised as infant sons) they nevertheless also believe in Christ's faithfulness—Paul does not use the phrase to refer to observing Torah per se (although for Jews, Torah enjoins the circumcision of their males sons), or even to ritual aspects of Torah practice per se, neither of which non-Jews are obliged to observe as if Jews. *Contra* Dunn's view, it also does not signify observance of special boundary-marking behavior such as Sabbath and food laws, which are for those already defined as Torah-people (Israelites, Jews), which Paul's addressees are not. At the same time, these non-Jews are being taught by Paul to behave according to Torah-based norms, which would have involved observing Sabbath and dietary norms to assemble in these Jewish subgroups. That reality turned a clear line of differentiation on technical terms into a less-than-clear one in practical terms, which likely contributed to the confusion that gave rise to the exigencies he sought to address in these letters, and to the (mis)understanding of his later interpreters that he was against Torah-observance per se. For detailed discussion why *erga nomou* specifically signified circumcision in Paul's argument and also as used by Josephus to describe the issue for Izates, see Nanos, "The Question of Conceptualization."

112. Often interpreters run together the categories of identity and behavior, of circumcision and Torah-observance for Jews as well as non-Jews, for example, when

Paul argues for the propositional views of this Jewish group in tension with the views that prevail among other Jewish groups, and in the larger non-Jewish society in which all of these Jewish groups functioned as minority groups and subgroups. His arguments often specifically deal with how to identify non-Jews as either guests or members, and thus with how they should be obliged to behave, including how Jews are to interact with them. It is to be according to the rules of the anticipated feast for all the nations who turn to worship God alongside Israel in the age to come, which has dawned, according to Paul, in Jesus the Messiah.

CONCLUSION

The investigation of Paul *and* Judaism has traditionally proceeded as if what was written was Paul *or* Judaism, with the understanding that these referents represent two different religious systems. That has not really changed with the development of the New Perspective on Paul. In the sense of Paul *within* or *for* or *representing* Judaism (or even a particular Jewish group), little work has been done to date. Interpreters do not often, if ever, write of converts to Paul's *Jewish communities* or *synagogues*, of Paul's *Judaism* or Pauline *Judaism*, of the *Judaism* of Paul,[113] or of the *Judaism* of Paul's communities.[114] Never do I remember reading of *Judaism's* Paul. The two [156] terms signify different and incompatible entities; something must be wrong with one or the other side of the equation, or else they would not be so essentially antithetical. This "essentializing" of difference between Paul and Judaism, and the concomitant requirement to find fault with one or the other, is influenced by the interpreter's ideological vantage point.[115] It will likely continue to be perpetuated implicitly when not explicitly to the degree that the ethnic differentiation that Paul upholds between Jews and non-Jews, between Israel and the other nations, is approached by his interpreters

---

discussing what Paul opposes in Galatia. But Paul's argument is not about Torah-observance, and he even appeals to it as that which follows after the identity-transformation involved in proselyte conversion (circumcision), as discussed above, indicating that it is not Torah-observance that is at issue in Galatia, but identity-transformation by the rites of the convention that makes it possible for non-Jews to become Jews in some Jewish groups.

113. In this direction, see Gager, "Paul, the Apostle of Judaism"; Frey, "Paul's Jewish Identity"; Barth, "St. Paul—A Good Jew."

114. In a forthcoming introduction to Paul, Anders Runesson and I have been working with the phrase "Apostolic Judaism" to denote the larger movement among Christ-followers, including Paul and his co-workers and communities as well as the other apostles such as James and Peter, and their communities.

115. See Eisenbaum, "Paul, Polemics, and the Problem of Essentialism."

as if drawn between Judaism and Christianity instead (whether using the term Christianity or not), or between Jewish and Pauline Christianities.[116]

Christianity has had much invested in the tradition of Paul *against* Judaism, providing a counter-narrative against which to measure its own unique fulfillment of God's expectations, whereas the Judaism it has fashioned in this meaning-making is portrayed to have failed. Interestingly, Jewish interpreters have become invested in the same construction of Paul, although turning the meaning upside down. This is all the more evident since the nineteenth-century reclamation of Jesus as a faithful Jewish figure, when Paul becomes the distorter of Jesus, the antagonist even of the Judaism that he had represented.[117] Since it is so obvious that Paul did not understand his former religion and no longer recognized its value, it was easy to trivialize and blame Paul for the misunderstandings and ill will that Christianity so often expressed toward Jewish people and religion. There was no reason to suppose that those who appealed to Paul's authority had misunderstood him, and certainly no reason to look for Judaism at work in the teachings and actions of the apostle, or in Paulinism.[118]

[157] I have argued that successfully challenging the implicit as well as explicit negative valuations of Judaism that arise in the study of Paul requires attending to the particular contexts of Paul's language, written to non-Jews. Instead of treating this language as if universal, as if it addressed everyone (for example, Jews in precisely the same way as non-Jews), we should approach his rhetoric as highly situational and specific and not designed to offer a balanced view for everyone, on everything, forever. Sufficient historical-critical work on Paul has made it clear that the particular should not be confused with the absolute anymore than prescriptive rhetoric should be construed to be descriptive. Instead of proceeding as if Paul finds fault with Judaism, we should test the hypothesis that to the degree that his rhetoric expresses fault, it is with other Jews and groups in position to influence the

---

116. Nanos, "How Inter-Christian Approaches."

117. See discussions of this dynamic by Heschel, *Abraham Geiger and the Jewish Jesus*; Langton, "The Myth of the 'Traditional View of Paul'"; Eisenbaum, "Following in the Footnotes of the Apostle Paul." The trend continues in recent works: e.g., Klinghoffer, *Why the Jews Rejected Jesus*; Levine, *The Misunderstood Jew*.

118. Interestingly, the traditional portrait of Paul against Torah has also played a role in disputes between Jewish groups about the relative merits and demerits of so-called progressive policies toward Torah (see Brumberg-Kraus, "A Jewish Ideological Perspective on the Study of Christian Scripture," 121–52; Langton, "Modern Jewish Identity and the Apostle Paul." The implications of reading Paul as a Torah-observant Jew for modern Jewish/Christian relations are addressed in Nanos, "The Myth of the 'Law-Free' Paul Standing between Christians and Jews," and other publications noted throughout this essay.

non-Jews he addressed in ways that he believed threatened their well-being in Christ. Like parental rhetoric regarding a teen's peers, it was designed to be prescriptive for his own, not descriptive of the others whose influence it was designed to undermine.

Paul's rhetoric, addressed to non-Jews, was often developed in conflict with rival Jewish groups and their interpretations of how to best live Jewishly, and usually, specifically emerged in the context of his Jewish coalition's claim that non-Jews, by way of their response to the gospel of Christ, have become included in the ways of life of the Jewish communities within which their Jewish subgroups operated. Claiming that these non-Jews were to now understand themselves living *within Judaism*, and with equal status to Jews apart from becoming Jews, that is, without undertaking proselyte conversion, was certainly a controversial claim.

We would expect different Jewish groups to define differently what faithfulness involves for Jews and what it entails for non-Jews, including any non-Jews who associate with Jews or want to become respected as fellow members of the people of God. Attending to this dynamic is critical to interpreting Paul's rhetoric and rivalries. His perspective on how to incorporate these non-Jews among the people of God because of his chronometrical convictions created a very unsettling environment for these non-Jews. The way Paul defined the faithful practice of Judaism for Christ-following non-Jews, which involved not becoming Jews, was contested by other Jewish groups. They presented the options for non-Jews seeking to express faithfulness differently. But Paul was not present to counter their influence. In the letters that we seek to interpret we encounter Paul's effort to (re)address the identification and behavioral concerns of the non-Jews within the Christ-following Jewish subgroups as they sought to become fully integrated into Jewish communities and ways of life, to access communal honor and goods. Paul needed to explain the positions of this coalition, and the price that might have to be paid to remain faithful to these propositional claims for the meaning of the gospel of Christ.

Paul faulted some Jews for failure to agree with him that the chronometrical expectations of Judaism were being realized in the work of proclamation in which he and his Jewish coalition were engaged, for failure to recognize that the end of the ages had dawned in Jesus Christ, and for not joining him in announcing this glad tiding to all of the scattered of Israel and those of the nations in which they were to be found (Rom 9–11; 15:30–32). Even more so, Paul found fault with those who sought to prevent him from making this announcement (1 Thess 2:15–16). He wished a curse upon those who marginalized his fellow non-Jew coalitionists for believing his message, for expecting communal inclusion on an unprecedented level

(Gal 1:8–9; 5:12). To me, this seems logically inconsistent with his own need to experience a personal revelation in order to be convinced of such claims (1:11–17), and it does not reflect the ideals to which he seemed to otherwise subscribe. But his polemical rhetoric is also qualified by the fact that he was not addressing his adversaries or developing a guidebook for the centuries; he was trying to persuade his disciples facing the temptation to comply with the apparently far more compelling claims of those whose influence was immediate, while his could only be delivered by letter. He feared that they would be persuaded to choose a path that subverted "his gospel" without perhaps recognizing that this was at stake.

Nevertheless, Paul's criticism was not of Judaism. It was of the failure of some Jews and Jewish groups to be all that Judaism promised to be when the end of the ages had dawned, which he was convinced had occurred.[119] He proclaimed this day to have arrived in the news of good in Jesus Christ, made manifest in the community of Jews and non-Jews who gathered as equal members to proclaim God's name in one voice. The awaited universal participation of all humankind in this joint praise [158] was what he believed all Jews should agree to now, at least respect—and that they would agree to in due time. That is very different from the later "Christian" concept of Jews "converting" from Jewish identity and behavior and community—from a Jewish way of life, Judaism—to a wholly different, if derivative religion, named "Christianity." In the meantime, he wanted the non-Jews who were Christ-followers to be respected as equal co-participants in Abraham's family, in the community of the righteous ones, and he wanted these non-Jews to live together with everyone else within the Jewish communities accordingly.

What separated Paul's particular way of practicing and promoting Judaism was that he believed everyone should be persuaded to respect the implications of this chronometrical proposition *now*. Many other Jews and Jewish groups (or Judaisms) did not believe that the awaited day had arrived. For them, the empirical evidence to warrant this conclusion was simply not experienced or observed (just as had been the case for Paul before his personal revelation). Many believed that non-Jews were welcome as guests, but to be included as equal members in the present age required membership in Israel, which involved completing the rite of proselyte conversion, if it could be facilitated at all. His chronometrical stance was thus, *mutatis mutandis*, just as ethnocentric and particularistic in its application of the universalistic proposition of the meaning of Christ for humanity as that of any Jewish group that did not believe this proposition to be verified,

---

119. Cf. Davies, "Paul and the People of Israel," 136, 142.

which thus logically maintained the particularistic requirement of proselyte standing for non-Jews to be included on equal terms. Neither proposition made sense independent of Judaism, independent of a particular people and way of living that proposes to know the will of the Creator, and thus to represent the ultimate interests of all humankind.

Paul explained in Romans 11, when confronting potential arrogance on the part of non-Jew Christ-followers, that he regarded his fellow Jews' failure to yet be persuaded of this message or its reception among the non-Jews to represent "stumbling," but that there was no doubt that they were still within the covenant, insisting that they have not fallen (vv. 11–36). He believed that within his lifetime his fellow Jews would eventually be steadied again as a result of his ministry. That ministry also included the role of the non-Jews to whom he wrote. He sought to make them realize that generosity of spirit rather than triumphalism or indignation was warranted. Their lives must represent the righteous ideals of the age to come that they proclaim to have dawned in Christ: Judaism as it should be lived. They are to understand the momentary out-of-balance-state of these Jewish brothers and sisters not to be a final judgment, but rather to represent vicarious suffering on their behalf. Paul believed that bringing this message to the rest of the nations would ultimately result in the restoration of all Israel, as well as the salvation of the other nations, even if he only came to that conclusion with the passing of time and the disclosure of a mystery (vv. 25–26, 33–36).[120]

Whether one judges *Paul's Judaism*—or Pauline Judaism, if you will—to be right about these claims, or in its criticisms of other Jews and Jewish [159] points of view, is another matter entirely. But in my view, what Paul would find wrong in Paulinism is this: *it is not Judaism*.

BIBLIOGRAPHY

Ascough, Richard S. "Paul, Synagogues, and Associations: Reframing the Question of Models for Pauline Christ Groups." *Journal of the Jesus Movement in its Jewish Setting* 2 (2015) 27–52. http://www.jjmjs.org/.

Barclay, John M. G. "'Do We Undermine the Law?': A Study of Romans 14.1—15.6." In *Paul and the Mosaic Law*, edited by James D. G. Dunn, 287–308. Grand Rapids: Eerdmans, 2001.

———. *Jews in the Mediterranean Diaspora: from Alexander to Trajan (323 BCE–117 CE)*. Edinburgh: T. & T. Clark, 1996.

———. "Paul among Diaspora Jews: Anomaly or Apostate?" *Journal for the Study of the New Testament* 60 (1995) 89–120.

Barrett, C. K., ed. *Essays on Paul*. Philadelphia: Westminster, 1982.

---

120. Nanos, *Mystery of Romans*, 239–88; Nanos, "Challenging the Limits That Continue to Define Paul's Perspective on Jews and Judaism."

Barth, Markus. "St. Paul—A Good Jew." *Horizons in Biblical Theology* 1 (1979) 7-45.
Baumgarten, Albert I. "The Pharisaic Paradosis." *Harvard Theological Review* 80 (1987) 63-77.
Baur, Ferdinand Christian. *Paul the Apostle of Jesus Christ: His Life and Works, His Epistles and Teachings: A Contribution to a Critical History of Primitive Christianity.* 2nd ed. Edited by Eduard Zeller; translated by Allan Menzies. 1873-75 (original German, 1845). Two vols in one vol. Reprint. Peabody, MA: Hendrickson, 2003.
Betz, Hans Dieter. *Galatians: A Commentary on Paul's Letter to the Churches in Galatia.* Hermeneia. Philadelphia: Fortress, 1979.
Bird, Michael F. *An Anomalous Jew: Paul among Jews, Greeks, and Romans.* Grand Rapids: Eerdmans, 2016.
———. "The New Perspective on Paul: A Bibliographical Essay." *The Paul Page*, webmaster Mark Mattison: http://www.thepaulpage.com/Bibliography.html.
———. *The Saving Righteousness of God: Studies on Paul, Justification and the New Perspective.* Paternoster Biblical Monographs. Milton Keynes, UK: Paternoster, 2007.
Boccaccini, Gabriele, and Carlos A. Segovia, eds. *Paul the Jew: Rereading the Apostle as a Figure of Second Temple Judaism.* Minneapolis: Fortress, 2016.
Boyarin, Daniel. *A Radical Jew: Paul and the Politics of Identity.* Contraversions 1. Berkeley: University of California Press, 1994.
Brumberg-Kraus, Jonathan D. "A Jewish Ideological Perspective on the Study of Christian Scripture." *Jewish Social Studies* 4 (1997) 121-52.
Buell, Denise Kimber, and Caroline Johnson Hodge. "The Politics of Interpretation: The Rhetoric of Race and Ethnicity in Paul." *Journal of Biblical Literature* 123 (2004) 235-51.
Caizzi, Fernanda Decleva, ed. *Antisthenis Fragmenta.* Milan: Instituto Editoriale Cisalpino, 1966.
Campbell, William S. *Paul and the Creation of Christian Identity.* Library of New Testament Studies 322. London: T. & T. Clark, 2006.
———. "Perceptions of Compatibility between Christianity and Judaism in Pauline Interpretation." *Biblical Interpretation* 13 (2005) 298-316.
Carson, D. A., Peter Thomas O'Brien, and Mark A. Seifrid, eds. *Justification and Variegated Nomism: Vol. 2: The Paradoxes of Paul.* Tübingen: Mohr Siebeck, 2004.
Chadwick, Henry. "'All Things to All Men' (1 Cor. IX.22)." *New Testament Studies* 1 (1954-55) 261-75.
———. "St. Paul and Philo of Alexandria." In *History and Thought of the Early Church*, edited by Henry Chadwick, 286-307. 1965-66. Reprint. London: Variorum Reprints, 1982.
Cheung, Alex T. *Idol Food in Corinth: Jewish Background and Pauline Legacy.* JSNTSup 176. Sheffield, UK: Sheffield Academic Press, 1999.
Cohen, Shaye J. D. *The Beginnings of Jewishness: Boundaries, Varieties, Uncertainties.* HCS 31. Berkeley: University of California Press, 1999.
Das, A. Andrew. *Paul, the Law, and the Covenant.* Peabody, MA: Hendrickson, 2001.
Davies, W. D. "Paul and the People of Israel." In *Jewish and Pauline Studies*, 123-52. Philadelphia: Fortress, 1984.
———. *Paul and Rabbinic Judaism: Some Rabbinic Elements in Pauline Theology.* Rev. ed. New York: Harper & Row, 1967.
Dodd, C. H. *The Epistle to the Romans.* London: Hodder and Stoughton, 1932.

Donaldson, Terence L. *Judaism and the Gentiles: Jewish Patterns of Universalism (to 135 CE)*. Waco, TX: Baylor University Press, 2007.

———. *Paul and the Gentiles: Remapping the Apostle's Convictional World*. Minneapolis: Fortress, 1997.

Dunn, James D. G. "Echoes of Intra-Jewish Polemic in Paul's Letter to the Galatians." *Journal of Biblical Literature* 112 (1993) 459–77.

———. "How New Was Paul's Gospel? The Problem of Continuity and Discontinuity." In *Gospel in Paul: Studies on Corinthians, Galatians, and Romans*, edited by L. Ann Jervis and Peter Richardson, 367–88. Sheffield, UK: Sheffield Academic Press, 1994.

———. "The New Perspective on Paul." *Bulletin of the John Rylands Library of Manchester* 65 (1983) 95–122 (reprinted with additional notes in James D. G. Dunn, *Jesus, Paul, and the Law: Studies in Mark and Galatians*, 183–214. Louisville: Westminster/John Knox, 1990).

———. *The Partings of the Ways: Between Christianity and Judaism and Their Significance for the Character of Christianity*. London: SCM, 1991.

———. *Romans 9–16*. WBC. Dallas: Word, 1988.

———. *The Theology of Paul the Apostle*. Grand Rapids: Eerdmans, 1997.

———. "Who Did Paul Think He Was? A Study of Jewish-Christian Identity." *New Testament Studies* 45 (1999) 174–93.

Ehrensperger, Kathy. "The Question(s) of Gender: Relocating Paul in Relation to Judaism." In *Paul within Judaism: Restoring the First-Century Context to the Apostle*, edited by Mark D. Nanos and Magnus Zetterholm, 245–76. Minneapolis: Fortress, 2015.

———. *That We May Be Mutually Encouraged: Feminism and the New Perspective in Pauline Studies*. London: T. & T. Clark, 2004.

Eisenbaum, Pamela. "Following in the Footnotes of the Apostle Paul." In *Identity and the Politics of Scholarship in the Study of Religion*, edited by Jose Ignacio Cabezon and Sheila Greeve Davaney, 77–97. New York: Routledge, 2004.

———. "Paul, Polemics, and the Problem of Essentialism." *Biblical Interpretation* 13 (2005) 224–38.

———. *Paul Was Not a Christian: The Real Message of a Misunderstood Apostle*. New York: HarperOne, 2009.

Elliott, Neil. *Liberating Paul: The Justice of God and the Politics of the Apostle*. Maryknoll, NY: Orbis, 1994.

———. "The Question of Politics: Paul as a Diaspora Jew under Roman Rule." In *Paul within Judaism: Restoring the First-Century Context to the Apostle*, edited by Mark D. Nanos and Magnus Zetterholm, 203–43. Minneapolis: Fortress, 2015.

Esler, Philip F. *Conflict and Identity in Romans: The Social Setting of Paul's Letter*. Minneapolis: Fortress, 2003.

Fee, Gordon D. *The First Epistle to the Corinthians*. NICNT. Grand Rapids: Eerdmans, 1987.

Fredriksen, Paula. "Judaism, the Circumcision of Gentiles, and Apocalyptic Hope: Another Look at Galatians 1 and 2." In *The Galatians Debate: Contemporary Issues in Rhetorical and Historical Interpretation*, edited by Mark D. Nanos, 235–60. Peabody, MA: Hendrickson, 2002.

———. "Judaizing the Nations: The Ritual Demands of Paul's Gospel." *New Testament Studies* 56 (2010) 232–52.

———. "The Question of Worship: Gods, Pagans, and the Redemption of Israel." In *Paul within Judaism: Restoring the First-Century Context to the Apostle*, edited by Mark D. Nanos and Magnus Zetterholm, 175–201. Minneapolis: Fortress, 2015.

Frey, Jörg. "Paul's Jewish Identity." In *Jewish Identity in the Greco-Roman World = Jüdische Identität in der griechisch-römischen Welt*, edited by Jörg Frey, Daniel R. Schwartz and Stephanie Gripentrog, 285–321. Ancient Judaism and early Christianity 71. Leiden: Brill, 2007.

Fuchs-Kreimer, Nancy. "The 'Essential Heresy': Paul's View of the Law according to Jewish Writers: 1886–1986." Ph.D. diss., Temple University, 1990.

Gager, John G. "Paul, the Apostle of Judaism." In *Jesus, Judaism, and Christian Anti-Judaism: Reading the New Testament after the Holocaust*, edited by Paula Fredriksen and Adele Reinhartz, 56–76. Louisville, KY: Westminster John Knox, 2002.

———. *Reinventing Paul*. Oxford: Oxford University Press, 2000.

Gaston, Lloyd. *Paul and the Torah*. Vancouver: University of British Columbia Press, 1987.

Gathercole, Simon J. *Where is Boasting? Early Jewish Soteriology and Paul's Response in Romans 1–5*. Grand Rapids: Eerdmans, 2002.

Gerdmar, Anders. *Roots of Theological Anti-Semitism: German Biblical Interpretation and the Jews, from Herder and Semler to Kittel and Bultmann*. Studies in Jewish History and Culture 20. Leiden: Brill, 2009.

Given, Mark D. *Paul's True Rhetoric: Ambiguity, Cunning, and Deception in Greece and Rome*. Emory Studies in Early Christianity 7. Harrisburg, PA: Trinity, 2001.

Glad, Clarence E. *Paul and Philodemus: Adaptability in Epicurean and Early Christian Psychagogy*. NovTSup 81. Leiden: Brill, 1995.

Goodblatt, David. *Elements of Ancient Jewish Nationalism*. Cambridge: Cambridge University Press, 2006.

Goodman, Martin. "A Note on Josephus, the Pharisees and Ancestral Tradition." *Journal of Jewish Studies* 1 (1999) 17–20.

———. *The Ruling Class of Judaea: The Origins of the Jewish Revolt against Rome, A.D. 66–70*. Cambridge: Cambridge University Press, 1987.

Hagner, Donald A. "Paul and Judaism—The Jewish Matrix of Early Christianity: Issues in the Current Debate." *Bulletin for Biblical Research* 3 (1993) 111–30.

———. "Paul as a Jewish Believer—According to his Letters." In *Jewish Believers in Jesus: The Early Centuries*, edited by Oskar Skarsaune and Reidar Hvalvik, 97–120. Peabody, MA: Hendrickson, 2007.

Harland, Philip. *Associations, Synagogues, and Congregations: Claiming a Place in Ancient Mediterranean Society*. Minneapolis: Fortress, 2003.

———. *Dynamics of Identity in the World of the Early Christians: Associations, Judeans, and Cultural Minorities*. London: T. & T. Clark, 2009.

Hayes, Christine. *What's Divine about Divine Law? Early Perspectives*. Princeton: Princeton University Press, 2015.

Hays, Richard B. *First Corinthians*. Interpretation. Louisville, KY: John Knox, 1997.

Hedner Zetterholm, Karin. "The Question of Assumptions: Torah Observance in the First Century." In *Paul within Judaism: Restoring the First-Century Context to the Apostle*, edited by Mark D. Nanos and Magnus Zetterholm, 79–103. Minneapolis: Fortress, 2015.

Heschel, Susannah. *Abraham Geiger and the Jewish Jesus*. Chicago Studies in the History of Judaism. Chicago: University of Chicago Press, 1998.

Hirshman, Marc. "Rabbinic Universalism in the Second and Third Centuries." *Harvard Theological Review* 93 (2000) 101–15.

Hogg, Michael A., and Dominic Abrams. *Social Identifications: A Social Psychology of Intergroup Relations and Group Processes.* London: Routledge, 1988.

Hvalvik, Reidar. "Paul as a Jewish Believer." In *Jewish Believers in Jesus: The Early Centuries*, edited by Oskar Skarsaune and Reidar Hvalvik, 121–53. Peabody, MA: Hendrickson, 2007.

Jackson-McCabe, Matt A., ed. *Jewish Christianity Reconsidered: Rethinking Ancient Groups and Texts.* Minneapolis: Fortress, 2007.

Johnson Hodge, Caroline. "Apostle to the Gentiles: Constructions of Paul's Identity." *Biblical Interpretation* 13 (2005) 270–88.

———. *If Sons, Then Heirs: A Study of Kinship and Ethnicity in the Letters of Paul.* New York: Oxford University Press, 2007.

———. "The Question of Identity: Gentiles as Gentiles—But Also Not—in Pauline Communities." In *Paul within Judaism: Restoring the First-Century Context to the Apostle*, edited by Mark D. Nanos and Magnus Zetterholm, 153–73. Minneapolis: Fortress, 2015.

Jones, F. Stanley, ed. *The Rediscovery of Jewish Christianity: From Toland to Baur.* History of Biblical Studies 5. Atlanta: Society of Biblical Literature, 2012.

Jones, Siân, and Sarah Pearce, eds. *Jewish Local Patriotism and Self-Identification in the Graeco-Roman Period.* JSPSup 31. Sheffield, UK: Sheffield Academic Press, 1998.

Kim, Seyoon. *Paul and the New Perspective: Second Thoughts on the Origin of Paul's Gospel.* Grand Rapids: Eerdmans, 2001.

Klinghoffer, David. *Why the Jews Rejected Jesus: The Turning Point in Western History.* New York: Doubleday, 2005.

Korner, Ralph J. "*Ekklēsia* as a Jewish Synagogue Term: Some Implications for Paul's Socio-Religious Location." *Journal of the Jesus Movement in its Jewish Setting* 2 (2015) 53–78. http://www.jjmjs.org/.

Lamm, Norman. *The Shema: Spirituality and Law in Judaism as Exemplified in the Shema, the Most Important Passage in the Torah.* Philadelphia: Jewish Publication Society, 2000.

Land, Christopher D. "'We Put No Stumbling Block in Anyone's Path, So That Our Ministry Will Not be Discredited': Paul's Response to an Idol Food Inquiry in 1 Corinthians 8:1–13." In *Paul and His Social Relations*, edited by Stanley E. Porter and Christopher D. Land, 229–83. Leiden: Brill, 2013.

Langton, Daniel R. *The Apostle Paul in the Jewish Imagination: A Study in Modern Jewish-Christian Relations.* New York: Cambridge University Press, 2010.

———. "Modern Jewish Identity and the Apostle Paul: Pauline Studies as an Intra-Jewish Ideological Battleground." *Journal for the Study of the New Testament* 28 (2005) 217–58.

———. "The Myth of the 'Traditional View of Paul' and the Role of the Apostle in Modern Jewish-Christian Polemics." *Journal for the Study of the New Testament* 28 (2005) 69–104.

Lapide, Pinchas. "The Rabbi from Tarsus." In *Paul, Rabbi and Apostle*, edited by Pinchas Lapide and Peter Stuhlmacher, 31–55. Minneapolis: Augsburg, 1984.

Last, Richard. *The Pauline Church and the Corinthian Ekklēsia: Greco-Roman Associations in Comparative Context.* SNTSMS 164. Cambridge: Cambridge University Press, 2016.

Paul and Judaism 55

Lee, Jae Won. *Paul and the Politics of Difference: A Contextual Study of the Jewish-Gentile Difference in Galatians and Romans*. Eugene, OR: Pickwick, 2014.
Levine, Amy-Jill. *The Misunderstood Jew: The Church and the Scandal of the Jewish Jesus*. New York: HarperSanFranscisco, 2006.
Longenecker, Richard Norman. *Paul, Apostle of Liberty*. New York: Harper & Row, 1964.
Maccoby, Hyam. *The Mythmaker: Paul and the Invention of Christianity*. New York: Harper & Row, 1986.
Malherbe, Abraham J. *Paul and the Popular Philosophers*. Minneapolis: Fortress, 1989.
Martin, Troy. "Pagan and Judeo-Christian Time-Keeping Schemes in Gal. 4:10 and Col. 2:16." *New Testament Studies* 42 (1996) 120–32.
Mason, Steve. "Jews, Judaeans, Judaizing, Judaism: Problems of Categorization in Ancient History." *Journal for the Study of Judaism in the Persian, Hellenistic, and Roman Periods* 38 (2007) 457–512.
Meißner, Stefan. *Die Heimholung des Ketzers: Studien zur jüdischen Auseinandersetzung mit Paulus*. WUNT 2.87. Tübingen: Mohr Siebeck, 1996.
Mitchell, Margaret M. "Pauline Accommodation and 'Condescension' (συγκατάβασις) 1 Cor 9:19–23 and the History of Influence." In *Paul Beyond the Judaism/Hellenism Divide*, edited by Troels Engberg-Pedersen, 197–214. Louisville, KY: Westminster John Knox, 2001.
Mitternacht, Dieter. "Foolish Galatians?—A Recipient-Oriented Assessment of Paul's Letter." In *The Galatians Debate: Contemporary Issues in Rhetorical and Historical Interpretation*, edited by Mark D. Nanos, 408–33. Peabody, MA: Hendrickson, 2002.
———. *Forum für Sprachlose: Eine kommunikationspsychologische und epistotarrhetorische Untersuchung des Galaterbriefs*. CBNT 30. Stockholm: Almqvist & Wiksell, 1999.
Nanos, Mark D. "Are Jews Outside of the Covenants If Not Confessing Jesus as Messiah? Questioning the Questions, the Options for the Answers Too." Paper presented at the "Paul within Judaism" session of the Society of Biblical Literature Annual Meeting, November 23, 2015.
———. "'Broken Branches': A Pauline Metaphor Gone Awry? (Romans 11:11–36)." In *Between Gospel and Election: Explorations in the Interpretation of Romans 9–11*, edited by Florian Wilk and J. Ross Wagner, 339–76. Tübingen: Mohr Siebeck, 2010. (See volume 2 in this series of collected essays.)
———. "'Callused,' Not 'Hardened': Paul's Revelation of Temporary Protection Until All Israel Can Be Healed." In *Reading Paul in Context: Explorations in Identity Formation*, edited by Kathy Ehrensperger and J. Brian Tucker, 52–73. London: T. & T. Clark, 2010. (See volume 2 in this series of collected essays.)
———. "Challenging the Limits That Continue to Define Paul's Perspective on Jews and Judaism." In *Reading Israel in Romans: Legitimacy and Plausibility of Divergent Interpretations*, edited by Cristina Grenholm and Daniel Patte, 217–29. Romans through History and Culture Series, vol. 1. Harrisburg, PA: Trinity, 2000. (See volume 2 in this series of collected essays.)
———. "'The Gifts and the Calling of God are Irrevocable' (Romans 11:29): If So, How Can Paul Declare that 'Not All Israelites Truly Belong to Israel' (9:6)?" *Studies in Christian-Jewish Relations* 11 (2016) 1–17. http://ejournals.bc.edu/ojs/index.php/scjr/article/view/9525. (See volume 2 in this series of collected essays.)

———. "Have Paul and His Communities Left Judaism for Christianity? A Review of the Paul-Related Chapters in *Jewish Believers in Jesus and Jewish Christianity Revisited*." Paper presented in the Jewish Christianity Consultation at the Annual Meeting of the Society of Biblical Literature, San Diego, CA, November 19, 2007. http://www.marknanos.com/SBL-07-Jewish-Chrstnty.pdf.

———. "How Could Paul Accuse Peter of 'Living *Ethné*-ishly' in Antioch (Gal 2:11–21) If Peter Was Eating according to Jewish Dietary Norms?" *Journal for the Study of Paul and His Letters* 6.2 (2016) 199–223. (See volume 3 in this series of collected essays.)

———. "How Inter-Christian Approaches to Paul's Rhetoric Can Perpetuate Negative Valuations of Jewishness—Although Proposing to Avoid that Outcome." *Biblical Interpretation* 13 (2005) 255–69. (See chapter 2 in this volume of collected essays.)

———. "Intruding 'Spies' and 'Pseudo-brethren': The Jewish Intra-Group Politics of Paul's Jerusalem Meeting (Gal 2:1–10)." In *Paul and His Opponents*, edited by Stanley E. Porter, 59–97. Pauline Studies 2. Leiden: Brill, 2005. (See volume 3 in this series of collected essays.)

———. *The Irony of Galatians: Paul's Letter in First-Century Context*. Minneapolis: Fortress, 2002.

———. "The Jewish Context of the Gentile Audience Addressed in Paul's Letter to the Romans." *Catholic Biblical Quarterly* 61 (1999) 283–304. (See volume 2 in this series of collected essays.)

———. "A Jewish View." In *Four Views on the Apostle Paul*, edited by Michael F. Bird, 159–93. Counterpoints. Grand Rapids: Zondervan, 2012.

———. *The Mystery of Romans: The Jewish Context of Paul's Letter*. Minneapolis: Fortress, 1996.

———. "The Myth of the 'Law-Free' Paul Standing between Christians and Jews." *Studies in Christian-Jewish Relations* 4 (2009) 1–21. https://ejournals.bc.edu/ojs/index.php/scjr/article/view/1511/1364. (See chapter 3 in this volume of collected essays.)

———. "Out-Howling the Cynics: Reconceptualizing the Concerns of Paul's Audience from His Polemics in Philippians 3." In *The People Beside Paul: The Philippian Assembly and History from Below*, edited by Joseph A. Marchal, 183–221. Early Christianity and Its Literature. Atlanta: SBL Press, 2015.

———. "Paul's Non-Jews Do Not Become 'Jews,' But Do They Become 'Jewish'?: Reading Romans 2:25–29 within Judaism, alongside Josephus." *Journal of the Jesus Movement in its Jewish Setting* 1 (2014) 26–53. http://www.jjmjs.org/uploads/1/1/9/0/11908749/nanos_pauls_non-jews.pdf (See chapter 5 in this volume of collected essays.)

———. "Paul's Polemic in Philippians 3 as Jewish-Subgroup Vilification of Local Non-Jewish Cultic and Philosophical Alternatives." *Journal for the Study of Paul and His Letters* 3 (2013) 47–91. (See volume 4 in this series of collected essays.)

———. "Paul's Relationship to Torah in Light of His Strategy 'to Become Everything to Everyone' (1 Corinthians 9:19–23)." In *Paul and Judaism: Crosscurrents in Pauline Exegesis and the Study of Jewish-Christian Relations*, edited by Didier Pollefeyt and Reimund Bieringer, 106–40. LNTS 463. London: T. & T. Clark, 2012. (See volume 4 in this series of collected essays.)

———. "Paul's Reversal of Jews Calling Gentiles 'Dogs' (Philippians 3:2): 1600 Years of an Ideological Tale Wagging an Exegetical Dog?" *Biblical Interpretation* 17 (2009) 448–82. (See volume 4 in this series of collected essays.)

———. "The Polytheist Identity of the 'Weak,' and Paul's Strategy to 'Gain' Them: A New Reading of 1 Corinthians 8:1—11:1." In *Paul: Jew, Greek, and Roman*, edited by Stanley E. Porter, 179–210. Pauline Studies 5. Leiden: Brill, 2008. (See volume 4 in this series of collected essays.)

———. "The Question of Conceptualization: Qualifying Paul's Position on Circumcision in Dialogue with Josephus's Advisors to King Izates." In *Paul within Judaism: Restoring the First-Century Context to the Apostle*, edited by Mark D. Nanos and Magnus Zetterholm, 105–52. Minneapolis: Fortress, 2015.

———. "Reading the Antioch Incident (Gal 2:11–21) as a Subversive Banquet Narrative." *Journal for the Study of Paul and his Letters* (forthcoming). (See volume 3 in this series of collected essays.)

———. "A Torah-Observant Paul? What Difference Could It Make for Christian/Jewish Relations Today?" Paper presented at the Christian Scholars Group for Christian/Jewish Relations, Boston, June 4–6, 2005. http://http://www.marknanos.com/Boston-Torah-Obs-5-9-05.pdf.

———. "Was Paul a 'Liar' for the Gospel? The Case for a New Interpretation of Paul's 'Becoming Everything to Everyone' in 1 Corinthians 9:19–23." *Review and Expositor* 110 (2013) 591–608. (See volume 4 in this series of collected essays.)

———. "What Was at Stake in Peter's 'Eating with Gentiles' at Antioch?" In *The Galatians Debate: Contemporary Issues in Rhetorical and Historical Interpretation*, edited by Mark D. Nanos, 282–318. Peabody, MA: Hendrickson, 2002. (See volume 3 in this series of collected essays.)

———. "Why the 'Weak' in 1 Corinthians 8—10 Were Not Christ-Believers." In *Saint Paul and Corinth: 1950 Years Since the Writing of the Epistles to the Corinthians: International Scholarly Conference Proceedings (Corinth, 23–25 September 2007)*, edited by Constantine J. Belezos, Sotirios Despotis and Christos Karakolis, 385–404. Athens: Psichogios, 2009. (See volume 4 in this series of collected essays.)

Nanos, Mark D., and Magnus Zetterholm, eds. *Paul within Judaism: Restoring the First-Century Context to the Apostle*. Minneapolis: Fortress, 2015.

Nickelsburg, G. W. E. "Revealed Wisdom as a Criterion for Inclusion and Exclusion: From Jewish Sectarianism to Early Christianity." In *To See Ourselves as Others See Us: Christians, Jews, Others in Late Antiquity*, edited by J. Neusner and E. Frerichs, 73–82. Chico, CA: Scholars, 1985.

Paget, James Carleton. "The Definition of the Terms Jewish Christian and Jewish Christianity in the History of Research." In *Jewish Believers in Jesus: The Early Centuries*, edited by Oskar Skarsaune and Reidar Hvalvik, 22–52. Peabody, MA: Hendrickson, 2007.

"The Paul Page." Website with a section dedicated to the discussion of Paul within Judaism: http://www.thepaulpage.com/paul-within-judaism/.

Räisänen, Heikki. *Paul and the Law*. Philadelphia: Fortress, 1986.

Richardson, Peter. "Pauline Inconsistency: 1 Corinthians 9:19–23 and Galatians 2:11–14." *New Testament Studies* 26 (1979) 347–62.

Robertson, Paul M. *Paul's Letters and Contemporary Greco-Roman Literature*. Leiden: Brill, 2016.

Rudolph, David J. *A Jew to the Jews: Jewish Contours of Pauline Flexibility in 1 Corinthians 9:19-23*. 2nd ed. Eugene, OR: Pickwick, 2016.
Runesson, Anders. "Inventing Christian Identity: Paul, Ignatius, and Theodosius I." In *Exploring Early Christian Identity*, edited by Bengt Holmberg, 59-92. WUNT 226. Tübingen: Mohr Siebeck, 2008.
———. "Particularistic Judaism and Universalistic Christianity? Some Critical Remarks on Terminology and Theology." *Studia Theologica* 54 (2000) 55-75.
———. "Placing Paul: Institutional Structures and Theological Strategy in the World of the Early Christ-believers." *Svensk exegetisk årsbok (SEÅ)* 80 (2015) 43-67.
———. "The Question of Terminology: The Architecture of Contemporary Discussions on Paul." In *Paul within Judaism: Restoring the First-Century Context to the Apostle*, edited by Mark D. Nanos and Magnus Zetterholm, 53-77. Minneapolis: Fortress, 2015.
Sanders, E. P. *Paul and Palestinian Judaism: A Comparison of Patterns of Religion*. Philadelphia: Fortress, 1977.
———. *Paul, the Law, and the Jewish People*. Philadelphia: Fortress, 1985.
Schoeps, Hans Joachim. *The Jewish-Christian Argument: A History of Theologies in Conflict*. Translated by David Green. London: Faber and Faber, 1965. (Published in German in 1961 as *Israel und Christenheit: Jüdisch-christliches Religionsgespräch in neunzehn Jahrhunderten* [original first edition: *Jüdisch-Christliches Religionsgespräch in 19 Jahrhunderten: Geschichte einer theologischen Auseinandersetzung* [Berlin: 1937])
———. *Paul: The Theology of the Apostle in the Light of Jewish Religious History*. Philadelphia: Westminster, 1961.
Schwartz, Daniel R. "'Judaean' or 'Jew'? How Should We Translate *Ioudaios* in Josephus?" In *Jewish Identity in the Greco-Roman World = Jüdische Identität in der griechisch-römischen Welt*, edited by Jörg Frey, Daniel R. Schwartz and Stephanie Gripentrog, 3-27. Ancient Judaism and early Christianity 71. Leiden: Brill, 2007.
———. *Judeans and Jews: Four Faces of Dichotomy in Ancient Jewish History*. Toronto: University of Toronto Press, 2014.
Scott, Bernard Brandon. *The Real Paul: Recovering His Radical Challenge*. Salem, OR: Polebridge, 2015.
Segal, Alan F. *Paul the Convert: The Apostolate and Apostasy of Saul the Pharisee*. New Haven: Yale University Press, 1990.
Stanford, W. B. *The Ulysses Theme: A Study in the Adaptability of a Traditional Hero*. Dallas: Spring, 1992.
Stendahl, Krister. "Biblical Theology, Contemporary." In *The Interpreter's Dictionary of the Bible*, edited by George Arthur Buttrick, 418-32. Nashville: Abingdon, 1962.
———. *Paul Among Jews and Gentiles, and Other Essays*. Philadelphia: Fortress, 1976.
Stowers, Stanley Kent. *A Rereading of Romans: Justice, Jews, and Gentiles*. New Haven: Yale University Press, 1994.
Thiessen, Matthew. *Contesting Conversion: Genealogy, Circumcision, and Identity in Ancient Judaism and Christianity*. New York: Oxford University Press, 2011.
———. *Paul and the Gentile Problem*. New York: Oxford University Press, 2015.
Thurén, Lauri. *Derhetorizing Paul: A Dynamic Perspective on Pauline Theology and the Law*. WUNT 124. Tübingen: Mohr Siebeck, 2000.
Tofighi, Fatima. *Paul's Letters and the Construction of the European Self*. Library of New Testament Studies Series 572. London: Bloomsbury T. & T. Clark, 2017.
Tomson, Peter J. *Paul and the Jewish Law: Halakha in the Letters of the Apostle to the Gentiles*. CRINT. Minneapolis: Fortress, 1990.

Tucker, J. Brian. *"Remain in Your Calling": Paul and the Continuation of Social Identities in 1 Corinthians*. Eugene, OR: Pickwick, 2011.

———. *You Belong to Christ: Paul and the Formation of Social Identity in 1 Corinthians 1–4*. Eugene, OR: Pickwick, 2010.

Wassen, Cecilia. "Do You Have to Be Pure in a Metaphorical Temple? Sanctuary Metaphors and Construction of Sacred Space in the Dead Sea Scrolls and Paul's Letters." In *Purity, Holiness, and Identity in Judaism and Christianity*, edited by Carl S. Ehrlich, Anders Runesson, and Eileen Schuller, 55–86. Tübingen: Mohr Siebeck, 2013.

Watson, Francis. *Paul, Judaism, and the Gentiles: A Sociological Approach*. SNTSMS 56. Cambridge: Cambridge University Press, 1989.

Wendt, Heidi. *At the Temple Gates: The Religion of Freelance Experts in the Roman Empire*. New York: Oxford University Press, 2016.

Westerholm, Stephen. *Perspectives Old and New on Paul: The "Lutheran" Paul and His Critics*. Grand Rapids: Eerdmans, 2004.

Williams, Margaret H. "The Meaning and Function of *Ioudaios* in Graeco-Roman Inscriptions." *Zeitschrift für Papyrologie und Epigraphik* 116 (1997) 249–62.

Wright, N. T. *Paul and the Faithfulness of God*. COQG 4. Minneapolis: Fortress, 2013.

Wyschogrod, Michael. *Abraham's Promise: Judaism and Jewish-Christian Relations*. Radical Traditions. Grand Rapids: Eerdmans, 2004.

Zetterholm, Magnus. *Approaches to Paul: A Student's Guide to Recent Scholarship*. Minneapolis: Fortress, 2009.

———. "Paul and the Missing Messiah." In *The Messiah: In Early Judaism and Christianity*, edited by Magnus Zetterholm, 33–55. Minneapolis: Fortress, 2007.

———. "Paul within Judaism: The State of the Questions." In *Paul within Judaism: Restoring the First-Century Context to the Apostle*, edited by Mark D. Nanos and Magnus Zetterholm, 31–51. Minneapolis: Fortress, 2015.

PART II

Exploring the Implications for Exegesis and Christian-Jewish Relations

2

How Inter-Christian Approaches to Paul's Rhetoric Can Perpetuate Negative Valuations of Jewishness—Although Proposing to Avoid That Outcome

[255] WHERE MATTERS OF Judaism are concerned, the discourse in Pauline studies has improved immensely in recent years, and the intention to do Christian theology in the light of the Shoah is evident in many contemporary projects. As monumental and welcome as some of these developments have been, for a Jewish reader or Jewish–Christian relations critic there is much that remains problematic in the discourse, and in the ideas upon which it depends. I aim to illustrate one of the areas where negative evaluations of Jewish*ness*—that is, the identity, ideas, motives, and behavior associated with the ideals of Jewish people and religious life—continue to arise in the interpretation of Paul's texts. I hope that focusing attention on a detail that represents the kind of matters that continue to permeate the language of the discipline will provide a useful example of broader trends that continue to undermine the effort to eliminate the traditional negative valuations of Judaism characteristic of the discourse in the past.

I do not have in view those scholars who are not concerned and do not express concern to avoid anti-Jewishness—that is a different matter altogether. Rather, the goal is to investigate how problematic judgments persist in the work of scholars who state clearly the intention to avoid expressing anti-Jewish sentiments by way of a specific move to read Paul within historical and rhetorical inter-mural Christian constructions of the situations his letters address. Appeal to its ability to undermine anti-Jewishness has become a common refrain. Although I think that this approach could be helpful, as supposed (and employed!) by several of my fellow-panelists,[1] I have found the results to date to be largely disappointing. [256] This construction does not have the power to accomplish the goal of eliminating anti-Jewish rhetoric if it is not consistently applied, and if the traditional privileging of positively valued non-Jewish Christianness over negatively valued Jewishness persists, for example, in the course of the exegetical discourse itself. It also makes it difficult to understand Paul's position as truly Jewish, and his rhetoric as intra-Jewish, as many of these proponents also simultaneously suggest.[2] Moreover, it needs to work especially hard at how it values the Jewishness of the Christ-believers it constructs, if it hopes to avoid the *a fortiori* inference that what is assessed negatively for them would logically apply all the more to the Jewishness of Jews and Judaisms that do not even share that faith in Christ.

For efficiency, I will focus on some examples that arise in the work of J. Louis Martyn, particularly related to the interpretation of Paul's voice in Galatians, and the construction of Jewishness they seem to imply.[3] I want to make it unmistakably clear that I am not questioning Martyn's intentions, only whether the exegesis conducted under this construction succeeds in the ways proposed.[4] To strengthen this point, I want to note that when beginning my own investigation of Galatians I was persuaded of the historical probability and ideological desirability of the intra- or inter-Christian proposition. Yet as my exegesis of the text proceeded, it became plain to me that Paul's rhetoric was probably not best understood to be intra-Christian, but intra-Jewish, involving a difference of opinion between his Jewish subgroups and non-Christ-believing Jewish authorities of the larger Jewish communities who were appealing to the traditional convention for incorporation of non-Jews by way of proselyte conversion. Each "Jewish" group [257] appealed to Torah, but to different conclusions based upon their belief about the relevance of the claimed meaning for Jesus Christ

1. Cf. Gaston, *Paul and the Torah*; Gager, *Reinventing Paul*, read Paul as dealing only with gentiles, which makes a substantial difference for how their interpretation of Paul's oppositional rhetoric is assessed.

2. E.g., Dunn, "Echoes of Intra-Jewish Polemic in Paul's Letter to the Galatians."

3. Many other examples can be provided from the work of scholars in the field developing the same basic lines of argument, and to varying degrees, could be subject to the same or similar criticism as that offered below.

4. In addition to the explicit statements to be surveyed to this effect, Martyn's efforts to promote positive Christian relations toward Jews in his work are evident in his discussions of Leo Baeck (see Martyn's essays in Rothschild [ed.], *Jewish Perspectives on Christianity*; and "Leo Baeck's Reading of Paul").

for the inclusion of non-Jews. That is, each proceeded with different views about whether the age to come—when such inclusion of the other nations as nations instead of by becoming members of Israel (and thus undertaking proselyte conversion) would be appropriate—had begun, or not.[5] As I pondered the dilemma created for me ideologically by moving the tension to a Christ-believing/non-Christ-believing line, I realized several problems with the presupposed advantages of the inter-Christian construct. Not only did I begin to recognize historical and rhetorical issues that this construction did not resolve, about which I have written a monograph, but I also saw that it did not necessarily hold the ideological promise I had supposed. This forum offers me the opportunity to explain some of the discoveries on the ideological front.

I will not deal here with agreements and disagreements I may have with the particulars of the interpretations discussed,[6] but with the paradigms within which they work. I hope that those mentioned will agree that the few examples dealt with in this brief essay are fair representations of statements they make.

In summary comments for a distinguished 1994 symposium on Paul and the Mosaic Law, James Dunn proposed that the consensus to be sought should be based upon finding the *"common ground between Paul and his fellow Christian Jews with whom he was in dispute"* (emphasis his).[7] This statement, coupled with several others of that nature, such as the perception that these Christian Jews opposed [258] Paul's gospel,[8] reveals an interpretive decision Dunn assumes to be largely if not entirely beyond debate among the participants. Its influence can be clearly traced in Pauline scholarship since it provided the basic framework for F. C. Baur's interpretation of early Christianity: the dispute is an inter-mural "Christian" one between "Pauline" and "Jewish" Christianity. Dunn makes explicit the ideological benefit that is central to the theme under discussion here: this inter-Christian approach, since it moves the dispute away from one with non-Christ-believing Jews, "cuts the nerve of much of the charge of anti-Judaism laid against Paul."[9]

---

5. The full argument is set out in Nanos, *The Irony of Galatians*.

6. That criticism is undertaken in my *Irony of Galatians*, especially pp. 110–92. For methodological reasons explained therein (pp. 62–72, 137–58), my interaction with interpretations of the Antioch Incident and Jerusalem meetings is detailed elsewhere ("What Was at Stake in Peter's 'Eating with Gentiles' at Antioch?"; "Intruding 'Spies' and 'Pseudo-Brethren': The Jewish Intra-Group Politics of Paul's Jerusalem Meeting [Gal 2:1–10]").

7. Dunn, "In Search of Common Ground," 309.

8. Ibid., 312.

9. Ibid., 310. This deduction resonates with a note in his 1993 Galatians volume

Two problems with this conclusion immediately come to mind. The first is manifest in the way that this approach failed to inhibit the intensely anti-Jewish rhetoric filling the work of F. C. Baur and, to various degrees, many other interpreters since him, making it at least suspect as the right tool for cutting this nerve. Baur's work, of course, is from a much different time and place than the works I wish to address, but it was also based upon constructing an inter-Christian template for interpreting Paul's rhetoric. For example, his assessment of the essential nature of Paul's opponents in Galatia, although identified as Jewish Christians, did not attempt to avoid anti-Jewishness, and provides a forum to express his negative assessment of non-Christian Judaism all the more: "the chief reason why their Judaistic position was so narrow was just their natural incapacity to raise themselves from the lower state of religious consciousness to a higher and freer one."[10] For him, "Christianity is the absolute religion, the religion of the spirit and of [259] freedom, with regard to which Judaism belongs to an inferior standpoint, from which it must be classed with heathenism" under the weak and worthless elements of the world (he quotes the Greek of Gal 4:9).[11] Not only was Baur's discourse anti-Jewish regardless of this inter-Christian construction, it was precisely the Jewishness remaining within Jewish-Christianity that was objectionable to him, because Jewishness was by nature a detrimental force (e.g., particularistic versus universalistic).[12]

The second problem has not been as clearly realized, but I propose that it arises from the permission that this position grants itself to express uninhibited negative evaluations of Christ-believing Jewishness, which logically extends all the more (*a fortiori*) to the Jewishness of those who do not even share the bond of Christ-faith, although this inference is often apparently not drawn, in fact, it appears to go generally unrecognized. Demonstrating

---

in the Black's New Testament Commentary series, where Dunn refers approvingly to Mussner's observation about the importance of recognizing "the conclusion that Paul was not attacking Jews as such, far less the Jews, but only Christian Jews, fellow Christians of Jewish origin," in the context of discussing Paul's rhetorical attacks in Galatians (*The Epistle to the Galatians*, 10 n. 1).

10. Baur, *Paul the Apostle of Jesus Christ*, 263. Baur further states that Galatians should be read with this point of view in mind: "It places us in the midst of the great excitement of the critical struggle which had begun between Judaism and Christianity, in the decision of the momentous question whether there should be a Christianity free from Judaism and essentially different from it, or whether Christianity should only exist as a form of Judaism, that is to say, as nothing else than a modified and extended Judaism" (p. 263).

11. Ibid., 265.

12. Cf. Elliott, *Liberating Paul*, 66–72; Ehrensperger, *That We May be Mutually Encouraged*, 123–25; Buell and Johnson Hodge, "The Politics of Interpretation: The Rhetoric of Race and Ethnicity in Paul," 242–43.

this problem will be the focus of this essay. No attempt will be made to discuss the variety of examples or the different kinds of advantages and disadvantages particular to each.

J. Louis Martyn's commentary on Galatians offers a significant window into recent trends in Pauline scholarship.[13] Not many commentaries receive the kind of praise granted by Richard Hays in his review, in which this volume is declared to provide "provocative scholarship, unmatched in its penetrating insight and theological depth by any NT commentary of our generation."[14] Moreover, the introduction directly addresses the significance of Paul's voice for Jewish–Christian relations in a section entitled "Galatians as Read by Jews and Christians Today."[15] Here Martyn observes that the reader will discover with him, against the traditional [260] interpretations, that "anti-Judaic intention on Paul's part ... is not present in the text."[16] The reasons given are several. The primary one is that "the ruling polarity is not that of Christianity versus Judaism, church versus synagogue," but "rather the cosmic antinomy of God's apocalyptic act in Christ versus religion, and thus the gospel versus religious tradition."[17] Religion here is defined by Martyn as "the various communal, cultic means ... by which human beings seek to know and to be happily related to the gods or God," in particular, it "is a human enterprise."

Martyn explains that what Paul and the church are about are different from anything that anyone or institution was about prior to or independent of them; "that, in the life of the church, worship of God is the corporate act in which the religious distinction of sacred from profane is confessed to have been abolished precisely by God's redemptive deed in Christ," and in this Christ "there is neither Jew nor Gentile," so that the church is the place where "God is planting his war of liberation from all religious differentiations."[18] That differentiation of Christ-believers of Pauline persuasion from the rest of the world seems to (a Jewish reader like) me to be of the same order as the scriptural basis of the Jewish claim made for differentiating God-believers of Mosaic persuasion from the rest of the world, which is also based upon a claim to divine revelation; yet Sinai is defined by Martyn instead as having *introduced* "the sacred/profane distinction" that God in

---

13. Martyn, *Galatians* (1997).
14. Hays in *Review of Biblical Literature*, 59.
15. Martyn, *Galatians*, 35–41.
16. Ibid., 36.
17. Ibid., 37.
18. Ibid., 37 n. 67.

Christ terminates.[19] I suppose the point is that Martyn's interpretation is not specifically anti-Judaic, it is anti-everything-but-its-own-differentiated-group-which-claims-no-differentiation-among-its-members—just as can result from Jewish claims to election. It is also a questionable judgment to make, since Paul's letters *do* distinguish between Jews/Greeks, masters/slaves, males/females, and so on, just as does rhetoric from other religious groups. Furthermore, Paul's letters would not have been written to address the kind of discrimination arising within these churches to which they attest in the first place, if it had been the case that such differences did not exist and lead, as they do in all social groups, to discrimination based upon categorical differences between people [261] and groups.[20] Anyway, I do not see how this approach by definition excludes anti-Jewishness.

The reader of this and other comments will find that Martyn's argument logically depends upon a denial of the claim to revelation that is at the heart of Judaism as well as to the claim to "God's invasive grace" that "is active in the love of neighbor," for outside of Paul's apocalyptic faith there is only "human being's superstitious effort to come to know and to influence God."[21] Martyn nevertheless claims that "Paul never presents it [i.e., his antinomy between apocalyptic and religion] as an attack on the practice of Judaism by Jews," because "the issue he poses is without exception internal to the church," that is, his polemic refers to "Jewish Christians, not to non-Christian Jews": "Paul always focuses this antinomy on issues that are internal to the church."[22]

In Martyn's interpretation, Paul is not engaged in religious activity, but in challenging "the emergence of religion *within* the church"; thus he can state that "the church is not a new religion set over against the old religion, Judaism."[23] Thus, Martyn takes issue with those who propose that Galatians expresses Paul's theory of the Jews: "one of the clearest indications that Galatians is not an anti-Judaic text lies in the fact that the letter contains no theory of the Jews, properly speaking."[24] Martyn's interpretation of Galatians postulates that there were no Jewish communities in the cities of Paul's addressees, no former Jews among their churches, and no Jews in view in Paul's rhetoric, except Christian Jews who had arrived from Jerusalem: "Paul had, in fact, no reason to think that the members of his Galatian

---

19. Ibid., 39.
20. Cf. Hogg and Abrams, *Social Identifications*.
21. Martyn, *Galatians*, 37 n. 67.
22. Ibid., 38.
23. Ibid., 39 (emphasis his).
24. Ibid., 37; cf. 40 n. 73.

churches would ever come into contact with non-Christian Jews. Thus, the subject of church and synagogue lies beyond the letter's horizon."[25]

Coupled with appeal to John Gager's observation that "anti-Judaic writings always speak *about* Jews,"[26] the claim is that Paul's [262] rhetoric— and by implication, Martyn's—cannot be interpreted to be anti-Jewish. A more thoroughgoing *inter-Christian* construction would be hard to imagine. But the logical implications of this definition of apocalyptic versus religion, including the way that the revelation is reserved by definition only for the Christian church—forget that Paul's Scriptures claim for Abraham the same basis for circumcision as well as for Moses the same basis for the giving of the commandments, to name just two examples—cannot help but reflect the view that not only is *Christian* Judaism bankrupt, but all the more, by implication, is *non-Christian* Judaism. Martyn's rhetoric reflects this *a fortiori* logic at various points.

Martyn senses a problem with the introductory claim that Judaism is never in view in Galatians when dealing with 1:13-14. This passage may "contain an *implication* with regard to Judaism," namely, that "Paul's zealous observance of the Law failed to liberate him from enslavement to the elements of the old cosmos," which Martyn arrives at by way of reference to 4:3-5;[27] nevertheless, it does not express anti-Judaic sentiments, for this reference to Paul's early life "causes Judaism to lie *just beyond* the letter's horizon."[28] But is that so? Then why is it stated within the letter's argument? But to stay on point, when Martyn discusses the exegesis of 1:13-14, he observes that "*Ioudaïsmos*, 'Judaism,' was coined in the Hellenistic period to refer to *the religion of the Jews* as distinct from the religions of other peoples," so we are witnessing Paul referring to non-Christian Jewish *religion*, in terms that Martyn has clearly defined in antinomy with revelation, and his comment soon after this one displays this logic: "Galatians is thus a letter in which Paul speaks directly and explicitly and repeatedly *about* Judaism as a *religion*. With these references, then, Paul clearly indicates that he *cannot give an account* of the path along which God has now led him *without addressing the issue of religion*."[29] And again, a few pages later, Martyn states, when writing

---

25. Ibid., 40. Elsewhere, Martyn pushes the point even further in a way important to his thesis with respect to the setting for interpreting Paul's rhetoric by arguing that "Paul is unlikely to have spoken in any detail of his life as a Jew or even of Judaism itself" (p. 153).

26. Ibid., 40 n. 70 (emphasis Martyn's).

27. Ibid., 38.

28. Ibid., 41, n. 75 (emphasis mine).

29. Ibid., 154 (one of the "religion" emphases his!; other emphases, including those using "religion," mine).

of the sharp contrast he understands Paul to be making between his former life as a Law-observant Jew and the next period as analogous to "the contrast between the present evil age and the new creation": "after his apocalyptic call at God's own hands . . . he saw that Judaism was now revealed [263] to be a *religion*, as distinguished from God's apocalyptic and new-creative act in Christ."[30] Surely these statements contradict his earlier denial that Galatians reflects a theory of the Jews. Moreover, Martyn here admits that Paul writes "about" Jewish religion, meeting the criterion he cited as necessary in order to qualify the rhetoric to be anti-Jewish.

Another element in Martyn's argument about 1:13-14 that undermines the claim that his interpretation of Paul's rhetoric is not anti-Judaic arises when discussing Paul's call for the Galatians to imitate himself in 4:12. Martyn states: "Not observant of the Law when he was among them, Paul became like them in that he could think of himself as a former Gentile (4:3). Now—given their temptation to credit the message of the Teachers—they are to become like him in regarding themselves as former Jews (4:5)."[31] But one wonders how the addressees as described by Martyn could understand such a proposition, since, according to Martyn, there were and are no Jews among the addressees, including Paul, who was no longer a Jew or behaving like one and did not discuss his former life as a Jew when among them, and no Jews are expected to arrive. Does this statement not exemplify the fact that the discourse and the ideas that have dominated the study of Paul overcome both the logic of new ideas and the ability to express different intentions consistently in the midst of the details of the exegetical process?[32] For here the addressees are to conceptualize their own state and their responsibility to follow Paul's advice in thoroughly Christian terms that require a shared negative valuation of what it meant to be a Jew in order to understand what it should mean to be a Christian. It is difficult not to hear with Daniel Boyarin an echo of the anti-Semitic legacy of labeling as "Jew" and "Jewish" and "Judaism" that which is negatively valued in European culture, to the degree that "the Jew within" symbolized human evil in Nazi propaganda. It is just this language that one discovers in Käsemann's work, such as when he states: "In and with Israel he [Paul] strikes at the hidden Jew in all of us, at the man who validates rights and demands over against God on the [264] basis of God's past dealings with him and to this extent is serving not God but an illusion."[33] That is notable because Martyn quotes

---

30. Ibid., 164 (emphasis on "religion" his!).
31. Ibid., 420.
32. Cf. Kelley, *Racializing Jesus*, for an excellent discussion of this problem.
33. Käsemann, "Paul and Israel," 186. See the critique of this and similar statements

from this Käsemann article favorably when defining religion as that which provides the human being with "an illusion of God."[34] In spite of Martyn's stated intentions, is there not at work here a Pauline discourse that is based on a theory of Jewishness, indeed, a negative assessment of a people and religious life that Paul's addressees as well as Martyn's readers are assumed to share knowledge "about"? Does such discourse substantiate the claim to have avoided anti-Jewishness, for Martyn, for his implied readers, or for the Paul for which Martyn's interpretation speaks?

To sum up the problem: this Jewish reader of Martyn's commentary cannot read it without seeing that the negative valuation of religion that it posits and applies to Christ-believing interest groups that maintain their Jewishness extends logically to the negative valuation of non-Christian Judaism, of Jewishness in general, in spite of contrary assertions and the expression of benevolent intentions. And I am not the only reader to recognize this problem. In the overall appreciative review of Martyn's commentary by Richard Hays, he similarly observes: "Nonetheless, the letter's slanderous statements about the Law and its radical negation (on Martyn's reading) of the election of Israel seemingly leave no room for the continuing existence of a Law-observant Jewish people."[35]

[265] Many scholars proceed with inter-Christian constructions for reading Paul, postulating a relatively if not entirely separate circle for Christianity, albeit a divided circle, within which they seek to interpret the conflict they imagine between Paul and Jewish Christianity, variously labeled. It is historically problematic, because, at the very least, such a circle

---

by Käsemann in Boyarin, *A Radical Jew*, 209–14.

34. Martyn, *Galatians*, 37 n. 67.

35. Hays, review in *Review of Biblical Literature*, 64. Similar concern is expressed in the review by John Barclay from the same review session in *Review of Biblical Literature*, 48. In view of Claudia Setzer's charge that my critique of Martyn involves anachronism ("Because Paul's Law-free mission has survived and won the day . . ." ["Does Paul Need to be Saved?" 296]), I want to point out that I disagree with the working assumptions of Martyn (and these reviewers and Setzer to the degree that they might share them) that Paul is understood to see the Law and Israel's election as terminated. I believe that these notions of a "*Law-free* Paul" and "*Law-free* gospel/mission," from which many Pauline interpreters work (and the stated basis for Setzer's criticism), express later interpretive constructions of Paul that are historically doubtful. They should be subject to critical distance from the later "Pauline" trajectories, and not assumed to represent the historical Paul instead of being themselves interpretive constructions. In other words, because this construction of Paul "won" does not mean that it represents Paul's voice. Martyn shows a similar concern to identify anachronism in the portrait of Paul with which Baeck worked: "The first flaw arises from Baeck's tendency to credit first-century authors with views that emerged only much later in the church's history" ("Leo Baeck's Reading of Paul," 61).

cannot be drawn independent of the Jewish communities and norms within which the early Christ-believers began as a Jewish subgroup or subgroups, anymore that it can be drawn independent of the Greco-Roman political and cultural world. The personal and group divisions imagined to exist within the circle correspond to similar personal and group divisions that existed outside of the circle. As I have sought to demonstrate, the usual result—unintentionally, to be sure—is that the inter-Christian constructions circumscribe a smaller scale circle *along the same axis*, thereby merely mimicking the disputes imagined to arise within the larger circle drawn in traditional constructions of Christianity versus Judaism.[36] It is based on a conceptualization of the world positively valuing the Christian component versus the negatively valued Jewish/others components, positively valuing Pauline (non-Jewish) Christianity versus Jewish or other kinds of (unacceptable forms of) Christianity. In other words, it does not change the perception that what is positively or negatively valued is to be analyzed along a non-Jewish/Jewish axis, because that axis divides the circle drawn, albeit a [266] smaller circle, Christianity, into two parts along the same line of differentiation: non-Jewish/Jewish.[37] Although this approach in principle leaves room for a different circle representing non-Jewish Christianity to exist independently, the way that the conflicting values are represented in the "Christian" circle suggests, *a fortiori*, a negative valuation of the norms represented within the Jewish circle, for its members have not even taken the positively valued step of faith in Jesus Christ.

---

36. Since presenting this essay I have become aware of an observation in a similar vein by Richard L. Rubenstein, *mutatis mutandis*: "Those who minimize the break between established Judaism and the primitive Church [i.e., referring to James and Peter, not Paul] tend to interpret Paul's relation with the Church, and especially with Peter, in terms of mutual antipathy. . . . *What is at stake in this interpretation is the question of Paul's relations with his own people.* Those who stress his hostility to those Jewish Christians who insisted on circumcision as a precondition to entry into their community usually picture him as turning his back on his own kin and creating a rival Gentile religion that was destined to maintain an antagonistic posture not only toward Judaism but toward Jewish Christianity as well. This view is consistent with the image of Paul as the turncoat and founder of Christian anti-semitism" ("The Apostle and the Seed of Abraham," 73–74; emphasis his; stated originally (!) in 1972 in *My Brother Paul*, 122–23).

37. The reformation discourse in a similar way negatively valued Roman Catholicism as symbolizing Jewishness, differentiating Christianity along an imposed Jewish/non-Jewish axis.

TOWARD AVOIDING THE PERPETUATION OF ANTI-JEWISHNESS IN PAULINE DISCOURSE

How might this cycle of persistent negative valuations of Jewishness within the discourse interpreting Paul's voice be broken? Here I can only sketch a few suggestions that come to mind for me, and hope for additional suggestions from fellow contributors and readers:

(1) Naturally, change begins with the conviction that things are not as others have supposed them to be. If an interpreter does not believe that Jewishness is a negative value, whether discussing Christ-believing Jews or those who do not share this faith, whether discussing Jewishness in Paul's time or one's own, then it is not something that should arise in his or her analysis. If an interpreter believes that Paul did negatively value Jewishness, but he or she does not, and does not want the potential impact of that interpretation of Paul's voice to perpetuate the harm traditionally caused, then he or she should offer some critical comment that distances what is attributed to Paul's voice from what is believed to be correct for those who share the values of the interpreter on the matter at hand. However, as just discussed, to some degree the problem may persist because it is obscured by the way the discourse itself normally proceeds,[38] which brings up the next point.

(2) Few would likely dispute that the discourse on Paul of previous generations was generally influenced by, when not influential to, [267] the anti-Jewishness that many scholars now seek to avoid and to challenge as mistaken and harmful. It was also not methodologically critical to the degree that is now expected in the field. The prevailing discourse perpetuates the questions and concerns of different times and people, which were of course built upon matters of concern and perspectives of yet earlier times and people. And some of that discourse is plainly anti-Jewish. Therefore, scholars should attempt to develop a new vocabulary and work independently of the language and ideas that dominate the exegetical tradition. New hypotheses for reading Paul need to be constructed and tested. And interpreters should work hard to remain consistent within the new paradigms developed; otherwise, their own potential is subverted.

(3) Scholars should consider approaching the historical and rhetorical situations for interpreting Paul's texts on thoroughly inter/intra-Jewish instead of inter/intra-Christian models, and they should be careful not to mix them, which can undermine the effort. There is good historical reason to explore these approaches, since Paul and the other early believers in Jesus were Jewish and probably understood what they were doing to be Judaism.

---

38. See especially the discussion by Kelley, *Racializing Jesus*.

I think it likely that they thought of themselves in terms of a coalition, a Jewish subgroup or subgroups engaged in a temporary task on behalf of Israel, and not founding a new religion or sect that was in some way less Jewish. These approaches have a better chance of yielding the desired ideological benefit, to the degree that they consistently recognize the issues at dispute in Paul's letters did not revolve around the question of *whether* or *to what extent* Jewish norms such as Torah applied, but to *how* they applied to the new reality he claimed his groups represented, for example, such as is understood to be the case when evaluating the idiosyncratic halakhot (rules) of the Dead Sea Scroll sectarians in view of their rejection of the current administration of the temple. In the case of the Christ-believing Jewish groups, at issue was the *Jewish* claim that the expected age to come consisting of the reconciliation of Israel and the nations had *begun* within the present age, so that members of the nation Israel *and* members of the other nations *now together* worshipped the Creator God of all humankind as one, as equals, without discrimination, although remaining distinguishably Israelites and representatives of the nations when doing so. Otherwise, if representatives of the nations were integrated into [268] the nation Israel by undertaking the rite of proselyte conversion, as was the common convention for full membership in the people of God upheld in the present age among other Jewish groups, that claim would be meaningless. In the language of Paul, "then Christ died gratuitously" (Gal 2:21).

When the shared term is Jewishness, as it is in intra-Jewish terms, the contrast shifts from discussing whether there is something problematic with *Jewishness*, to whether or not a person or group *believes in Jesus Christ*, and the associated claims for what difference that makes. The focus becomes christological. In other words, unlike when the shared term is Christ, the difference between two groups does not fall along a line differentiating levels of respect for Jewish identity and Torah, since Jewish identity and behavior is likely upheld to be of unquestionable value by Jewish groups. Imagining the dispute between and within Jewish group boundaries keeps the focus on the meaning of faith in Jesus for themselves, and others, as Jewish groups. The different rules developed to accommodate the inclusion of non-Jews as equal members would be based upon interpretations of Jewish communal identity and behavior that these Jewish groups believe to be consistent with their faith decision in Jesus Christ. They did not seek the elimination of Jewishness, but the proper expression of Judaism for Jewish and non-Jewish members joined as one in the conviction that what God was in Christ *now* doing in the world was that which was promised to Abraham: his seed would be a blessing to all of the nations.

Another benefit of this conceptualization is that difference is respected. An intra-Jewish construction allows the historical participants as well as the interpreter to respect that having a different opinion about the meaning of Jesus Christ or of appeals to him to legitimate social change within Jewish groups need not represent value judgments that one decision or the other is better; it is just different. It is the one in which you and your group chooses to believe. As I understand Paul, he upheld the Jewish notion that although social (and biological) differences remain in the present age, that is, there remain Jews and non-Jews (and males and females) in Christ, the discrimination usually associated with such differences should not prevail, just as is expected to be the case in the age to come, when even the wolf and the lamb will dwell together. This seems to me to be a sensible and noble ideal for how to approach each other today in Jewish–Christian relations [269] terms, whether sharing his belief that the awaited age has dawned in Jesus Christ, or not.

BIBLIOGRAPHY

Barclay, John. Review of *Galatians* by J. Louis Martyn. *Review of Biblical Literature* (2001). https://www.bookreviews.org/pdf/2064_1356.pdf.

Baur, F. C. *Paul the Apostle of Jesus Christ: His Life and Works, His Epistles and Teachings.* Edited by E. Zellers; translated by A. Menzies. 2nd ed. Peabody, MA: Hendrickson, 2003.

Buell, Denis K., and Caroline J. Johnson Hodge. "The Politics of Interpretation: The Rhetoric of Race and Ethnicity in Paul." *Journal of Biblical Literature* 123.2 (2004) 235–51.

Dunn, James D. G. "Echoes of Intra-Jewish Polemic in Paul's Letter to the Galatians." *Journal of Biblical Literature* 112.3 (1993) 459–77.

———. *The Epistle to the Galatians.* Peabody, MA: Hendrickson, 1993.

———. "In Search of Common Ground." In *Paul and the Mosaic Law,* 309–34. Rev. ed. Grand Rapids: Eerdmans, 2001.

Ehrensperger, Kathy. *That We May be Mutually Encouraged: Feminism and the New Perspective in Pauline Studies.* London: T. & T. Clark, 2004.

Elliott, Neil. *Liberating Paul: The Justice of God and the Politics of the Apostle.* Maryknoll, NY: Orbis, 1994.

Gager, John G. *Reinventing Paul.* Oxford: Oxford University Press, 2000.

Gaston, Lloyd. *Paul and the Torah.* Vancouver, BC: University of British Columbia Press, 1987.

Hays, Richard B. Review of *Galatians* by J. Louis Martyn. *Review of Biblical Literature* (2001). https://www.bookreviews.org/pdf/2064_1359.pdf.

Hogg, Michael A., and Dominic Abrams. *Social Identifications: A Social Psychology of Intergroup Relations and Group Processes.* New York: Routledge, 1986.

Käsemann, Ernst. "Paul and Israel." In *New Testament Questions of Today,* 183–87. Philadelphia: Fortress, 1969.

Kelley, Shawn. *Racializing Jesus: Race, Ideology and the Formation of Modern Biblical Scholarship*. London: Routledge, 2002.

Martyn, J. Louis. *Galatians: A New Translation with Introduction and Commentary*. AB 33. New York: Doubleday, 1997.

———. "Leo Baeck's Reading of Paul." In *Theological Issues in the Letters of Paul*, 47–69. Nashville: Abingdon, 1997.

Nanos, Mark D. "Intruding 'Spies' and 'Pseudo-Brethren': The Jewish Intra-Group Politics of Paul's Jerusalem Meeting (Gal 2:1–10)." In *Paul and His Opponents*, edited by Stanley Porter, 59–97. Pauline Studies 2. Brill, 2005. (See volume 3 in this series of collected essays.)

———. *The Irony of Galatians: Paul's Letter in First-Century Context*. Minneapolis: Fortress, 2002.

———. "What Was at Stake in Peter's 'Eating with Gentiles' at Antioch?" In *The Galatians Debate: Contemporary Issues in Rhetorical and Historical Interpretation*, edited by Mark D. Nanos, 282–318. Peabody, MA: Hendrickson, 2002. (See volume 3 in this series of collected essays.)

Rothschild, Fritz A., ed. *Jewish Perspectives on Christianity*. New York: Continuum, 1996.

Rubenstein, Richard L. "The Apostle and the Seed of Abraham." In *A Shadow of Glory: Reading the New Testament after the Holocaust*, edited by Todd Linafelt, 68–88. New York: Routledge, 2002.

———. *My Brother Paul*. New York: Harper & Row, 1972.

Setzer, Claudia. "Does Paul Need to be Saved?" *Biblical Interpretations* 13.3 (2005) 289–97.

3

The Myth of the "Law-Free" Paul Standing between Christians and Jews[1]

[2] SINCE THE EMERGENCE of historical criticism, many Christian and Jewish scholars have concluded that Jesus was Torah positive, upholding that not even a jot or tittle of the Torah is to be removed (Matt 5:18). Thus, any ostensible disagreements Jesus had with Pharisees or other rival Jewish interest groups were not about the continued role of Torah per se, but over competing interpretations of how to apply Torah. But this new approach does not extend to the apostle Paul. In fact, this new understanding about Jesus has magnified exponentially the tendency to represent Paul as one who devalued Torah and founded Christianity.[2] Now Paul, not Jesus, by his ostensible conversion from Torah to Christ, substantiates the differences between these faith communities.[3] Jesus practiced Judaism, however different his halakhah may have been from that of his rivals; Paul

---

1. This essay is dedicated to Krister Stendahl, may his memory be for a blessing. Special thanks to Andy Johnson, David May, and Bill Stancil for comments on earlier versions of this paper, which was presented as a guest at the Evangelical Theological Society (ETS) Annual Meeting, Providence, RI, November 21, 2008.

2. Surveys of modern Jewish views of Paul include: Fuchs-Kreimer, "The 'Essential Heresy'"; Meißner, *Die Heimholung des Ketzers*; Heschel, *Abraham Geiger and the Jewish Jesus*; Eisenbaum, "Following in the Footnotes of the Apostle Paul"; Langton, "The Myth of the 'Traditional View of Paul' and the Role of the Apostle in Modern Jewish-Christian Polemics"; Langton, "Modern Jewish Identity and the Apostle Paul"; Segal, "Paul's Religious Experience in the Eyes of Jewish Scholars."

3. Rubenstein, *My Brother Paul*, 114, put the matter succinctly: "'Jesus, yes; Paul, never!' would seem to be the watchword of much of the thoughtful Jewish New Testament scholarship in modern times."

did not. With his announcement of the arrival of the kingdom of God, Jesus sought to refine prevailing interpretations of Torah; Paul altogether abandoned it. Thus ironically, a central proposition of Christianity, that it is "not-Judaism," and of Judaism, that it is "not-Christianity," revolves around the prevailing portrait of the "Law-free" (or better, "Torah-free") Paul and his supposedly "Law-free gospel" (or better, "Torah-free gospel"), instead of around Jesus and his teachings.[4]

When Christians celebrate Paul as the apostle of "the gospel of freedom from law," this nomenclature highlights the problem of polemic at work at the level of ideology. "Torah" means "Teaching" rather than "Law." Torah is not simply the teaching of commandments or rituals, but of a way of life that prizes the interests of God and God's creation. The "love command" quoted by Paul (and Jesus) is from the heart of Torah, Lev 19:17–18. Torah includes the teaching of *freedom*, a core value for Judaism just as it is for Christianity. Freedom is at the heart of the celebrations of Sabbath and Pesach, of many commandments enjoining the humane treatment of others, reasoning that extends to the treatment of animals.[5] It is because of freedom that responsibility to God and to each other are magnified in Torah. And the word "gospel" also communicates a central concept of Judaism, the message of good for Israel, and that news which the heralds [3] from Israel will bring to all of the other nations (e.g., Isa 52:6–10; cf. Rom 10:15).[6]

In response to the way that Judaism is portrayed in Christian interpretations of Paul, Jews traditionally characterize him as an apostate who either failed to understand Torah, or rejected it because of his own inadequacies. Even generous treatments of Paul today conclude that his teachings on Torah indicate a religious way of life that does not represent Judaism, instead perhaps advocating its mirror opposite.[7] Yet the Tanakh itself, as well as later forms of Judaism, emphasize God's grace and faith, just as Paul did. We find this view even among extreme halakhists like the community of the Dead Sea Scrolls, and this emphasis continues in Judaism

---

4. This characterization of Paul's attitude toward Torah and Judaism is so widely held that annotation would be superfluous, and inevitably incomplete.

5. See, for example, Lev 26:13; Deut 5:15; 15:1–15; 16:1–12; 24:17–22. I do not mean to discount the weight of the responsibility to do the commandments, which rabbinic Judaism characterizes as the "yoke of the commandments," referring to the Shema (Deut 11:13–21; B. Ber. 2.2), but this is the responsibility of those who are in a covenant relationship with the God who delivered Israel from Egypt, which is also a central element of the *Ge'ulah* (redemption) blessing recited following the *Shema*; similarly, Paul bases the call to keep the commandments on covenant identity in Christ (e.g., 1 Cor 7:19; Gal 5:13—6:10).

6. For more detail, see Nanos, *Irony of Galatians*, 288–96.

7. See, for example, 1QS XI; 1QM XI.4; 1QH VIII.11–18; VII.29–39; XV.15–25.

to this day. One need but consult the rabbinic morning prayers to recognize that while responding to God's call to responsibility, Jews also look to God's lovingkindness, grace, and forgiveness.[8] The actions undertaken, just as for Christians, are in grateful response to God's kindness and the covenant relationship into which this people have entered.

Both of these polemical viewpoints about the other depend upon certain interpretations of Paul's language and intentions. Each community relies upon these choices to protect themselves, to make them different from the other, to show their own religious impulses and systems to be superior. What Christians might celebrate as freedom, Jews might deride as antinomian, illogical, and harmful; what Jews might celebrate as a special calling and sacred obligation, Christians might deride as bondage, self-serving, and passé. Members of both communities want it to be clear that Christianity is not like Judaism, and Judaism is not like Christianity. Consequently, it is difficult and threatening to consider seriously a different reading of Paul regarding Torah that might undermine this dichotomy; that it is ideologically relevant to do so in an age of Christian-Jewish reconciliation is self-evident.

I submit that the prevailing portrayal of Paul's heralding a "Law-free gospel" and teaching a life "freed from Law" for all Christ-followers represents a profound *mis*reading of his texts. For Jews, such as himself, Paul did not teach the end of Torah, including Jewish dietary norms. But he did uphold that Christ-believing *non-Jews* were not to *become Jews*, that they should never be under Torah in the same way that Jews were and remained. Paul himself observed Torah as a matter of faith, as incumbent upon himself as a faithful *Jewish* believer in Christ. He also affirmed Torah unambiguously, proclaiming that the good news in Christ "established" it (Rom 3:31); he went so far as to declare the Torah "spiritual" (Rom 7:14). At issue in his letters to non-Jews was how they were to become members of Judaism, of a politico-religious community and its way of life, without becoming Jews ethnically, that is, without becoming members of Israel. They thus remained without the "advantages" Torah offered (Rom 3:1-2; 9:4-5), but also without the responsibility "fully" to observe Torah like him and other Christ-believing Jews (1 Cor 7:17-24; Gal 5:3). This mixing of different people while retaining their different religio-ethnic identities and thus different relationships to Torah confused some of his original audiences, provoking him to write letters intended to clarify this proposition, but they have misled later interpreters reading his instructions to non-Jews in particular as if universal truths Paul applied without distinction to every person, including Jews.

---

8. See Scherman, *The Complete ArtScroll Siddur*, 24-27, 70-71, 82-83 (Ps 130).

[4] There are viable alternative interpretations for each text upon which the traditional and still prevailing myth of the Torah-free Paul and his supposed Torah-free gospel has been constructed. Thus these traditional portrayals of Paul need not delimit the possibilities for each community's ongoing conceptualizations of the other; there are new perspectives that promise more positive relations going forward. I will demonstrate this in an examination of Paul's treatment of the Jewish dietary commandments, a topic that is central to the traditional and still prevailing constructions of Paul as "Torah-free." First, we turn to a general discussion of Paul's Jewish identity and behavior.

PAUL AS A TORAH-OBSERVANT JEW

That Paul observed Torah according to the halakhic conventions for a Jew of his time and place—including dietary norms—would be in keeping with the logic of his rhetoric. He claims to be a Jew, indeed a Jew beyond reproach (2 Cor 11:22; Gal 2:15; Phil 3:3-6).[9] He argues in 1 Cor 7:17-24 that everyone is to remain in the state in which one was before responding to the gospel message, and thus, in his own case, he should be expected to remain in a circumcised state.[10] He argues that what matters above all for everyone is not their different states of identity, but "keeping the commandments of God" (v. 19).[11]

How does this logic apply to Gal 3:28, where Paul declares that among those who are in Christ there is oneness, and thus that there "is neither Jew nor Greek, neither slave nor free, neither male and female"? In the traditional view, this indicates that Paul eliminates religio-ethnic difference. Yet Paul and his communities know full well that there are differences between slaves and freepersons, between men and women, and that he gave different instructions for each. Instead, in this text, Paul is elaborating on his theme of eliminating discrimination among Christ-followers, and not ignoring

---

9. Stendahl, "The Apostle Paul and the Introspective Conscience of the West."

10. Rabbi Jacob Emden (1697-1776), made a similar point. See Falk, "Rabbi Jacob Emden's Views on Christianity."

11. Regardless of its historical accuracy, Acts bears witness to this interpretation of Paul by his earliest extant biographer. In Acts 21:15-26, Paul takes a Nazarite vow in the temple to deny the rumors that he teaches Jews not to observe Torah, an act that involves a burnt offering. In chs. 21-26, he affirms his identity as a Torah-observant Jew, indeed, as a Pharisee not guilty of charges of breaching the Torah or desecrating the temple. In 15:30 and 16:4, Paul represents the Jerusalem church decision that gentiles are to observe the apostolic decree, and in 16:1-13, he circumcises Timothy.

the fact that differences remain for these dyads, including the religio-ethnic distinction between Jew and Greek.

Paul's argument in Gal 5:3 similarly derives from Paul's maintaining his own Jewish identity. There, following their decision to be faithful to Christ, he argues against his non-Jewish audience's becoming Jewish proselytes, asserting that if one is circumcised, one is obliged "to observe the whole Torah." That argument would not have made sense, to the point of undermining his authority, had his audience thought that he, a circumcised Jew, did not himself observe Torah fully.

Some may argue that the very fact that Paul tries to dissuade the Galatians from circumcision on these terms shows his distaste for Torah. On the contrary, Paul's intent is to subvert not the Torah, but rather the authority of those his audience might suppose represent its ideals. He criticizes his competition, suggesting that they trivialize the advantages of Torah-based identity when they avoid making plain the cost that is involved. From Paul's perspective, the supposedly good news that they present as a complement to faithfulness to Christ, namely, proselyte conversion, is rather a rival "good news" to the "good news" in Christ for non-Jews, who should not become Jews or members of Israel according to Paul's gospel. Although proselyte [5] conversion ostensibly would solve their socio-religious dilemma by making them not mere guests but proselytes—and thus full members of the Jewish community in religio-*ethnic* terms—it actually compromises the gospel proposition that the end of the ages has begun with gathering of the nations alongside of Israel. In addition, proselyte conversion incurs the obligation fully to observe Torah. Paul thus plants here seeds of distrust in the reliability of his competitors' motives and teachings.[12]

In other words, Paul is engaged in intra-Jewish polemic about precisely how to interpret Torah and *not* in disparagement of Torah. The rabbis similarly warn potential proselytes of the enormous responsibility involved in the privilege of Torah observance that comes with this identity transformation.[13] Paul understands that obscuring this fact is itself not righteous; it

---

12. Interpreters miss the point of Galatians when conflating Torah-observance with Torah-identification, as if those whose influence Paul opposes were teaching those without Torah-identification of the need to undertake Torah-observance. But 5:3 makes plain that is not the case. Circumcision of non-Jews is not about Torah-observance, but about Torah-identification. Paul does not challenge Torah-observance at any point in the letter. In *Irony of Galatians*, 267–69, I challenge Paul's usually supposed opposition to Jewish food norms and calendar, leaving only his opposition to proselyte conversion, symbolized in the language of circumcision and works of Torah (that work being specifically the entrance requirement for gaining Torah/Jewish identity).

13. Yebam. 47a-b; Cohen, *The Beginnings of Jewishness*, 198–238.

fails to uphold a central ideal of Torah, the imperative to love one's neighbor as oneself (Lev 19:18; Rom 13:8; Gal 5:14).

There were significant differences between the Judaism of Paul and his disciples and the other Jewish groups which did not profess commitment to Jesus Christ. But these differences did not find expression in derogatory views of Torah, or in reactions to such views. Instead, they focused on the meaning of Christ, both for the people of Israel who observe Torah and for the people of the rest of the nations to whom Israel is to proclaim Christ. The tensions over the interpretation of Torah primarily arise over Paul's claim that the people from the other nations are full co-members of the people of God and yet not under Torah because they are not members of Israel, even after they decide for faith in Christ. For Paul, whether Jesus is the promised one is a question independent of whether Torah continues to define what was promised, and why, and how those of Israel who define themselves by Torah will live.

At issue in Paul's letters is how to portray righteousness for those from the other nations. The dominant Pauline interpretive tradition de-emphasizes this continued ethnic differentiation between the nations and Israel.[14] Often citing as evidence Gal 3:28, it interprets Paul to have universalized all religio-ethnic difference, so as to apply his every instruction to everyone equally, making immaterial any distinction, including Jewishness as an identity and as a way of life.[15] When combined with [6] the traditional interpretation of Gal 4:8-10, which understands Paul to be constructing an analogy between Jewish calendrical observances (including the Sabbath) and idolatry, this logically generates a Pauline teaching that privileges non-Jewish identity and behavioral norms for Christ-followers.[16] They present "Torah-free" as the ideal state universally for all Christ-believing

---

14. Challenging this tradition, see Gaston, *Paul and the Torah*; Gager, *Reinventing Paul*; Runesson, "Particularistic Judaism and Universalistic Christianity?"; Ehrensperger, *That We May Be Mutually Encouraged*; Campbell, *Paul and the Creation of Christian Identity*; Johnson Hodge, *If Sons, Then Heirs*.

15. See, for example, Boyarin, *A Radical Jew*, 4–12, *passim*. Amy-Jill Levine, *The Misunderstood Jew*, 84 (cf. 114, 159), writes: ". . . (Gal 3:28) is not good for Jews, whose identity is then erased. In the church, the vision came true." Closer to my view on this passage are Pinchas Lapide, "The Rabbi From Tarsus"; Segal, *Paul the Convert*, 146; Wyschogrod, *Abraham's Promise*, 188–201; and those listed in the immediately previous note.

16. This widely held interpretation has been challenged by Martin, "Pagan and Judeo-Christian Time-Keeping Schemes in Gal. 4:10 and Col. 2:16"; Nanos, *Irony of Galatians*, 267–69. The calendar Paul mentions lacks the one element that would signify a Jewish way of marking time, namely "weeks." This suggests that Paul is writing about the Roman and local idolatrous calendars, not the Jewish calendar, consistent with his challenge here to those returning to idolatry.

humankind, and not as something applicable to gentiles in ways that do not apply to Jewish believers in Christ.[17] Thus, they assert that Pauline teaching by definition undermines the very essence of Jewish and Israelite identity as set apart by God from that of other peoples and nations, and non-Jewish becomes equivalent to universal. At the same time, logically, Christ-faith now becomes a religio-ethnic identity marker that separates Christ-followers from all others, including Jews, making it no more universal than the Judaism with which the traditional as well as "New Perspective" interpretations find fault for drawing religio-ethnic boundaries between Israel and the nations.

The Acts of the Apostles and the Epistle of James[18] confirm that Paul teaches that Torah is established by Christ, that Christ's faithfulness exemplifies righteousness, that this righteousness was first Israel's, and that now it is Israel's special role to declare this righteousness also to the nations. Anyone who believes in Christ is obligated to live righteously, as is anyone who believes in Torah. In neither case is the goal of pursuing righteousness undertaken to initiate God's favor.[19]

Both Jews and Christ-followers decide to be faithful in order to retain right standing in a covenant relationship that presents obligations to both parties. Anything other than the pursuit of what is right would represent continuing bondage to sin, when bondage to God, the righteous one—the one who does right and judges accordingly—is the desired alternative (cf. Rom 6–8).

The threats to the non-Jews within the Christ-believing Jewish communities founded by Paul were, on the one hand, from their local "pagan" community's hostile reactions to their avoidance of participation in civic and familial cults, tempting [7] these non-Jews to continue in or return to practicing idol rites to avoid such hostilities (e.g., 1 Thess 2; 1 Cor 8–10,

---

17. For more on this matter, including fuller bibliography, see Nanos, "Paul and Judaism: Why Not Paul's Judaism?"

18. James agrees with rather than corrects Paul, although perhaps he challenges a misrepresentation of Paul's teaching.

19. This insight is central to the "New Perspective on Paul." See Sanders, *Paul and Palestinian Judaism*; Dunn, *Jesus, Paul, and the Law*, 183–214; Dunn, "The New Perspective on Paul," especially 185–86. It has been frequently noted by Jews writing about Paul since the mid-nineteenth century. See, for instance, Schoeps, *The Jewish-Christian Argument*, 41–44, 165; Schoeps, *Jüdisch-Christliches Religionsgespräch in 19 Jahrhunderten*, 49–61, 152; Herberg, "Judaism and Christianity: Their Unity and Difference." Some other earlier examples are discussed in Sanders, *Paul and Palestinian Judaism*, 33–59, which also explains the traditional viewpoint that Sanders challenges. It is now a point commonly made; see the discussions listed in footnote 2.

discussed below; Gal 4:8–10;[20] Phil 3[21]), and on the other hand, from the temptation to overcome such religio-ethnic identity problems by undertaking proselyte conversion into Israel in addition to confessing Christ. These social identity conundrums arose to a large degree from Paul's way of teaching non-Jews that they were no longer idolaters and yet they were not becoming Jews either, but rather fellow members of Jewish groups out of the other nations, representing the assembly of the righteous from all of the nations at the dawning of the age to come (Rom 15:7–12).

Why did Paul oppose this religio-ethnic identity-transformation into Jews and Israelites by way of proselyte conversion, which would have probably eased if not eliminated much of the gentile Christ-followers' suffering and confusion? The traditional interpretive approach to Paul argues that in addition to obstructing the universal appeal of the gospel, he considered Israel/Jew to be an inferior identity bound to Torah and thus passé. It would trap these Christ-followers into works-righteousness. It would enslave them to Torah. These non-Jews are instead members of true or spiritual Israel, which is superior to carnal Israel. The "New Perspective" view argues that it is because the ethnic or boundary-marking elements of Torah—such as circumcision, Sabbath observance, and dietary rules—were passé, and observing these would trap these non-Jews in the ostensibly essential Jewish problem of ethnocentric exclusivism. By definition, only universalization in the church could free carnal Israel from this problem, leaving in Christ neither Jew nor Greek.[22] Even though proponents of this perspective have otherwise largely undermined the traditional Christian basis for the negative valuation of Judaism and Torah, they continue to suggest that attaining Jewish proselyte standing would enslave Christ-followers to a lifestyle that is immature, because they are ideally to be "free" from Torah in their supposed

---

20. Nanos, *Irony of Galatians*, 267–71.

21. Nanos, "Paul's Reversal of Jews Calling Gentiles 'Dogs' (Philippians 3:2)."

22. Cf. Dunn, "Who Did Paul Think He Was? A Study of Jewish-Christian Identity," who, on 192, argues that Paul would not give a straight "No" to his identity as a Jew, as long as it was qualified "to come from within and not from without, and that the trappings of Jewish identity, most explicitly the practice of circumcision and food laws, could be equally taken on or put off without affecting the integrity of that Jewishness either way." But Paul would give a clear "No" to being "in Judaism": "the term had become too much identified with ethnicity and separation from other nations; and Paul's self-understanding on just these points had been too radically transformed by his conversion . . . for 'Judaism' to continue to define and identify himself or his apostolic work." See also Dunn, "New Perspective," 198. For critique of this view, see Elliott, *Liberating Paul*, 66–72, 108.

new religion, Christianity.[23] These are aspects of the "New Perspective" view that I seek to challenge.

Instead, I submit, Paul insisted that non-Jews must remain non-Jews, and thus not come under Torah on the same terms as Jews, because it would compromise the propositional truth of the gospel of Christ that the end of the ages has dawned. That proposition maintains that with the resurrection of Christ and arrival of the Spirit the awaited age has begun, when all of the other nations will recognize Israel's God as the One God, the Creator God of all humankind. In this age, Christ-following non-Jews are obligated to bear witness to the righteousness expressed in Torah, that is, the love of God and neighbor, but as representatives of the *other* nations, and not as members of [8] Israel and her Mosaic covenant. This age represents the fulfillment of God's covenant with Abraham, bringing blessing to all of the nations through his seed. But non-Jews becoming Jews by proselyte conversion, symbolized by "circumcision" for males—which in Paul's letters serves as a metonym for completion of the rite of proselyte conversion, just as does "works of law"—would undermine the message that the awaited good for Israel *and* the nations had arrived *now* in Christ Jesus.[24] The proclamation of this proposition was Paul's vocation: unlike his "former" understanding that non-Jews must become members of Israel to become members of the family of Abraham (Gal 5:11; cf. 1:23; Rom 3:28—4:25), this is the new-age "way of living in Judaism" to which he was called by Christ (Gal 1:13-16).

This position was simple, but confusing, and led to many problems for the first non-Jewish believers in the gospel of Christ, and for the Jews proclaiming this message as well. It created the need for a new religio-ethnic category to identify these believers. They were no longer idolaters, and thus no longer represented the *status quo* of the nations from which they came. But they were not Israelites, not Jews, and thus, not worshipers of the God of Israel on the same terms as Jews. Neither ethnic Jews who did not share their faith in Christ, nor their own idolatrous families and neighbors perceived them as full members. Rather they were merely guests of or sympathizers with the socio-ethnic community practicing Judaism. Yet they were to understand themselves as fellow members of the Jewish way of life, of Judaism, of the people of God (cf. Acts 15). Their equal standing with Jews was legitimated by faith in Christ, the faithful representative of God's plan

---

23. Dunn, *Romans 9–16*, 798; in my *The Mystery of Romans*, 88–95, I provide other examples of this phenomenon, and discuss the process of "Luther's trap" for the prevailing interpretations of the "weak" in Romans 14; see also my "Paul and Judaism."

24. For details of this position, see my *Mystery of Romans*, esp. 179–87, and "Paul and the Jewish Tradition: The Ideology of the *Shema*."

to reconcile *all* of the nations equally.²⁵ They were thus not Jews or Israelites, but members of a certain Judaism, of a Jewish subgroup, of a Jewish coalition, of Christ-faith Judaism, the Judaism of Paul post-Damascus.²⁶

This nuanced and controversial way of incorporating non-Jews into the communal life of this Jewish subgroup led to many social problems, as well as confusion in these gentiles' own sense of self. It is in this context that we can understand Paul's relativizing of all identities to the shared identity of Christ-faith. This includes his own highly esteemed and honored identity as a Jew (e.g., Phil 3:4–16), a socio-religiously advantageous identity within the Jewish community, and one that provides for respectful avoidance of idolatrous cults within the broader community, including those related to imperial cult, but an identity that he denies to his non-Jewish audience, since they cannot become proselytes according to his teaching. The category "Christian" does not yet exist, yet he must make these non-Jews realize that they are neither identified any longer with the gods of the other nations, nor are they on the way to becoming members of the nation Israel, even though they now worship Israel's God as the only God of all humankind. This amorphous identity, which does not correspond with the communal lines defining socio-religious identity on either side of the Jewish/gentile divide, creates confusion and marginalization on both sides. It is one that non-Jews in Christ-believing communities seek to make sense of or escape, some by seeking to become proselytes (in Galatia), others by supposing to have replaced Jews (in Rome, independent of Paul's instruction). Paul responded to these developments in his letters. He addressed some of the problems that arose among them from this controversial proposition of the "truth of the [9] gospel": that these Christ-following non-Jews are now members of Judaism, of the socio-religious people of the God of Israel, who the One God of all the nations incorporates in the *ekklesia* without re-identifying them religio-ethnically as Jews or members of the nation Israel. They are thus without the same relationship to Torah that applies to the Jewish members. At the same time, because these gentiles are now members of the Jewish community, they are not without a relationship to Torah-defined norms for living, including dietary practices when among Jews.

PAUL AND JEWISH DIETARY NORMS

It is not possible in this context to discuss all of the relevant passages about Paul's Torah observance, or the vast corpus of secondary literature that

25. Cf. Stendahl, *Paul*.
26. Nanos, "Paul and Judaism."

overwhelmingly assumes (when it does not explicitly argue) that Paul left Judaism, was Law-free, and taught a Law-free gospel. Instead, I will focus on the topic most often discussed in this context, one of the matters that highlights what is at issue in the discussion of Paul and Torah, or better, Paul's version of Christ-believing Judaism: did Paul eat according to Jewish dietary norms or believe that other Jewish Christ-followers should? What about gentile Christ-followers; were they to observe Jewish dietary norms? The primary texts for this discussion include Gal 2:11-15, the so-called Antioch Incident, when Peter withdrew from eating with gentiles because he feared "the ones from circumcision" following the arrival of "certain ones from James"; 1 Corinthians 8-10, the matter of eating in idolatrous settings or of food that had been used in idol rites; and Romans 14-15, concerning how the "strong" ought to behave with respect to the "weak" in faith.[27]

The Antioch Incident

In Gal 2:11-15, Paul informs his audience about an earlier incident in Syrian Antioch when he confronted Peter for lacking faithfulness to the truth of the gospel, because Peter, followed by the rest of the Jews, withdrew from eating with the gentiles after the arrival of "certain ones from James."[28] Thus, for Paul, the mixed meals that they celebrated prior to this breach of communal conduct signified the theological "truth of the message of good" in Christ.

The traditional reading of this text, which continues in the "New Perspective" analyses, understands the "certain ones from James" to represent the ideological view of the Jerusalem church that the Christ-faith movement continues to be a subset of Jewish communal life, of Judaism, in a way that supposedly clashes with Paul's viewpoint.[29] Accordingly, James and the Jerusalem church, so-called Jewish or Palestinian Christianity,[30] held that meals were to be conducted according to prevailing halakhic dietary norms. Moreover, they maintained that gentile believers in Christ should become Jewish proselytes; alternatively, if they wished to follow instead Paul's [10]

---

27. The order of this discussion is based on the consensus view for the chronological order of these texts.

28. A more complete discussion is available in my "What Was at Stake in Peter's 'Eating with Gentiles' at Antioch?"; *Mystery of Romans*, 337-71; "Peter's Hypocrisy in the Light of Paul's Anxiety." The related matter of the Jerusalem meeting in the prior passage is the topic of my "Intruding 'Spies' and 'Pseudo-brethren.'"

29. Dunn, "The Incident at Antioch (Gal 2:11-18)."

30. Problems of terminology and definition are discussed in Jackson-McCabe, ed., *Jewish Christianity Reconsidered*.

conviction that they should not become Jews, then this gentilized, so-called Pauline Christianity should remain separate from Jewish Christianity. Any joint meetings, such as to celebrate the Lord's Supper, should be conducted according to the standards of Jewish Christianity.[31] In contrast, in Antioch, Paul had denounced this position in no uncertain terms, asserting that when joint meetings took place, it was Torah-free standards that should be applied. Christianity was not Judaism; it was to be free from "bondage" to Torah. Anyone proclaiming otherwise subverted the gospel of Christ.

This traditional reading, in its various forms, depends upon several decisions. The following are a few of the most fundamental ones.

First, it bases its interpretation on the notion that what "the ones from circumcision" found objectionable about the mixed meals was that they were not conducted according to prevailing halakhic dietary standards.[32] Paul's accusation that Peter was compelling the gentiles to "judaize," although Peter was himself "living like a gentile," has been understood to mean that Peter had been eating Torah-free, and that he implicitly, if not explicitly, was teaching faith plus proselyte conversion and Torah-observance for gentile Christ-followers.[33] That interpretation supposes that Christ-followers met independently of the Jewish community and according to Torah-free norms, so that by definition the Jews present were not behaving Jewishly.

Second, this reading understands the "certain ones from James" to represent James' viewpoint and presumes that these people are those whom Paul says Peter feared, namely, "the ones from circumcision."[34] Since it

---

31. For the "commensality" alternative, see Zetterholm, "Purity and Anger: Gentiles and Idolatry in Antioch."

32. Naturally, for a variety of reasons, including local constraints, there were various interpretations of halakhic standards, inside and outside of Judea, and between communities in each location. Dunn holds that the standards at issue were those for Noahides, which lessens the matter of degree. However, this does not alter the traditional view that the issue was halakhic, having to do with laws governing food preparation. It also does not work because Paul was accusing Peter of (implicitly) compelling "judaizing," not "noahidizing"; see my "What Was at Stake?" 282–318.

33. Commentators have not usually differentiated adequately between circumcision, that is, proselyte conversion, which has to do with identity transformation, and Torah-observance, which applies only to Jews and those who have completed or who are in the process of completing proselyte conversion. Circumcision is for the male children of Israelites, slaves, and strangers living among them, and for the non-Israelite wishing to become an Israelite. I suggest that Paul's metonym *ergon nomou* ("works/deeds of Law") denotes "rites of Torah," specifically, those deeds/acts involved in a non-Jew becoming a Jewish proselyte.

34. A minority position upholds that the "certain ones from James," although coming from James, misrepresented his policies, or perhaps his ideals; see Howard, *Paul: Crisis in Galatia*.

was the influence of the "certain ones from James" that led Peter as well as Barnabas and other unnamed Jews to adopt (or return to) this position regarding gentile Christ-followers, the traditional interpreters thus infer that it represents the view of James, of Jewish Christianity, or of a significant element of that movement.

Third, these interpreters conclude that Paul's opposition is thus not only to proselyte conversion for Christ-believing gentiles, but also to Torah-defined dietary behavior. By extension, he also then objected to Torah-observance as a way of life for Jews as well as gentiles, at least when they mixed in church, which would seemingly apply to all cases in Pauline assemblies, and probably most other Christ-believing groups as well.[35]

[11] I disagree with each of these decisions.

On the first point, when Paul says Peter is living like a gentile, or "gentilely," Paul is not accusing him of a Torah-free lifestyle, but of living *justified* by Christ just like the gentiles are, not also by his standing as a Jew.[36] According to Paul, drawing on Hab 2:4, "the just shall *live* by faithfulness" (3:11, 16–21; cf. Rom 1:17). Thus, non-Jews were *living* equal *in standing* before God with Jews, without the conferral of ethnic identity and concomitant advantage of being a Jew within the Jewish community (cf. Gal 2:15; Rom 3:1-2; 9:3-5). Because these gentiles have attained equal standing with Jews before God, naturally, they should be treated as equal in standing among each other (cf. Gal 2:16; 3:28-29; Rom 3:27—4:25; 15:5-12).

Paul's accusation that Peter's behavior implicitly compels the gentile Christ-followers to become Jews (*ioudaïzien*),[37] does not derive from Peter

35. There are some interpreters who maintain that Paul allowed Jews not engaged in the gentile mission to observe Torah fully, although he himself could not because of his close affiliation with gentiles (e.g., Johnson Hodge, *If Sons, Then Heirs*, 123). But this does not square with Paul's logic, which is based on principle. He either believed that Torah-observance still applied to Christ-believing Jews as a part of covenant faithfulness, or it did not; he himself was committed to living consistently, and he accuses Peter precisely for failing to do so. What would Christ-believing Jews be expected to do according to Paul's standards when a gentile was present in their congregations, regardless of whether they had engaged in an active gentile mission leading to this circumstance? The consensus view is that, like Paul, who is understood to "live like a gentile" (interpreted to mean he does not live Torah-observantly), any Christ-believing Jews would be expected to compromise Torah when in the company of Christ-believing Gentiles. Cf. Sanders, *Paul, the Law, and the Jewish People*, 185–87.

36. Nanos, "What Was at Stake?" 312–16.

37. Cf. my "What Was at Stake?," 306–12, where I challenge the arguments that *ioudaïzein* in general as well as here refers only to behaving like a Jew, and not to proselyte conversion. It is also important to note that this verb does not signify Jewish missionary behavior, but is a reflexive verb, denoting a non-Jew becoming a Jew (or behaving Jewishly). In other words, it is synonymous with references to the proselyte, not to those conducting non-Jews in the rites of proselyte conversion, or in some way

teaching non-Jews to become proselytes or adopt some kind of change in dietary behavior. This is implicit in Paul's accusation of "*hypocrisy*" rather than of "apostasy" or "heresy." He accused Peter of masking the conviction that Paul still believes Peter shares with him, that gentile Christ-followers were to not become proselytes. But because of the exigencies of the moment and his fear of those who do advocate proselyte conversion, Peter is not behaving consistently with that conviction. His expedient behavior is undermining "the truth of the gospel" that he otherwise upholds, that gentiles in Christ *live* as equal members of the people of God already, descendants of Abraham, without becoming members of Israel. This is what distinguishes this Christ-following Jewish coalition from all other Jewish groups.

Moreover, Peter, and everyone else at the table, including the non-Jews, had been eating according to Torah-defined dietary norms. Paul does not accuse Peter of eating like a gentile and then ceasing to eat in this manner; he does not accuse him of withdrawing for "fear of the ones advocating dietary norms." Rather, he relates that Peter fears "the ones from circumcision," that is, presumably, those advocating the need for gentiles to become circumcised to be welcome at this table on the terms being upheld at it.

In other words, Paul describes Peter as withdrawing from eating *with* gentiles, not from eating like a gentile. If "the ones from circumcision" Peter feared had been advocating a change of menu, then Peter, and the other Jews present, including "certain ones from James," were in a position to change that menu and to expect the gentiles either to accept this or to be the ones who withdrew. It makes little sense for the Jews, including important figures like the "certain ones from James," Peter, and Barnabas, to do the withdrawing. And again, the issue is about "those *from circumcision*," not "those from the kosher menu committee." A change of diet certainly would be a less threatening option, and one that non-Jewish men should [12] be expected to accommodate more gladly than the alternative of circumcision—but that is not what Paul states to be at issue.

The issue Paul addresses concerns *with whom* Peter was eating, and what his withdrawal from eating *with* them implies about their standing. Other Jewish groups also included non-Jews at meals without compromising Jewish dietary norms, everyone eating according to Jewish dietary rules.[38] However, in this group, which also ate according to Jewish dietary norms, there was something about their eating together that was distinctive. They sought to demonstrate through their table fellowship together

---

seeking to persuade non-Jews to adopt such a course of action.

38. Cf. Sanders, "Jewish Association with Gentiles and Galatians 2:11–14"; Fredrikson, "Judaism, the Circumcision of Gentiles, and Apocalyptic Hope."

as equals, Israelites and members from the other nations, that the awaited "age to come" had dawned in Christ, that the messianic banquet had begun in their midst. They thus likely arranged the seating and distributed food and drink according to non-hierarchical arrangements, whereas it was likely normal in Jewish groups, as in Greco-Roman groups in general, to discriminate in such matters according to rank.[39]

In other Jewish groups, non-Jewish guests would be distinguishable as guests, however welcome. But not in these groups, where equality of Jew and Greek in Christ was being celebrated. That would account for the threat from the ones advocating that circumcision of these gentiles was necessary, if they were to be treated as if equal members of the people of God within the Jewish community of Antioch. But according to the truth of the message of good that Paul and Peter proclaim, they are to be treated as religio-ethnic equals without proselyte conversion, that is, without religio-ethnic sameness. Thus, to avoid seating and serving people from the other nations equally would compromise the very proposition around which this Christ-following Jewish subgroup exists, and for which purpose it meets together to remember Jesus.

Second, Paul does not equate the "certain ones from James" with "the ones from circumcision." The arrival of the "certain ones from James" represents a time marker: it is *after* their arrival that Peter and "the rest of the Jews" withdrew. Paul also does not equate these "certain ones from James" with "the ones from circumcision" Peter feared. It could be that the two are synonymous, but Paul has just finished an argument in vv. 1–10 in which he concluded that James and the Jerusalem leaders were in *full agreement* with Paul that gentile Christ-followers should not be circumcised (similarly, Acts 15).

Where many interpreters argue that James and the Jerusalem church now reversed their agreement with Paul in Jerusalem, Paul does not in fact signal any reversal in principle, and does not accuse the "certain ones from James," or James himself, of anything. Moreover, as already noted, he does not accuse Peter or the rest of apostasy or heresy, but only of "hypocrisy." An accusation of hypocrisy (of "masking") implies continued theoretical agreement with and teaching of "the truth of the gospel" proposition that gentiles are to remain gentiles within this movement. Otherwise, one should conclude that the Jerusalem church leaders reneged on this agreement,[40] in

---

39. Nanos, "What Was at Stake?" 304 n. 75.

40. Based on recognizing the logic of this route: if one adopts the prevailing view that Paul was Torah-free and the other apostles were Torah-observant, then Philip F. Esler's case is cogent. See his "Making and Breaking an Agreement Mediterranean Style: A New Reading of Galatians 2:1–14."

spite of Paul's failure to state the matter in those terms. Yet Paul chose to introduce this example. Presumably he did so to [13] persuade his audience that his position was normative for Christ-faithfulness, and thus the only legitimate one for them to consider in their own situation in Galatia.

There are other more logical identifications of the "certain ones from James." They may be James' representatives, and thus, like him, they join in mixed table fellowships and arouse a heightened objection from local Antiochene Jews who were already upset with such practices. Their joining this mixed table fellowship represented the last straw for those in the Jewish communities of Antioch who opposed such developments within these Christ-following subgroups. Those who came from James' coalition in Jerusalem were reinforcing the claim of local Antiochene Christ-believing Jews that these gentiles were now equal members of the people of God, welcome as full members of table fellowships being otherwise conducted according to normal Jewish dietary laws. Antiochene Jews could not doubt that this was the position of all members of the Christ-believing movement, and it was high time to oppose it vehemently. In response, the Christ-believing Jewish members sought to dissipate the heat by a temporary, expedient withdrawal, but without changing their teachings. Presumably, in due time, they would return to the mixed table.

Or it may be that the "certain ones from James" represented those who were outsiders to the Christ-believing movement, as related in the prior Jerusalem meeting passage (2:1–10). They were "inspectors" whom James allowed to be present at the Christ-believing coalition's otherwise private meetings in Jerusalem.[41] In either case, Paul judged them to be "informants" who gained access in Jerusalem, and now were allowed to travel to Antioch to investigate matters there also. If so, then they might well be synonymous with "the ones from circumcision" whom Peter feared. They objected to the Christ- movement's standards for equal fellowship with non-Jews, and Peter worried that it might be unclear just how important it was in Antioch, as in Jerusalem, that Torah standards be upheld within these mixed meals. Thus, rather than permit ambiguity, he withdrew to avoid any problems while these informants were seeking to find some reason to report back to Jerusalem that things were not as they should be. Perhaps the inspectors' purpose was to bring greater pressure upon James and the Jerusalem church to respond to supposed transgressions within the spreading network under their supervision, including Antioch, and Peter reasoned that avoiding normal behavior for a while would be a strategic way to avert their intentions.

---

41. Nanos, "Intruding 'Spies' and 'Pseudo-brethren.'"

None of these alternatives for the identity of the "certain ones from James" concerning their role in Antioch and for their relationship to "the ones from circumcision" implies that James differed from Peter and Paul in his expectations of proselyte conversion for gentile Christ-followers or Torah-observance for Jews, or participation in joint meals. This challenges the third major point of the prevailing views.

Galatians 2:11–15 thus shows that Paul objected neither to Torah-observance in his assemblies, nor to prevailing halakhic standards for dietary behavior. The issue at Antioch had to do not with the food being served, but instead with how it was being shared with non-Jews as if equal members of the fellowship rather than as non-Jewish guests or proselyte candidates. This was unlike the practice of all other Jewish groups of which we are aware. For while gentiles were welcome in other Jewish groups, they remained distinguishable as non-Jewish guests, and likely were not treated as members unless they chose to become proselytes. Not so in the Christ-believing groups in Antioch and in Jerusalem.

That is the message that Paul wanted to communicate to the Galatians, who were under similar pressure from their own local Jewish communities. He expected them to resist these [14] pressures, just as he insisted on such resistance elsewhere.[42] When Jewish apostles and leaders like Peter and Barnabas erred, Paul criticized them too. "The truth of the gospel" was at issue; the entrance of members of the other nations to the messianic meal was fundamental to the propositional truth claims they sought to substantiate. Non-Jews join Judaism, but they do not become Jews through the "works of Torah" that alter their religio-ethnic identity to make them Jews. For that they would need to complete the rites of proselyte conversion, which involves circumcision for males. Thus, they are not under Torah in the fullest sense, as are Jews. But gentile Christ-followers are nevertheless under the Torah (i.e., teaching, principles) of Christ, which includes the halakhic codes of behavior for guests, which cohere with the Noahide commandments, as witnessed in the so-called Apostolic decree (Acts 15).[43]

In short, the Antioch Incident does not substantiate that Paul ate Torah-free on any occasion, or that he taught that Jews or even gentiles should eat free of Jewish dietary norms. The implications of Paul's argument run in exactly the opposite direction. He teaches that gentile Christ-followers must be proselyte-conversion free. They do not undertake the "works/actions of Torah" that create Jewish religio-ethnic identity and thus they are not under

---

42. For the setting and message of Galatians, see my *Irony of Galatians*; and my, "The Inter- and Intra-Jewish Political Context of Paul's Letter to the Galatians."

43. Cf. Nanos, *Mystery of Romans*, 50–57, 192–207.

Torah; they do not become Israelites, although they become enslaved to the love of neighbor that is the essence of Torah, and thus Israelite covenant life (Gal 5:13–14). And since their groups are Jewish, being Christ-believing subgroups of the larger Jewish communities, these non-Jews will eat and live together according to prevailing Jewish communal regulations that govern the lifestyle of the righteous non-Jew.

Food Offered to Idols

1 Corinthians 8–10 is Paul's response to apparent queries from his Corinthian disciples about whether they might participate in idolatrous rites, or eat food that had been sacrificed to idols.[44] Interpretations of this passage logically must be consistent with interpretations of the Antioch Incident. If one maintains that Paul did keep the kosher dietary laws, then he certainly would not eat food from idolatrous sacrifices. But if one argues that Paul did permit and even ate idolatrous food in some circumstances, then it follows that he would not keep kosher regulations regarding other food.

The consensus view is that Paul permits the eating of idolatrous food in principle, but not when it would bother the "sensibilities" (*syneidesis*: "conscience," or better, "consciousness") of the *asthenes* ("weak," or better, "impaired"). The "weak" are understood to be Christ-followers who are not secure enough in their faith to internalize fully the Torah-free principles of the gospel of Christ. They thus hesitate to eat idolatrous food, or when eating it, are conscious in some way of participating in idolatry. They misunderstand the gospel proposition (according to the "knowledgeable") that there are no real [15] gods represented by these idols.[45] The food dedicated to them is really profane (ordinary) food and should be of no real concern.

It is widely maintained, even by those who understand Paul to accept eating idolatrous food in certain circumstances, that he did not permit participation in idolatrous rites.[46] This would seem to suggest that Paul does indeed argue from certain basic Torah-inspired sensibilities. Nevertheless, those maintaining the consensus view hold inconsistently that unless Paul is opposed to eating idolatrous food because it is intrinsically impure, he

---

44. A full discussion of the prevailing views and my interpretation is available in my "The Polytheist Identity of the 'Weak,' And Paul's Strategy to 'Gain' Them"; and "Why the 'Weak' in 1 Corinthians 8–10 Were Not Christ-believers."

45. This observation also applies to those who define these two groups by their different socio-economic backgrounds; cf. Thiessen, *The Social Setting of Pauline Christianity*, 121–43.

46. Barrett, ed., *Essays on Paul*, 50–52.

cannot be a Torah-observant Jew, or one teaching a Torah-based approach to Christ-faith. They combine this with their decision to interpret 1 Cor 9:19–22 to mean that Paul adapted his *behavior* equally to the Torah-observant and to those free of Torah.[47] Depending upon which group he was among, he sought to proclaim his gospel free of such supposedly non-essential requirements, since Torah is for Paul *adiaphora*, a matter of indifference.

While the overwhelming consensus agrees that Paul was against keeping Jewish dietary norms in Antioch, some interpreters recognize that the logic of Paul's argument in 1 Corinthians signals both that he disapproved of other's eating of food known to be idolatrous, and that he did not eat idolatrous food himself, for example, when evangelizing among idolaters.[48] My own work strengthens this second case.[49] The "weak" or "impaired" in 1 Corinthians 8–10 are probably not Christ-followers, but polytheists (pagans), those who still practice idolatrous rites as a matter of principle. Unlike Paul's audience, who are the "we" who know the One God and who "all have knowledge" that these statues do not represent real gods (8:1–6), "they" are the "some" who lack this knowledge of the One God, who until now have been accustomed to eating idolatrous food without sensing that it is not right to do so (v. 7). And why would they if they are not Christ-followers but idolaters?

The issue raised by the Corinthian Christ-followers is whether they may eat food that was being or had been sacrificed to idols. They reason that since they no longer believe that these idols represent gods and lords, food offered to them has no holiness. Eating idol-related food with indifference would have the advantage of bearing witness to their gospel convictions and at the same time not giving offense to their polytheist neighbors. Withdrawal from all contexts where it was being served and from buying it in the marketplace, in contrast, would be akin to social suicide, to dwelling apart from the world. How were they to live when virtually every social engagement and much of the food available for meals involved [16] some association with the idolatry of their polytheistic families, neighbors, and fellow workers, with civic life in general?

However, Paul sees things from a Jewish Torah-based point of view, and the logic of their appeal to eat idolatrous food escapes him. Their

47. Richardson, "Pauline Inconsistency," 347; Segal, *Paul*, 228, 229–40; Klinghoffer, *Why the Jews Rejected Jesus*, 106–10.

48. Tomson, *Paul and the Jewish Law*; Gooch, *Dangerous Food*; Cheung, *Idol Food in Corinth*; Fotopoulos, *Food Offered to Idols in Roman Corinth*.

49. Nanos, "Polytheist Identity"; Nanos, "Paul's Relationship to Torah in Light of His Strategy 'to Become Everything to Everyone' (1 Corinthians 9:19–23)" sets out this case in detail.

reasoning probably surprises him, for Israelites have long upheld that idols were merely statues, ones that should not have been built. Those who worshiped the gods through "idols" were regarded to be misguided, at the very least. But it does not follow that one could participate with indifference in idolatrous rites or even eat food that had been used in any such rites, including when it was later available in the marketplace. Rather, it must be avoided as if infected with powers that seek to rival God and to harm his people.[50] So Paul argues that rather than bearing witness to their polytheist neighbors, eating this idolatrous food may serve as a scandal for them, leading them to continue in idolatry under the impression that Christ-faith sanctions such behavior. They will remain ignorant of the proposition of the One God that is at the heart of the confession of this Jewish subgroup community's faith in Christ.

But why doesn't Paul just come right out and say that the Torah teaches the "knowledgeable" about Christ not to eat idolatrous food? Because his intended audience is not composed of Jews; thus, they are not under Torah on the same terms as Israelites. Paul's understanding of the logic of the truth of the gospel constrains him—to a point. So he begins 1 Corinthians 8 with first principles. He agrees with the Christ-followers who "know" that there is no such thing as the gods and lords these statues seek to represent (v. 4). Yet he adds, as part of his logical appeal to the Shema—the proclamation that God is the One and Only God for Israel, and for the Christ-believing gentiles too—that there are such things as other gods and lords, whom he will identify as daemons (v. 5; 10:20–21). Then he writes in the balance of chapter 8 that, because some do not have this knowledge, being "weak/impaired," the "knowledgeable" should refrain from behaving as if all things related to idols should be considered profane. To do so will harm the "weak" polytheists, for they think these things to be sacred to the gods and lords to which they are dedicated. It would not send the message to these "impaired," not *yet* Christ-believing "brother[s] for whose sake Christ died" (8:11–12; cf. Rom 5:6–10), that they, together with these Christ-followers and all Israelites, should desist from any such behavior and turn to the One God alone.[51]

50. Paradoxically, Scripture trivializes idols as not gods and meaningless and yet proscribed as demonic and dangerous for those in covenant with the One God (e.g., compare Deut 32:21 with vv. 16–17; Isa 8:19 and 19:3 with chapters 40 and 44; cf. Wisdom 13–16; see also Ps 106:36–39; 1 Enoch 19; Jub. 11.4–6); other gods and lords are implicitly recognized to exist, albeit to be lower than Israel's God, and they are not to be honored by Israelites (Exod 15:11; 20:2–6; 22:28; Deut 4:19; 29:26; 32:8–9; Ps 82:1; Mic 4:5; Jas 2:19); images of other gods are to be destroyed in the Land (Exod 23:24; Deut 7:5). See Tomson, *Paul*, 151–77, 208–20; Cheung, *Idol Food*, 39–81, 152–64, 300–301.

51. Cf. Nanos, "Polytheist Identity," for full discussion of the logic for understanding

After a digression in chapter 9 to explain Paul's own self-sacrificial way of living, including how he adapts his rhetoric to each group he seeks to win, Paul moves the argument against [17] eating idol food to the next stage in chapter 10. Although to some degree avoiding direct appeal to Torah injunctions, he invokes examples from Torah to make clear that one who eats at the table of the Lord cannot also eat at the table of other gods, the so-called daemons. In other words, he admits that there are powers associated with idols, undermining the theoretical concession with which he began this argument that apparently shared these gentile Christ-believers' premise that there were no such things as other gods and lords. Thus, regardless of the fact that God made all things to be eaten with sanctifying prayer, not all things can be eaten. Purity is not inherent to the food, but imputed by the command of God. Any food *known* to be idolatrous food, whether available in the marketplace, or offered in a host's home, may not be consumed. Christ-believers, like biblical Israelites, must flee idolatry, both for their own sakes and for the sake of their polytheist neighbors, their brothers and sisters in the created order whom God in Christ seeks to redeem through them.

Paul did not permit the eating of food known to be idolatrous food, and there is no indication that he himself ever ate it. Quite the opposite is the case. Moreover, the teaching of the early church for centuries was that Christians were not to consume idolatrous food, in part, based on their reading of this text.[52] Paul's argument, including that contained in 1 Cor 9:19–22, confirms that his audience knew him to be not only one who would not eat such food, but also one who would not expect them to do so

---

the *asthenes* ("weak/impaired") "brothers" to be non-Christ-believing idolaters, and of the letter's concern with winning them to Christ. Note that church fathers continued to operate according to this understanding of constructing outsiders as kin. Ignatius (late first/early second century) calls upon his addressees to pray for outsiders to the church, and to conduct themselves as "brothers/sisters [*adelphoi*]" to them, as expressed by imitating how Christ lived humbly with his neighbor, including choosing to be wronged rather than to wrong them (*Eph.* 10; cf. *Mart. Pol.* 1.2). And although Chrysostom (late fourth century) understood the impaired in 1 Corinthians 8–10 to be Christ-followers, he argued that on socio-economic grounds the Christian in his own audience ought to regard as *brother* the fellow-laborer more than the elite or wealthy (*Cor.* 117 [Homily XX]). For non-Christian examples of concern for those outside of one's own philosophical group, see Epictetus, *Diatr.* 1.9.4–6; 1.13.4, on the Cynics in particular, *Diatr.* 3.22.81–82; Marcus Aurelius, 2.1; 7.22; 9.22–23.

52. Acts 15:20, 29; 21:25; Rev 2:14, 19–20; Didache 6.3; Ignatius, *Magn.* 8–10; Pliny, *Letters* 10.96; Aristides, *Apology* 15.4; 12; Justin, *Dial.* 34.8; 35.1–2; Tertullian, *Apol.* 9.13–14; *Cor.* 10.4–7; 11.3; *Spect.* 13.2–4; *Jejun.* 2.4; 15.5; *Mon.* 5.3; Clement, *Strom.* 4.15.97.3; Tomson, *Paul*, 177–86; Gooch, *Dangerous Food*, 122–27, 131–33; Cheung, *Idol Food*, 165–295; Freidenreich, "Foreign Food," 123–41. Barnabas 10.9, may suggest an early group that does eat anything, but it is not specific about idolatrous food; and see Tertullian, *Apol.* 42.1–5.

either. Thus, although they knew him to be Torah-observant when he had been among them in Corinth, their query protests the cost to their civic life and standing caused by Paul's denying this food to them as gentiles. They knew that by the defining terms of Paul's own proclamation of the truth of the gospel, he understood that they remained non-Jews and were not subject to Torah.

In 9:19–22, Paul declares that to win Jews he "became like a Jew," to win the "ones under *nomos*" (law/convention/Torah?) he "became like the one under *nomos*," but also to win the lawless he "became like a lawless one" (*anomos*), and to win the "weak" that he "became weak," who are understood to be insecure in their freedom in Christ, and thus to avoid eating idolatrous food.[53] This statement has been universally understood to mean that Paul regards Torah-observance, including the value of Jewish identity itself, to be only a matter of evangelistic expedience. That interpretation, which for analytical purposes may be called "lifestyle adaptability," depends on understanding "causing myself to become like" (*egenomen hos*) members of each of the various groups to signify "causing myself to *mimic the conduct*" of each of them. In the consensus view, Paul does not share the various groups' propositional truths, but rather he merely copies certain aspects of their behavior, presumably, in order to gain a hearing among them by making them (mistakenly) suppose that he might actually share their convictions. This applies to such conduct as eating according to Torah when with those who eat halakhically and with no regard for Torah when with those who do not eat according to Jewish dietary norms. In other words, Paul does not actually "become" or "become like" each referent, but [18] instead merely "pretends on the surface to live like" each one when among each. Then he abandons that conduct and lives like the other ones when among them. But there is another way to understand Paul's argument here, one that both avoids implying that he is indifferent to Torah and also one that does not compromise his morality by ascribing to him a "bait and switch" strategy.

Rather than suggesting that he relates to each person or group by *mimicking* their *lifestyle*, Paul is referring instead, I propose, to his *rhetorical strategy* for *persuading* them. His "*becoming* like" signifies not "*behaving* like," but rather "*arguing* like," or "*reasoning* like." He employs a strategy of "rhetorical adaptability" widely upheld in the philosophical traditions

---

53. It is unclear how the reference to those "under law" differs from "Jews," for example. Perhaps it refers to proselytes or to those representing stricter standards like Pharisees; alternatively, it may refer to being under Roman or other laws or conventions. Likewise, it is not clear whether *anomos* refers to lawless (perhaps non-practicing) Jews as well as to non-Jews, or only to non-Jews, as if he had written *xoris nomos* ("without law"). See my "Paul's Relationship to Torah" and "Paul and Judaism."

of his time wherein speakers begin with the premises of those whom they seek to persuade, whether or not they intend ultimately to undermine these premises.[54] It was the way of Socrates, and it is still employed as one of the best methods for teaching students. Paul routinely begins with his audience's propositional truths, whether he shares them, like he does with Jews and those who are Torah-observant, or not, like in the cases of those he calls lawless, or the impaired who engage in idolatry as a matter of conviction. He does not behave like them, but he makes his arguments in ways that adapt to the propositional thinking of each group he seeks to persuade to the gospel. So too here, he approaches the knowledgeable in Corinth about idolatrous food by appearing to uphold premises with which he may disagree in order to lead them to different conclusions than those they have drawn.

Luke portrays Paul preaching to the philosophers in Athens in just this manner (Acts 17:16-34). Paul begins from their premise that there is an "Unknown God" to whom they dedicated a statue. Paul does not begin by declaring there is no such thing as polytheist gods, but builds on their (mistaken) conviction that this "idol" symbolizes a god. Then he declares the identity of that god as really the God of Israel. He next proceeds to inform them that this God does not approve of building statues to himself, or to any other supposed god or lord. Paul does not make this criticism obvious in the beginning of his address, but it becomes transparent as he moves toward his conclusion that the God of Israel is the one and only Creator God of all humankind. In this way Paul "became like" an idolater to gain idolaters. He does not conduct himself idolatrously or mimic idolater's conduct; rather, he remains like a Torah-observant Jew while arguing from the premises of the polytheists he seeks to persuade.

My reading not only avoids the negative characterization of Paul and his methods as intentionally deceptive, with a questionable commitment to righteousness, truth, and justice, but it also challenges the long-standing notion that 1 Corinthians 8–10 shows clearly that Paul is by definition Torah-free. Instead it substantiates that he is Torah-observant and that he constructs his arguments assuming that his audience is aware of this fact. Subsequent interpreters, assuming that his contemporary audiences shared the later understanding that Paul was Torah-free, have not only mischaracterized him, but they have missed the thrust of his teaching.

---

54. Stanford, *The Ulysses Theme*, 90–101.

Instructions to the Strong about the Weak

In Romans 14:1—15:7, Paul exhorts the ones who are "strong" or "able" (*dynatoi*) to respect the "weak" or "stumbling" (*asthenes*), who are "unable" (*adynatoi*) in faith.[55] To whom [19] each label refers is a matter of debate. Paul's argument, directed to the "strong," characterizes the "weak" by their convictions about the value of certain foods, drink, and days. These characteristics appear to be typical norms for Jewish behavior, such as eating vegetables when properly koshered meat is not available, avoiding wine that may have been offered as a libation to the gods according to normal Greco-Roman practice, and observing the holy days of the Jewish calendar, including the Sabbath.

According to the prevailing views, the "strong" are Christ-followers of Pauline persuasion, that is, they are "Torah-free" whether gentiles or Jews. The "weak" are also Christ-followers, but in contrast, they still observe Torah and probably consist mostly of Jews, perhaps with some "God-fearing" non-Jews included among them. Thus, the conflicting identities turn around their relative valuation of Torah, for all of them are Christ-followers.

These interpreters take the fact that Paul includes himself among the "strong" as support for the notion that Paul is Torah-free, but their logic is circular. If instead the Romans believe Paul to be Torah-observant, then their shared strength would be presumed to have nothing to do with Torah, but with shared faith in Christ. The prevailing view couples this assumption of Torah-freeness with Paul's declaration that he is "convinced in the Lord Jesus that nothing is impure in itself" (14:14), meaning that what makes something impure is someone's perception that it is, not something intrinsic to it. They understand Paul to define categories of purity and impurity not according to Torah, but rather according to Christ-based personal or group convictions as if inherently different from those defined by Torah for Jewish people and groups. Thus, Paul is not Torah-observant, or even Torah-respectful, except in concession to the convictions of others, whom he accommodates to advance more important matters like peace in the assembly and the witness of the gospel. I disagree with such readings.

I propose that the distinctions Paul makes between "strong" (or "unable") and "weak" (or "stumbling") do not revolve around their observance of Torah-based norms, the "strong" rejecting them and the "weak" observing them with this signifying an inferior choice (weaker faith) according to the ideals of Pauline Christianity. Nor does Paul's appeal to the inherent purity

---

55. For more detail, see my *Mystery of Romans*, 85–165; "The Jewish Context of the Gentile Audience Addressed in Paul's Letter to the Romans"; and "A Rejoinder to Robert A. J. Gagnon's 'Why the "Weak" at Rome Cannot Be Non-Christian Jews.'"

or even goodness of everything God created indicate a rejection of halakhic behavior. Rather, the distinction between the groups arises from their present level of "ability" or "inability" to believe in the gospel proposition.[56] At issue is whether or not they are "stumbling" over the proclamation of the message of good in Christ to the nations. They are in this way "weak" or "impaired" or "stumbling,"[57] but they are not non-believers in God. They do [20] not lack faith in general terms, but faith that God is bringing to pass what was promised in Christ.[58]

But does Paul's ostensible relativizing of the value of pure and impure, for example, imply that he does not respect, observe, or teach Torah as a matter of conviction? No, it does not. Rabbinic tradition relativizes these categories, making them apply only to Israel.[59] According to the Bible, God created everything good. The foods that are proscribed as impure are *not inherently* impure; rather, they are impure for Israel because God has designated them to be so in the Torah. Impurity or purity is an *imputed*, not an inherent characteristic. Paul appeals to the same notion here (and in 1 Cor 10:19—11:1) as does the (presumably Torah-observant) Psalmist whom he quotes (Pss 24:1; 50:12, in 1 Cor 10:26). However, Paul raises this as an argument, not its conclusion. He presumes his audience will identify positively with this premise—but characteristic of his rhetorical tactics, he subverts this argumentative concession in his subsequent conclusions. Regardless of whether the "strong" should identify something as pure or not, they are obliged to respect the sensibilities of those who conclude it to be impure, and to behave accordingly. Anything less is sin, and contributes not to testimony to their faith, but to their faithlessness, and to the ostensibly legitimate derision of their faith claims, i.e., to blasphemy itself. They can have no part in behavior that might lead to such results.

---

56. Note how Paul works around *dynatos* in 15:1

57. For further explanation, see my "Broken Branches" and *Mystery of Romans*, 239–88. Paul saw himself, like the prophets, engaged in restoring Israel. He viewed some of his fellow Israelites in a temporary state of discipline for disobeying this truth claim. They are "stumbling" but not "fallen," within the covenant standing of Israel, having the certainty of the gifts and calling of God promised to their fathers (Rom 9:4–5; 11:25–29). In due time, as a result of his successful ministry among the nations, Paul maintains that they will come to share his point of view and be restored to standing upright. I am pleased to say that Krister Stendahl embraced my argument when he first heard it at the 1998 Society of Biblical Literature Annual Meeting, now available in "Challenging the Limits That Continue to Define Paul's Perspective on Jews and Judaism."

58. Abraham's level of faith is described in similar terms in 4:18–20.

59. Sipra Aharei 93d; Gen. Rab. 44.1; Lev. Rab. 13.3; Grunfeld, *The Jewish Dietary Laws*, 5, 12–19, 28–29; Tomson, *Paul*, 249.

Therefore, I propose that the divisions between these groups arise around their expression or lack thereof of the identity markers of Christ-faith ("strong" = "able" to believe in versus "weak" = "stumbling" over the message of Christ), and not around their relative degree of Torah-observance ("strong" = free from Torah versus "weak" = observing Torah). Whether or not one accepts my view, this passage does not provide enough information to support the traditional case that Paul did not observe Torah in matters of diet, or that he taught against it. Moreover, even according to the consensus view, Paul defends the Torah-observant, or at least calls for respectful behavior toward them. Paul also explicitly proscribes the very judgmentalism towards the weak that this view imputes to him in understanding "weakness" to be stumbling over trusting God enough to abrogate Torah. But I submit that Paul instead argues here from the premises of a Torah-observant Jew, a faithful Israelite who believes that Jesus is the Messiah of Israel, and the Savior of the nations too.

CONCLUSIONS AND IMPLICATIONS

Those promoting the prevailing portrait of Paul's Torah-free gospel and lifestyle do not depend exclusively on these texts and topics, but they usually appeal to them first as the ostensibly most self-evident sources that contradict the proposition of a Torah-observant Paul. In each case, I question their readings. At this point, I am unaware of any reason to doubt that the approach I suggest, which I have only been able to briefly describe here, is the most historically probable, helpful, and useful way to read Paul, and the best place from which to seek to apply his messages to the issues that arise today. My understanding can lead to a heightened recognition of the similarities between first-century Judaism and Christian foundational texts and traditions. Moreover, combined with appropriate awareness of the differences that exist today between these faith traditions, it can also encourage a new level of respect in relationships.

These implications extend to include how each characterizes the other, which is so instrumental in the perpetuation of stereotypes. For even when these are ostensibly not encouraged outright, they often nevertheless travel implicitly in [21] the interpretations we present. They are carried on in the ways that each explains the viewpoint of the other, often by appeal to the apostle Paul, to Paulinism as traditionally understood. For Christians, it is exemplified in celebrating how different this special apostle's values supposedly were from those of other Jews, including the other apostles, even from those of Jesus, although sometimes this supposed difference seems to be retained without reconciling the tension it produces. For Jews, it is expressed in undermining such notions and values, not necessarily by denying the claims that Christians make in Paul's name, but rather, by turning them upside down: It is obvious that an apostate representing such teachings, one who did not get Judaism or even Jesus right, is not a rival worthy of respect, much less painstaking exegesis.

Some Christians may sense a deep and reprehensible threat to the very essence of Christianity at work in the notion of a Torah-observant Paul, a threat that undermines elements considered essential to highlighting Christianity's difference from Judaism. I believe that this concern is mistaken and unnecessary. When we examine the details of Paul's propositional truths, there is no need for Torah to be abrogated in order for Christ-faith to be central to Paul's theology. It is widely recognized that indifference to Torah was not the norm either for Jesus or for James and the other apostles of this movement. For them, there was no dichotomy between Torah and Christ. Why *must* there be for Paul?

If we take seriously a portrayal of Paul as Torah-observant, one that is consistent with his own self-witness and confirmed by his earliest biographer in the Acts of the Apostles, might not the Jewish and Christian communities find themselves to be more similar than different? Should not the differences become more clearly related to how each community values the identity and meaning of Jesus, a Judean martyr of the Roman regime, and not to their shared concern for the "teaching" of faithfulness in response to the gracious calling of God? This is not an appeal to disregard differences, but to get them right.

I hope each community will give this critical approach a hearing, not only in the interest of seeking to read these texts in the most historically viable way possible, but for the sake of our welfare today, and for the generations to come.

BIBLIOGRAPHY

Barrett, C. K., ed. *Essays on Paul*. Philadelphia: Westminster, 1982.
Boyarin, Daniel. *A Radical Jew: Paul and the Politics of Identity*. Contraversions 1. Berkeley: University of California Press, 1994.
Campbell, William S. *Paul and the Creation of Christian Identity*. Library of New Testament Studies 322. London: T. & T. Clark, 2006.
Cheung, Alex T. *Idol Food in Corinth: Jewish Background and Pauline Legacy*. JSNT Sup 176. Sheffield, UK: Sheffield Academic Press, 1999.
Cohen, Shaye J. D. *The Beginnings of Jewishness: Boundaries, Varieties, Uncertainties*. HCS 31. Berkeley: University of California Press, 1999.

Dunn, James D. G. "The Incident at Antioch (Gal 2:11–18)." In *The Galatians Debate: Contemporary Issues in Rhetorical and Historical Interpretation*, edited by Mark D. Nanos, 225–30. Peabody, MA: Hendrickson, 2002.

———. "The New Perspective on Paul." In *Jesus, Paul, and the Law: Studies in Mark and Galatians*, 183–214. Louisville: Westminster/John Knox, 1990.

———. *Romans 9–16*. WBC 38b. Dallas: Word, 1988.

———. "Who Did Paul Think He Was? A Study of Jewish-Christian Identity." *New Testament Studies* 45 (1999) 174–93.

Ehrensperger, Kathy. *That We May Be Mutually Encouraged: Feminism and the New Perspective in Pauline Studies*. London: T. & T. Clark, 2004.

Eisenbaum, Pamela. "Following in the Footnotes of the Apostle Paul." In *Identity and the Politics of Scholarship in the Study of Religion*, edited by Jose Ignacio Cabezon and Sheila Greeve Davaney, 77–97. London: Routledge, 2004.

Elliott, Neil. *Liberating Paul: The Justice of God and the Politics of the Apostle*. Maryknoll, NY: Orbis, 1994.

Esler, Philip F. "Making and Breaking an Agreement Mediterranean Style: A New Reading of Galatians 2:1–14." In *The Galatians Debate: Contemporary Issues in Rhetorical and Historical Interpretation*, edited by Mark D. Nanos, 261–81. Peabody, MA: Hendrickson, 2002.

Falk, Harvey. "Rabbi Jacob Emden's Views on Christianity." *Journal of Ecumenical Studies* 19.1 (1982) 107–9.

Fotopoulos, John. *Food Offered to Idols in Roman Corinth: A Social-rhetorical Reconsideration of 1 Corinthians 8:1—11:1*. WUNT 2.151. Tübingen: Mohr Siebeck, 2003.

Fredrikson, Paula. "Judaism, the Circumcision of Gentiles, and Apocalyptic Hope: Another Look at Galatians 1 and 2." In *The Galatians Debate: Contemporary Issues in Rhetorical and Historical Interpretation*, edited by Mark D. Nanos, 235–60. Peabody, MA: Hendrickson, 2002.

Freidenreich, David Moshe. "Foreign Food: A Comparatively-enriched Analysis of Jewish, Christian, and Islamic Law." PhD diss., Columbia University, 2006.

Fuchs-Kreimer, Nancy. "The 'Essential Heresy': Paul's View of the Law according to Jewish Writers: 1886–1986." PhD diss., Temple University, 1990.

Gager, John G. *Reinventing Paul*. Oxford: Oxford University Press, 2000.

Gaston, Lloyd. *Paul and the Torah*. Vancouver, BC: University of British Columbia Press, 1987.

Gooch, Peter David. *Dangerous Food: I Corinthians 8–10 in Its Context*. SCJ 5. Waterloo, ON: Wilfrid Laurier University Press, 1993.

Grunfeld, I. *The Jewish Dietary Laws*. 2 vols. London: Soncino, 1972.

Herberg, Will. "Judaism and Christianity: Their Unity and Difference" [1953]. In *Jewish Perspectives on Christianity: Leo Baeck, Martin Buber, Franz Rosenzweig, Will Herberg, and Abraham J. Heschel*, edited by Fritz A. Rothschild, 249–50. New York: Crossroad, 1990.

Heschel, Susannah. *Abraham Geiger and the Jewish Jesus*. Chicago Studies in the History of Judaism. Chicago: University of Chicago Press, 1998.

Howard, George. *Paul: Crisis in Galatia: A Study in Early Christian Theology*. 2nd ed. SNTSMS 35. Cambridge: Cambridge University Press, 1990.

Jackson-McCabe, Matt A., ed. *Jewish Christianity Reconsidered: Rethinking Ancient Groups and Texts*. Minneapolis: Fortress, 2007.

Johnson Hodge, Caroline. *If Sons, Then Heirs: A Study of Kinship and Ethnicity in the Letters of Paul*. Oxford: Oxford University Press, 2007.
Klinghoffer, David. *Why the Jews Rejected Jesus: The Turning Point in Western History*. New York: Doubleday, 2005.
Langton, Daniel R. "Modern Jewish Identity and the Apostle Paul: Pauline Studies as an Intra-Jewish Ideological Battleground," *Journal for the Study of the New Testament* 28.2 (2005) 217–58.
———. "The Myth of the 'Traditional View of Paul' and the Role of the Apostle in Modern Jewish-Christian Polemics." *Journal for the Study of the New Testament* 28.1 (2005) 69–104.
Lapide, Pinchas. "The Rabbi From Tarsus." In *Paul, Rabbi and Apostle*, edited by Pinchas Lapide and Peter Stuhlmacher, 31–55, 64–74. Minneapolis: Augsburg, 1984.
Levine, Amy-Jill. *The Misunderstood Jew: The Church and the Scandal of the Jewish Jesus*. San Francisco: HarperSanFranscisco, 2006.
Martin, Troy. "Pagan and Judeo-Christian Time-Keeping Schemes in Gal. 4:10 and Col. 2:16." *New Testament Studies* 42 (1996) 120–32.
Meißner, Stefan. *Die Heimholung des Ketzers: Studien zur jüdischen Auseinandersetzung mit Paulus*. WUNT 2.87. Tübingen: Mohr Siebeck, 1996.
Nanos, Mark D. "Broken Branches: A Pauline Metaphor Gone Awry? (Romans 11:11–36)." In *Between Gospel and Election: Explorations in the Interpretation of Romans 9–11*, edited by Florian Wilk and J. Ross Wagner, 339–76. Tübingen: Mohr Siebeck, 2010. (See volume 2 in this series of collected essays.)
———. "Challenging the Limits That Continue to Define Paul's Perspective on Jews and Judaism." In *Reading Israel in Romans: Legitimacy and Plausibility of Divergent Interpretations*, edited by Cristina Grenholm and Daniel Patte, 217–29. Romans through History and Culture Series. Harrisburg, PA: Trinity, 2000. (See volume 2 in this series of collected essays.)
———. "The Inter- and Intra-Jewish Political Context of Paul's Letter to the Galatians." In *The Galatians Debate: Contemporary Issues in Rhetorical and Historical Interpretation*, edited by Mark D. Nanos, 396–407. Peabody, MA: Hendrickson, 2002. (See volume 3 in this series of collected essays.)
———. "Intruding 'Spies' and 'Pseudo-Brethren': The Jewish Intra-Group Politics of Paul's Jerusalem Meeting (Gal. 2:1–10)." In *Paul and His Opponents*, edited by Stanley E. Porter, 59–97. Pauline Studies 2. Leiden: Brill, 2005. (See volume 3 in this series of collected essays.)
———. *The Irony of Galatians: Paul's Letter in First-Century Context*. Minneapolis: Fortress, 2002.
———. *The Mystery of Romans: The Jewish Context of Paul's Letter*. Minneapolis: Fortress, 1996.
———. "Paul and the Jewish Tradition: The Ideology of the Shema." In *Celebrating Paul. Festschrift in Honor of Jerome Murphy-O'Connor, O.P., and Joseph A. Fitzmyer, S.J.*, edited by Peter Spitaler, 62–80. CBQMS 48. Washington, DC: Catholic Biblical Association of America, 2012. (See chapter 4 in this volume of collected essays.)
———. "Paul and Judaism: Why Not Paul's Judaism?" In *Paul Unbound: Other Perspectives on the Apostle*, edited by Mark Given, 117–60. Peabody, MA: Hendrickson, 2009. (See chapter 1 in this volume of collected essays.)
———. "Paul's Relationship to Torah in Light of His Strategy 'to Become Everything to Everyone' (1 Corinthians 9:19–23)." In *Paul and Judaism: Crosscurrents in Pauline*

Exegesis and the Study of Jewish-Christian Relations, edited by Reimund Bieringer and Didier Pollefeyt, 106–40. Library of New Testament Studies 463. London: T. & T. Clark, 2012. (See volume 4 in this series of collected essays.)

———. "Paul's Reversal of Jews Calling Gentiles 'Dogs' (Philippians 3:2): 1600 Years of an Ideological Tale Wagging an Exegetical Dog?" *Biblical Interpretation* 17.4 (2009) 448–82. (See volume 4 in this series of collected essays.)

———. "Peter's Hypocrisy in the Light of Paul's Anxiety." In *The Mystery of Romans: The Jewish Context of Paul's Letter*, 337–71. Minneapolis: Fortress, 1996.

———. "The Polytheist Identity of the 'Weak,' and Paul's Strategy to 'Gain' Them: A New Reading of 1 Corinthians 8:1—11:1." In *Paul: Jew, Greek, and Roman*, edited by Stanley E. Porter, 179–210. Pauline Studies 5. Leiden: Brill, 2008. (See volume 4 in this series of collected essays.)

———. "A Rejoinder to Robert A. J. Gagnon's 'Why the "Weak" at Rome Cannot Be Non-Christian Jews.'" Available at http://www.marknanos.com/Gagnon-rejoinder-6-20-03.pdf. (See volume 2 in this series of collected essays.)

———. "What Was at Stake in Peter's 'Eating with Gentiles' at Antioch?" In *The Galatians Debate: Contemporary Issues in Rhetorical and Historical Interpretation*, edited by Mark D. Nanos, 282–318. Peabody, MA: Hendrickson, 2002. (See volume 3 in this series of collected essays.)

———. "Why the 'Weak' in 1 Corinthians 8–10 Were Not Christ-believers." In *Saint Paul and Corinth: 1950 Years Since the Writing of the Epistles to the Corinthians: International Scholarly Conference Proceedings (Corinth, 23–25 September 2007)*, edited by Constantine J. Belezos, Sotirios Despotis, and Christos Karakolis, 385–404. Athens: Psichogios, 2009. (See volume 4 in this series of collected essays.)

Richardson, Peter. "Pauline Inconsistency: 1 Corinthians 9:19–23 and Galatians 2:11–14." *New Testament Studies* 26 (1979) 347–62.

Rubenstein, Richard L. *My Brother Paul*. 1st ed. New York: Harper & Row, 1972.

Runesson, Anders. "Particularistic Judaism and Universalistic Christianity?: Some Critical Remarks on Terminology and Theology." *Studia Theologica* 54 (2000) 55–75.

Sanders, E. P. "Jewish Association with Gentiles and Galatians 2:11–14." In *The Conversation Continues: Studies in Paul & John In Honor of J. Louis Martyn*, edited by Robert T. Fortna and Beverly R. Gaventa, 170–88. Nashville: Abingdon, 1990.

———. *Paul, the Law, and the Jewish People*. Philadelphia: Fortress, 1985.

———. *Paul and Palestinian Judaism: A Comparison of Patterns of Religion*. Philadelphia: Fortress, 1977.

Scherman, Nosson. *The Complete ArtScroll Siddur: Weekday/Sabbath/Festival: A New Translation and Anthologized Commentary*. ArtScroll Mesorah Series. The Rabbinical Council of America ed. Brooklyn, NY: Mesorah, 1990.

Schoeps, Hans Joachim. *The Jewish-Christian Argument: A History of Theologies in Conflict*. Translated by David E. Green. London: Faber & Faber, 1963.

———. *Jüdisch-Christliches Religionsgespräch in 19 Jahrhunderten: Geschichte einer theologischen Auseinandersetzung*. Berlin: Vortrupp, 1937.

Segal, Alan F. *Paul the Convert: The Apostolate and Apostasy of Saul the Pharisee*. New Haven: Yale University Press, 1990.

———. "Paul's Religious Experience in the Eyes of Jewish Scholars." In *Israel's God and Rebecca's Children: Christology and Community in Early Judaism and Christianity: Essays in Honor of Larry W. Hurtado and Alan F. Segal*, edited by David B. Capes,

April D. DeConick, Helen K. Bond and Troy A. Miller, 321–43. Waco, TX: Baylor University Press, 2007.
Stanford, W. B. *The Ulysses Theme: A Study in the Adaptability of a Traditional Hero.* Dallas: Spring, 1992.
Stendahl, Krister. "The Apostle Paul and the Introspective Conscience of the West." In *Paul among Jews and Gentiles, and Other Essays*, 78–96. Philadelphia: Fortress, 1976.
Thiessen, Gerd. *The Social Setting of Pauline Christianity: Essays on Corinth.* Translated by John H. Schütz. Philadelphia: Fortress, 1982.
Tomson, Peter J. *Paul and the Jewish Law: Halakha in the Letters of the Apostle to the Gentiles.* CRINT. Minneapolis: Fortress, 1990.
Wyschogrod, Michael. *Abraham's Promise: Judaism and Jewish-Christian Relations.* Radical Traditions. Grand Rapids: Eerdmans, 2004.
Zetterholm, Magnus. "Purity and Anger: Gentiles and Idolatry in Antioch." *Interdisciplinary Journal of Research on Religion* 1 (2005) 1–24.

4

Paul and the Jewish Tradition
The Ideology of the *Shema*

Sh'ma Yisra'eil Adonai Eloheinu Adonai echad
"Hear, O Israel, the LORD is our God, the LORD is One"

[62]THE *SHEMA ISRAEL* IS arguably the most important ideological claim of Judaism in early Israelite history.[1] This call to listen to God is followed by the injunction to love God, that is, to be loyal and serve with all of the effort one can summon.[2] It includes observance and reflection, *kavannah*, the intention of the heart. It captures the very essence of Torah, the Teachings of God that Israel is privileged to have on behalf of all humankind, but also responsible to listen to and embody.[3]

The *Shema Israel* is uttered in sacred prayer twice a day. Jewish children learn it as their first prayer, and Jews hope that it will be the last words on their lips. R. Akiva recited the *Shema* when executed by the Romans following the failed second revolt against Rome, understanding the

---

1. This essay was originally delivered as a lecture at Villanova University, Jubilee Year of Paul Lecture Series, October 23, 2008, and updated for publication.

2. The *Shema* includes Deut 6:4–8; 11:13–21; Num 15:37–41. For a discussion of all of the elements of the prayer, see Hoffman, *My People's Prayer Book*. My reflections on the *Shema* are informed by the observations of many others, e.g., Heschel, *Between God and Man*, 102–7; Lamm, *The Shema*.

3. m. 'Abot. 3.14.

commandment [63] to loyalty "with all thy soul" to signify "even if He takes thy soul," and the call to martyrdom is repeated in subsequent interpretive tradition.[4]

The claim that God is "One" affirms Israel's choice of her God "alone," or "only" in response to God's choice of Israel, regardless of the claims of other nations on their gods, or their gods on those nations. The natural sense of the declaration of Deuteronomy 6:4 in its own context is not the denial of the existence of other gods, but the prescription for Israel to only look to her God (see Exod 15:11). It is analogous to a person declaring that a certain mate is the only one for him or her.[5] Such a proposition does not rest upon denying the existence of other men or women, but affirming, in spite of their existence, that the one in view is singularly of interest to him or her, the one he or she loves like no one else, to whom he or she will be loyal, regardless of the circumstances. Marriage rituals are constructed around just this dynamic—so too is the Israelite conception of the covenant relationship between God and Israel.

Although the *Shema* is mentioned only once in Torah, the redactor of the Mishnah, R. Judah the Prince, made it the opening *halakah* for the Talmud.[6] The call to hear is a call to obey. Yet, we do not always "do" as we ought to do according to what we have "heard" to be right. Thus, Midrash Deuteronomy Rabbah 3.11 reminds that even when Israel failed to "do" (*na'ăśeh*) what it ought to do by making the Golden Calf, it was nevertheless still responsible to "hear" (*nišmā'*), to "listen" (see Exod 24:7). The *Shema* thus includes the call to obedience and to reflection on the meaning of that calling despite falling short of perfection, for as Ecclesiastes 7:20 recognizes, "there is not a just person on earth who does good and sins not."[7] Yet Israel is called—on behalf of all humankind—to attend to the doing of that which is right. Hence, the Talmudic expression, the *Shema* is *qābbalāt 'ôl malkût šāmayim*, "the *acceptance* of the yoke of the kingdom of heaven."[8]

The *Shema* reminds Israel not only of God's loyalty and promises but also of the love of God that is central to Jewish identity. It encompasses [64] the responsibility to do God's will and serve one's neighbors (see Mal 2:10). It embodies the ideals of Jewish spirituality. In biblical Hebrew, there is—surprisingly, for a religious tradition so attentive to the obligation of

---

4. b. Ber. 61b; y. Ber. 9.5; Lamm, *The Shema*, 135–40.

5. Maimonides, *Hilkhot Teshuvah* 10.3 (see Lamm, *The Shema* 162; Moberly, "Toward an Interpretation of the Shema," 132–33).

6. Lamm, *The Shema*, 9.

7. Ibid., 9–10.

8. See, e.g., y. Ber. 2.1.

obedience—no specific word for obedience, but rather words such as *šěma'* (hear). In English, it is highlighted when a parent rebukes a child with, "Did you *hear* what I said?"—an ironic turn of phrase from one who knows the child heard what was said, yet feigns ignorance to rebuke the child indirectly. The ironic approach nevertheless communicates that "you did not respect my intentions," or, "you *understood* the responsibility to which hearing what was said, by definition, committed you as a member of this family unit, yet you eschewed your obligation." Indeed, the Sages ruled that the recitation of the *Shema* is more concerned with "understanding" than "hearing." Thus, while the ideal is to annunciate the *Shema* with intention, nevertheless, even if it is recited inaudibly, one can fulfill this halakhic requirement.[9] Obedience is intended to express heartfelt commitment to the ideals embedded in the action, even when the heart is heavy, or distant.

Defining the "oneness" of God is the subject of a rich interpretive tradition. Deuteronomy 4:39 tells how Moses taught the people to "realize today and turn it over in your mind: the LORD is indeed God, in heaven above and on earth below; there is no other." Maimonides (*ca.* 1135–1204) emphasized that God is incorporeal, indivisible, and completely unique. Rashi (*ca.* 1040–1105) observed that oneness includes the recognition that Israel's God is the only God of all the nations. The *Shema* became the rallying cry for Israelites in the face of polytheism. The call is to hear, not to see. There is no statue to behold. The sense of hearing involves not only cultivating hearing apart from seeing, but also commitment to that which others have not similarly witnessed. When Isaiah proclaimed that Israel's God declares, "I form the light and create darkness; I make peace and create evil" (45:7), he formulated a polemical challenge to the regime of the Persians, with the two gods of Zoroastrianism, one of light and goodness, the other of darkness and evil. Later, this declaration naturally expressed a polemical sense of singularity in the face of Christian Trinitarian claims. The *Shema* functions not only theologically, but also socially. It defines group identity and values.

WHAT DOES THE JEWISH TRADITION ABOUT GOD'S ONENESS HAVE TO DO WITH PAUL?

[65] Most interpreters of Paul, and most discussions of the topic, "Paul and the Jewish tradition," explain how Paul emerged from the Judaism of his time. The Paul conceptualized is no longer a representative of Judaism; he exemplifies a new religion, Christianity. I maintain instead that Paul and his

---

9. Lamm, *The Shema*, 15–16.

audiences practiced Judaism,[10] that his groups represented a Jewish coalition upholding that the end of the ages had dawned, the awaited day when members of the other nations would turn to Israel's God as the one God of all humankind. He spoke for a Jewish subgroup that upheld faith in Christ, to be sure, but this was not a new religion, nor did he imagine that it would ever be one. He was involved in the restoration of Israel and the gathering of the nations initiated thereby.

I submit that the *Shema Israel* is the central conviction of Paul's theology.[11] He often refers to God's oneness at critical points in arguments. It functions theologically and polemically in the cases he makes; but Paul does not really explain the *Shema* as much as appeal to it, which suggests that for him the concept of God's oneness functioned at the ideological level. He assumed its explanatory power was self-evident. This assumption was true not only for himself, but his arguments also presume his audiences would understand the logic of this theological proposition without explanation. Yet that would not work for those unfamiliar with its propositional bases or its importance in Jewish communal life and liturgy. Paul presumes that his audiences perceive reality in Jewish communal terms, either as a direct result of his own teaching or the teaching of others that is to be [66] expected in their communal life, which presupposes that they live and worship within Jewish communities, that they are being socialized into Jewish ideological patterns of thought and life as normative.

If we turn to Paul's letter to the Romans, we can see Paul's direct appeal to the *Shema* as the basis for his judgment about the standing of non-Jews within the community of the people of God. The text of Romans 3:29–31 reads:

> Or is God the God of Jews only? Not the God of members of the other nations also? Yes, of members of the other nations also, since God is one, who will justify the circumcised out of faithfulness and the foreskinned through the faithfulness [of Christ]. Do we then nullify the Torah by the faithfulness [of Christ]? By no means! On the contrary, we establish the Torah.[12]

---

10. For a detailed discussion of this topic, see Nanos, "Paul and Judaism: Why Not Paul's Judaism?"; Nanos, "The Myth of the 'Law-Free' Paul Standing between Christians and Jews."

11. For reflections on the oneness of God theme in Paul, from which I have benefited, see e.g., Dahl, *Studies in Paul*, 178–91; Guerra, "The One God Topos in *Spec. Leg.* 1.52"; Wright, "One God, One Lord, One People"; Wright, *The Climax of the Covenant*, 125–36.

12. The translation of ἔθνη as "members of the other nations" instead of "gentiles" emphasizes that Paul's logic works around a contrast between Israel and the other

One might expect Paul to reason from the oneness of humankind that we are all one, or to elaborate at least that because God is one therefore humankind is one, neither Jewish nor non-Jewish, which would reflect the way that Paul's theology has been most often presented, as if he believed that ethnic difference was nullified; but he does neither of these things. Rather, Paul simply appeals to the logic of God's oneness without further explanation. Paul pronounces a statement that is at once simple and complex—one that, for a Jew, is almost too close to the bone to be able to explain because it is self-evident, and at the same time, it is one that is too all-encompassing to ever finish explaining.

The discovery of the *Shema Israel* as central to Paul's theology was a profound moment for me as a Jewish reader of these texts, and has shaped my reading of him ever since. If I were to write a theology of Paul, it would be the center around which all the other topics turned. Here we see Paul employ it at a pivotal point in his argument in Romans for why non-Jewish [67] believers in Christ must remain non-Jews and not become proselytes, and by the implication of his logic, why Jews remain Jews after faith in Christ: "since God is one."[13]

Someone unfamiliar with Jewish logic based on this "oneness of God" theme might find it difficult to follow Paul's reasoning.[14] After all, what does "God is one" have to do with the warrant for the inclusion of non-Jews? If they become proselytes, that is, Jewish converts, how does it follow that God would not be one? But for Paul and other Christ-followers, with the coming of Christ to redeem Israel *and* the nations, the logical answer is, "No, that would undermine God's oneness." Why? Because it would signify that even in the awaited age—which they claim has begun—God is only the one God of Israelites. Thus, all others would have to join the people Israel by way of proselyte conversion, leaving the members of the rest of the nations turn-

---

nations. The choice of "faithfulness" for πίστις without the article in the case of the circumcised, and "the faithfulness [of Christ]" for the case of the foreskinned, which has the article, is based on Paul's grammar and argument here and throughout the letter (see esp. Rom 15:8–9 and discussion of that passage below). From Paul's perspective, a Jew faithful to Torah will undertake to declare the faith of Christ to the nations, and thus be faithful to the covenant obligation and privilege of being entrusted with the oracles of God for the nations (3:2), which is the way of life to which Torah points.

13. See Nanos, *The Mystery of Romans*, 179–201.

14. One should also consider the Greco-Roman idea of a supreme deity emerging among Stoics and other philosophical groups (see, e.g., Brenk, "'We Are of His Race': Paul and the Philosophy of His Time," 402–40); but telling are the differences between features of those traditions compared to the very similar elements and developments of themes in Paul and in the rabbinic tradition; see Lamm, *The Shema*; Dahl, *Studies in Paul*, 178–91.

ing to God in Christ without a legitimate claim on Israel's God apart from becoming Israelites, as if there were some other god for those who are not members of Israel.

THE RELATIONSHIP OF CHRIST-FOLLOWERS TO JEWISH IDENTITY AND CONDUCT

A critical issue in Christian theology arises concerning the relationship of its members to Jewish identity and behavior. For the original audiences of Paul's letters, that concern about identity arose from their self-understanding as participants in Judaism, a Jewish communal way of life that applied even to the non-Jewish members who joined themselves to these communities as guests, members from the other nations. In Paul's time, although no longer, for Christ-followers who were not Jews the first question was whether they could or should become members of Israel, Jews, which is [68] accomplished by completion of the rite of proselyte conversion. For males, this includes circumcision at the conclusion of the conversion process. Circumcision thus functions in Paul's time as a metonym for the rite of proselyte conversion. It is a rite or work or deed prescribed by Torah to become a member of Israel, and thereafter, a person is obliged to observe Torah, that is, responsible to practice Jewish behavior on the same terms as naturally born Jews.

Since the church fathers, the traditional Christian answer to whether proselyte conversion should be undertaken by Christ-followers has been a definitive "No." The traditional reason offered is that the time of Judaism and Torah has ended with the coming of Christ. They are finished—at least for Christ-followers—and Christians should not, indeed, cannot become Jews or observe Torah as a matter of faithfulness. This has been applied to Jewish believers in Christ as well as to non-Jewish believers.[15] It has been universalized so that Christianity has no place for Jewish identity or Torah-defined lifestyles.[16] It is thereby made clear that Christianity is not Judaism.

---

15. The exception proving the rule is Augustine's proposal that the first generation of apostles continued to practice Judaism (related to their habits when becoming Christians, and to their mission to Jews, as long as it was not as an element of their salvation), although this was not to be extended to subsequent generations of Christians (Augustine *ep.* 40.4.6; in Trigg, *Biblical Interpretation*, 250–95). But even this concession for the first generation was strongly opposed by Jerome on the grounds that it would have compromised Christianity to allow any level of Jewish practice to continue in the church beside the pretense necessary to move among Jews to persuade them of the gospel message (Jerome, *ep.* 104.13, 17; in Trigg, *Interpretation*, 285, 289).

16. For confessions extracted from Jews converting to Christianity that they would

Jewish tradition has answered that ideological stance in kind, making it clear that Judaism is not Christianity. And these communities and their religious practices have become very different, indeed. Obviously, then, when the topic, "Paul and the Jewish tradition," arises, it posits an essential contrast and refers to Paul's former religion—one that perhaps continues to surface in his life and teachings because of his past, or occasionally when seeking to mimic Jews in order to evangelize among them—but not to a religious way of life or community to which he still seeks to be faithful in his "Christian" life.

[69] I suggest that the traditional approach conceptualizes Paul and his contemporaries anachronistically, including the members of his communities. Yes, Paul did teach non-Jews believing in Christ that they could not become Jews, members of Israel, but he did so for a very different reason than is usually proposed. Paul argues not on the basis that Jewish identity and Torah are detrimental to Christian life, or passé, but rather that their role is specifically designed for Israelites and not for the members of the other nations. In terms of the *Shema*, Paul is developing a tension between the special privilege of being Israel because the LORD is *our* God—the God of the covenants made with *our* fathers—and God's role as the creator of all humankind: the LORD *alone*. God is the God of all the nations, in whose service God has called and set apart the people of Israel to demonstrate righteousness and express lovingkindness or grace, as well as to declare God's words to all of the other nations. Here we meet so-called particularism and universalism in unison, not as binary opposites, as they are so often treated. We can thus understand Paul's sharp denial that faithfulness to God in Christ nullified Torah or, rather, his claim that it established Torah. Torah (God's "Teaching") guides Israel to live faithfully to the one God, a way of living that includes bearing witness of God's faithfulness to the nations; for Paul, that includes declaring the good news of God's rescue of the nations in Jesus Christ.

THE *SHEMA* AND ESCHATOLOGICAL EXPECTATIONS

Paul's argument is consistent with other Jewish interpretations of the *Shema* not connected to Christ-faith. Consider the language of the *Sifre* on Deuteronomy 6:4 (*Piska* 31) discussing why the Scripture says the LORD is both "our God" as well as "One." The rabbis conclude first that "'our God' serves

---

never return to any Jewish practices or assemblies, see Parkes, *The Conflict of the Church and the Synagogue*, 394–400. See also Nicea II, Canon 8, in Lamberz, ed., *Concilium Universale Nicaenum Secundum*.

to teach us that His name rests in greater measure upon us ... upon Israel," and then offer this interpretation:

> "The LORD, our God," over us (the children of Israel); "the LORD is one," over all the creatures of the world. "The LORD, our God," in this world; "the LORD is one," in the world to come, as it is said, "[T]he LORD shall be king over all the earth. In that day shall the LORD be one and His name one" (Zech 14:9).[17]

[70] The concern for the universal as well as the particular is contextualized in terms of the awaited future. Israel presently has a special relationship with the One God, who is the master not just of Israel, but of all of the other nations, too.

Similarly, roughly halfway between Paul's time and our own, Rashi explained the repetition of "The Name" (*Haššêm*, a rabbinic circumlocution for YHWH/LORD) in the *Shema* as follows:

> The LORD who is our God now, but not (yet) the God of the (other) nations, is destined to be the One LORD, as it is said, "For then will I give to the peoples a pure language, that they may all call upon the name of the LORD, to serve Him with one consent" (Zeph 3:9). And (likewise) it is said, "And the LORD shall be king over all the earth; on that day shall the LORD be One and His name One" (Zech 14:9).[18]

The eschatological expectation expressed by Rashi also explains the confession that Israelites make today, and ultimately also the confession that all the other nations will make; but they do not do so "yet."

Paul's argument is based upon the same logic, but to a different conclusion, because of his understanding that Jesus Christ has brought the dawning of that awaited day. As Paul brings his argument in Romans to a close, he sets out a graphic social portrait of non-Jews joining together with Jews in praise of the One God with one voice that mirrors the language of Rashi, although predating it by a millennium. In Romans 15:5-12, drawing from Torah, the Writings, and the Prophets, Paul exclaims:

> May the God of steadfastness and encouragement grant you to live in harmony with one another, in accordance with Christ Jesus, so that together you may with one voice glorify the God and Father of our Lord Jesus Christ. Welcome one another, therefore, just as Christ has welcomed you, for the glory of God. For I tell you that Christ has become a servant of the circumcised

---

17. Hammer, *Sifre: A Tannaitic Commentary on the Book of Deuteronomy*, 58–59.
18. Lamm, *The Shema*, 31–37.

on behalf of the truth of God in order that he might confirm the promises given to the patriarchs, and in order that the Gentiles might glorify God for his mercy. As it is written, "Therefore, I will confess you among the gentiles, and sing praises to your name"; and again he says, "Rejoice, O Gentiles, with his people"; and again, [71] "Praise the Lord, all you Gentiles, and let all the peoples praise him"; and again Isaiah says, "The root of Jesse shall come, the one who rises to rule the gentiles; in him the Gentiles shall hope." (NRSV)

For Paul, if non-Jews "in Christ" would become Jewish proselytes, and thereby Israelites, they would not bear witness to the arrival of the day when representatives from all of the nations are expected to turn from idols to the worship of the One God, but simply to the truth that, for them, in the present age Israel represents the righteous ones of God, which members from the other nations also can become by proselyte conversion. That identity transformation for non-Jews is available apart from the confession of faith in Jesus Christ in most other Jewish groups of Paul's time. They provide for proselyte conversion to join the family of Abraham, of God, within the present age, and await with Israel the hope of the day of the reconciliation of the nations.[19] Then the "wolf" (such as is Rome) will lie down to eat with the "lamb" (Israel) without devouring her (Isa 11:6; 65:25);[20] but *until that time* such behavior would be foolish for "lambs" to indulge.

Paul's logic is this: If all who worship the One God are Israelites or become Israelites, then God is only the God of one nation, not of all the nations. But if the non-Jews who turn to Israel's God do so while remaining non-Jews, not as members of the nation Israel, then they worship the God of Israel as the one God of all the nations *also*. *That* is the point of Paul's argument. No matter how many difficulties this poses for these members from the other nations and the Jews who affiliate with them as co-members of this Jewish coalition, God's oneness must not be compromised by the proselyte conversion of non-Jews who turn to God by way of Jesus Christ. For Paul, that they remain members from the other nations joining alongside of Israelites constitutes an important proof of the propositional claims of the gospel; it signals the arrival of the awaited day when all of the nations will worship the Creator God together.

Most other Jewish groups probably would not disagree with Paul's proposition that such reconciliation will occur when that day arrives, when members of other nations will not join Israel but will join *alongside* Israel

---

19. See Philo, *Spec.* 2.164–66.
20. Maimonides *Hilkhot Melakhim* 12.1.

in worship of the One Creator God of all humankind. Paul most likely held this [72] view even before he was called to proclaim Christ, when he was involved in seeking to stamp out these communities, which was presumably in reaction to the earliest Christ-followers' inclusive policies toward these non-Jews apart from proselyte conversion, which were based on the very same propositional claims for the gospel that he later promoted, and for which he similarly suffered (see Gal 1:12-16 with 5:11). In addition, some Jews may have believed that day would be accompanied by the conversion of the nations in the sense of proselyte conversion to Israel; others might have awaited the destruction of the other nations. These expectations and others can be gleaned from the Scriptures and other writings of Paul's time.[21]

THE UNIQUE CHARACTER OF PAUL'S GROUPS AMONG JEWISH GROUPS

The important point to stress here is that although members of other Jewish groups similarly hoped for reconciliation with the nations and expected them to remain non-Israelites at that time, unless they shared the conviction of Paul and other Christ-following Jews that this moment had *already arrived* through Jesus Christ, or had begun to arrive and to be witnessed in the lives of the communities of believers in that proposition, they would not have agreed with this change of policy, that is, to including these non-Jewish Christ-followers as full members of the Jewish communities apart from proselyte conversion. In their groups, the religio-ethnic distinction between gentiles (however welcome as friends and guests) and Jews or Israelites, a category that included proselytes, was important to maintain. For them, any non-Jews who turned from idolatry to worship the One God and thus now seek full membership in the Jewish community would complete [73] the rite of conversion so that they are no longer regarded as mere guests. It is on *this* matter of *timing*, that is, where Israel and the nations stand on God's timetable—at the dawning of the awaited day, and thus making halakhic decisions appropriate to its arrival, or not—that

---

21. See Donaldson (*Paul and the Gentiles*, 60-74) for a discussion of various expectations for non-Jews, including a natural law non-Jew who turns from idolatry but is not identified with circumcision and other special laws for Israelites (e.g., observing dietary customs), righteous gentiles, and eschatological pilgrimage scenarios. Examples include Josephus, *A.J.* 20.41 (34-48); Philo, *Q.E.* 2.2; *Mos.* 2.4; *Abr.* 3-6, 60-61; *Virt.* 102, 181-82, 212-19; *Spec.* 1.51; 2.42-48; 4.178; Jos. Asen.; t. Sanh. 13.2. See Fredriksen, "Judaism, the Circumcision of Gentiles, and Apocalyptic Hope," 236-47; Wyschogrod, *Abraham's Promise*, 162-63, 190-95; Lamm, *The Shema*, 31-37.

Paul's (and other Christ-following) groups appear to have been "unique" among Jewish groups of his time.

That decision carried profound implications. Paul sought to proclaim this "truth" and bring his communities into conformity with his teaching so that they would exemplify its merits. In his view, it required subordination to the Spirit of God to live in the present age according to the dynamics of the age to come, a spiritual way of life that is available to gentiles in Christ on the same terms as Israelites and apart from them becoming Israelites. In particular, the challenge for Christ-following Jewish communities is to live out the "truth of the gospel" proposition that, among them, discrimination is no longer practiced even though social difference remains among them in this age. Of course, since they were but humans—and in human society, where discrimination often arises when there is difference, as Social Identity Theory demonstrates[22]—Paul recognizes that this ideal can only be achieved by dedication to God according to this proposition, and by yielding to God's Spirit in their lives together.

I disagree with the view of many interpreters of Paul—Jewish as well as Christian—that Paul taught the dissolution of religio-ethnic differences among Christ-followers, that there were no longer Jews and gentiles in Christ, but a kind of new, third race, as some have phrased it. Paul does write famously in Galatians 3:28, "There is not Jew or Greek, there is not slave or free, there is not male and female; for you are all one in Christ Jesus." Whereas here we see again the theme of oneness, Paul *cannot* mean that these different identities no longer exist among Christ-followers. There are very real biological, cultural, and socio-economic differences that are not dissolved. Slaves are not by definition freed in these groups, and Jews do not become gentiles any more than gentiles become Jews. There remain fundamental biological differences between women and men, for example, and a man has either been circumcised or remains in his foreskinned state.

Paul recognizes these differences in his arguments. In his letters, he addresses people and groups composed of these different identities specifically, [74] and with different instructions for each. He explains the world from an Israelite-based conceptualization of reality: he does not address anyone as "Christian," but as Jew or non-Jew, circumcised or foreskinned. Apart from an Israelite worldview, such categories do not carry meaning; and it is only within these categories that being named a loyal follower of Jesus Christ (Messiah), or not, arises meaningfully. Thus, his rhetoric must signify something other than the end of religio-ethnic difference. Rather, it signals that these different people and groups, although different, are not to continue to discriminate

---

22. Hogg and Abrams, *Social Identifications*.

among themselves based on prevailing cultural valuations of those present differences, as they had previously done "in the present evil age." They are to live in community, to eat together at the messianic banquet of the awaited age, bearing witness to the propositional claim of the gospel that the age to come has arrived with Christ in the midst of the present age. That is the truth of the gospel to which they are called (see Gal 2:14–16).

Paul's position in Romans 3 and Galatians 3 is in keeping with his argument in 1 Corinthians 7:17–24, that everyone who comes into the Christ-following subgroups should remain in the state in which they were when called. Thus, those circumcised remain Jews obligated to observe Torah, on the logic of Paul's own declaration of this concomitant obligation in Galatians 5:3, that those who are circumcised are responsible to observe the whole Torah. At the same time, those who are not Jews remain not-Jews and not under obligation to observe Torah as if they were Jews. What is paramount, Paul declares, which may surprise many, is not one's relative social identity or status, but that everyone put first "keeping the commandments of God." It is hard to believe that this Paul has become the apostle of freedom polemically juxtaposed with the value of faithful action, including the observance of Torah; the champion of faith alone, rather than of faithfulness.

It should also be recognized that, in the Christian tradition, the notion that Christians are neither Jews nor gentiles, circumcised nor foreskinned, has actually meant that they are not to be Jews or circumcised. For Paul, Christians did not constitute a third ethnicity, but in later theological developments of Paul's argument Christians in effect privilege the ideal of gentile identity; consequently, the notions of "gentile" and "Christian" are conflated in contrast to Jew and non-Christian. This conflation has created a struggle with Jewish identity and behavior, including how—and, in some cases (such as for Marcion), even whether—Christians should use the [75] Tanakh. In sharp contrast to Paul's argument and the implicit logic that God is the God of Jews, the logic of the Christian abrogation of Jewish identity and Torah-based lifestyles for Jews (as if both Torah and Mosaic covenant-based identity has ended in Christ) is that God is only the God of non-Jews, that Christianity is a gentile religion.

But this assumption turns Paul's argument from the *Shema* on its head. That God is the God of Jews was the logical premise for his question (Rom 3:29) about whether God is *also* the God of non-Jews. He argued for the inclusion of non-Jews as equal co-members in the people of God, as children of Abraham but not of Israel—not for the exclusion of Jews thereby! He argued for the unequivocal continuation of all Israelites in the family of God as "beloved," including those who did not share Paul's faith in Christ, because of the gifts and promises made to the fathers (Rom 9:4–5).[23] Indeed, concern to nip in the bud any potential arrogance toward those presently "stumbling" Israelites was one of Paul's central messages throughout the letter, made explicit in the olive tree allegory of 11:11–36.[24]

For Paul, what sets this Jewish community and the practice of Judaism by its non-Jewish members apart from all other Jewish groups is the maintenance of religio-ethnic difference without hierarchical advantage among them because of the reconciliation of all humankind in Jesus Christ. These non-Jews are not merely guests of the Jewish communities or practitioners of some religious way of life other than Judaism. By being "in Christ" they have become children of Abraham, children of the One God of all humankind as proclaimed in Israelite terms for the awaited age to come. It is the truth of this proclamation's claims in Jesus Christ to which they must be dedicated in all of their thinking and behavior by the "renewal of their minds" (see, e.g., 12:1–2). Otherwise, this claim's witness to the Jewish people and the rest of the nations in Israelite-based terms will not be borne out. In the meantime, these gentiles—regardless of their disputed identity (in Jewish communities, in which their subgroups dwell) because of their failure to become proselytes—must not think of themselves, or [76] try to gain standing in this-age terms, as either Jews, or alternatively, as mere guests still obliged to participate in idolatrous practices when among family and fellow townspeople. Rather, they must stand fast in the truth of their identity in the new-age terms of Christ, and thus "out of faithfulness to the Spirit, wait for the hope of righteousness" (Gal 5:5)—which is the argumentative goal of Galatians, in my view.[25]

---

23. Note the present tense possession of these gifts; see Rom 11:26–29.

24. Nanos, *Mystery*, 239–88; Nanos, "'Broken Branches': A Pauline Metaphor Gone Awry?"

25. Nanos, *The Irony of Galatians*. There are other texts in which Paul explicitly or implicitly appeals to the *Shema* that do not bear as directly on this discussion. In Galatians 3:20 (NRSV), Paul writes, "Now a mediator involves more than one party; but God is one." The oneness of God is also central to the argument in 1 Corinthians 8:4–6 (NRSV): "Hence, as to the eating of food offered to idols, we know that 'no idol in the world really exists,' and that 'there is no God but one.' Indeed, even though there may be so-called gods in heaven or on earth—as in fact there are many gods and many lords—yet for us there is one God, the Father, from whom are all things and for whom we exist, and one Lord, Jesus Christ, through whom are all things and through whom we exist."

CONCLUSION

In a title like I have chosen for my essay, "Paul and the Jewish Tradition," the conjunction usually serves to mark a contrast between Paul, the Christian apostle and founder of a new religion, Christianity, *and* the Jewish tradition that he supposedly left following his "conversion." While interpreters might note some similarities, the focus frequently is on how different these groups were, and how different they continue to be precisely *because of* Paul's influence. But Paul's arguments indicate that after his "calling" to proclaim Christ to the nations he continued to live and teach from within Judaism, albeit from within a specific group affiliation based on a shared conviction about the meaning of Jesus Christ. Paul still thought and argued and acted from the ideology of the *Shema*, appealing to Judaism's ideals and seeking to embody them, and he called for the members of his groups to do so as well.

In short, Paul and his groups practiced Judaism, even though, for subsequent generations representing the tradition known as Paulinism, and in the religion that became Christianity, this proposition was so fundamentally out of step with what Paul represented that it might have seemed impossible to imagine, much less maintain. Nevertheless, I conclude by highlighting eight dynamics of this interpretation.

(1) [77] Paul supposes that appeal to Judaism's ideals—in the case of this essay, the *Shema*—will carry authority with his Christ-following audiences, whether or not he has founded and worked among them. He does not explain the theological foundations for such an important assertion as the *Shema*, around which his arguments turn, although he apparently expects his audiences to respond positively to this way of seeing the world, and to behave accordingly.

(2) Paul was not against social difference in the lives of Christ-followers, including gender, ethnicity, economic means, cultural norms, location, or Jewish identity and concomitant observance of Torah. Rather, social difference played a role in expressing the fundamental truth of his gospel proposition that the Creator God was not confined to one people or culture. Although God is the God of Israel and best characterized by the righteousness expressed in Torah, the ideals of Torah (of God's Teachings for Israel) could be expressed in other cultural ways too. What Paul disallowed among Christ-followers was the hierarchical discrimination that social difference normally represented in cultures of the present age. Social difference was to remain; but because God is one, in the communities of those devoted to God, there is to be no intra-group discrimination based upon difference. This particular matter makes the interpretation of Paul advanced here

relevant for Christians today, not only with respect to the religio-ethnic categories of Jew and non-Jew, but for all relationships that take place across lines of social difference.

(3) The *Shema* was a central element in Paul's *eschatological* reasoning. Although Paul aspired to the universal hope for the future restoration of the nations before he came to believe in Christ, until that day arrived he believed that Israel alone represented the righteous family of God's people, and anyone from the other nations must join Israel to claim such identity. He now understood that ideal to be dawning already among Christ-followers. For him, the age to come has begun with the resurrection of Christ; the messianic banquet has started. Both Israel and the other nations turn to the One God equally. When the Christ-believing sub-groups of the Jewish community meet, they represent the demonstration of this propositional truth—or they should. It is from this propositional base that his specific teaching of Jewish values in cross-cultural terms proceeds. Thus, we find him explaining the theological premises from which they should think, and by which their behavior should be guided. The *Shema* involves not only a statement of central theological truths, but also offers guidance for how to [78] live in the present evil age as if they already were members of the community of the blessed age to come.

(4) Reasoning from these points, rather than from the premise that he regarded Jewish identity and behavior to be inferior or obsolete and, thus, undesirable for Christ-followers, helps explain why Paul opposed the circumcision or proselyte conversion of his non-Jewish audiences. Paul was not the champion of Christian universalism versus Jewish particularism. Paul's gospel and teaching were formulated around Jewish as well as non-Jewish particularism based on age-to-come Jewish universalistic aspirations. It is not the case that Paul argued gentiles *need not* become Jews, as if it represented an option if undertaken for the right reasons instead of, for example, to gain salvation (as normally formulated); rather, he insisted that gentiles in Christ *cannot* become Jews (Gal 5:2–6). They were, and were to remain, non-Jews, and thus not to undertake the rite of proselyte conversion. In this sense, they were not to become identified *under* Torah, obliged to observe it on the same terms as Jews. They must represent the nations turning to God with the arrival of the awaited age. At the same time, it follows that Jews were to continue to circumcise their sons and to observe Torah as Jews (1 Cor 7:17–24 with Gal 5:3), just as did Paul, who continued to practice prevailing Jewish dietary norms as a matter of covenant faithfulness.[26] They

---

26. Details available in my *Mystery of Romans*; "The Myth of the 'Law-free' Paul"; "What Was at Stake in Peter's 'Eating with Gentiles' at Antioch?"; "The Polytheist Identity of the 'Weak' and Paul's Strategy to 'Gain' Them"; and "Paul's Relationship to Torah

were the ones announcing this good news to the nations precisely as representatives of the nation Israel, the nation who God called and gave the gift of Torah, the nation entrusted with the words of God to be announced (Rom 1:1–5; 3:2, 31; 9:3–5; 10:15–18; 15:8–12). Thus, the non-Jewish Christ-followers were to respect the righteousness embodied in these Teachings (Rom 13:8–14; Gal 5:13–14), and to respect their explicit practice in the lives of Jews; non-Jews were to practice Jewish communal ways of living developed for non-Jewish guests (Rom 14:1—15:13).[27]

(5) [79] Paul wrote his letters to resolve the uncertainties and difficulties resulting from the application of this Jewish utopian ideal to the people in his groups, non-Jews in particular. We have a very limited and highly contextualized corpus of literature upon which to construct our portrayals of Paul as well as our histories of the origins of this movement. The explanatory phrase, "for non-Jews 'in Christ,'" should be added to most of Paul's statements to retain the specific, historical focus of his teachings. Particular care must be taken when one moves across the line that extends between the world of Paul and his assemblies, which were still part of Judaism, and the movement that sprung from them, which became Christianity. Exegesis (or historically oriented interpretation) and hermeneutics (or contemporary application-oriented interpretation) are both cross-cultural enterprises.

(6) That Paul works from the *Shema* and the ideals of Judaism has profound implications for Christian identity, for the ways with which Christians look at their own sense of self and ideals for living in the present age. Christian foundational truths, as far as the voice of Paul is concerned, arise from within Judaism, not to oppose it or begin a new religion, but to exemplify its ideals. Granted, within roughly fifty years of Paul's death, Ignatius declared that anyone not named a Christian does not belong to God, and more pointedly, that "[i]t is utterly absurd to profess Jesus Christ and to practice Judaism. For Christianity did not believe in Judaism, but Judaism in Christianity, in which 'every tongue' believed and 'was brought together' to God" (*Magn.* 10.3).[28] That central religious ideals, including God's oneness, were developed in this way should provide reason for pause, and reconsideration. If this was not the probable intended result of Paul's thought and teaching, then it should be the subject of investigation when and how this change came about. Instead of attributing to Paul the found- ing of Christianity as a new religion free of Judaism, it is time to seek to discover

---

in Light of His Strategy 'to Become Everything to Everyone.'"

27. See Nanos, *Mystery of Romans*, 166–238.

28. "To the Magnesians," in *The Apostolic Fathers: Greek Texts and English Translations*, 202–13, here 209.

just how and why this change occurred, and to reconsider these decisions and their implications. Paul's values and the values embodied in Paulinism are not one and the same.

(7) Similarly, this historical challenge to the meaning of Paul and the interpretation of Christian origins calls for a reconsideration of the voice of Paul in *Jewish* historiography. Jews should become aware of so-called Paulinism, which represents an interpretive trajectory in Christian teaching [80] to which Jews have responded without adequate recognition of the historical gap between Paul himself and the later schools of thought that claim to represent him. Jews need not agree with Paul to seek to translate his language and its meaning in historical context, including where the results might differ from the prevailing Christian translations and interpretations of him. Just as in the study of Jesus, the study of Paul offers data that is important for filling in the map of the Judaism (or Judaisms) of this critical period, the time just before the final destruction of the Second Temple and the subsequent emergence of rabbinic Judaism. Jesus is studied by Jews as well as Christians attentive to the difference between the study of the historical figure and the religious traditions that emerged thereafter: should Paul not be studied attentive to this dynamic?

(8) It follows that, in addition to calling for historical reevaluation of the Judaism of Paul's time and his own expression thereof, the reading proposed here overcomes the obstacle Paul's voice has represented to date for Christian-Jewish dialogue and relations. Today, there are significant differences between these two faith traditions, but the origins of Paul's faith were not based on a fundamental rejection of Judaism in the way so often imagined and taught. What was at issue was whether this propositional "truth of the gospel" was to be expressed in *age-to-come* terms in the *present age*.

What stood between these originally Jewish groups continues to be the main difference between the two present-day religions, one Jewish, and the other no longer so. Their foundational ideals are not in dispute, but the meaning of Jesus Christ. The point is not to ignore all the differences that now exist between the members of these two religions, but to get the differences right. The approach offered here provides a way to recognize and seize upon the similarities from which we can work together to bring about mutual respect—a level of much-needed *shalom* arising from shared identity in the present age as fellow witnesses to the One God, in spite of different opinions about whether the awaited age has dawned in Jesus Christ, or not.

BIBLIOGRAPHY

The Apostolic Fathers: Greek Texts and English Translations. Translated by M. W. Holmes. 3rd ed. Grand Rapids: Baker, 2007.

Brenk, Frederick E. "'We Are of His Race': Paul and the Philosophy of His Time." In *Unperfumed Voice: Studies in Plutarch, in Greek Literature, Religion and Philosophy, and in the New Testament Background*, edited by K. E. Brenk, 402–40. Potsdamer Altertumswissenschaftliche Beiträge 21. Stuttgart: Steiner, 2007.

Dahl, Nils Alstrup. *Studies in Paul: Theology for the Early Christian Mission.* Minneapolis, MN: Augsburg, 1977.

Donaldson, Terence L. *Paul and the Gentiles: Remapping the Apostle's Convictional World.* Minneapolis, MN: Fortress, 1997.

Fredriksen, Paula. "Judaism, the Circumcision of Gentiles, and Apocalyptic Hope: Another Look at Galatians 1 and 2." In *The Galatians Debate*, edited by M. D. Nanos, 235–60. Peabody, MA: Hendrickson, 2002.

Guerra, Anthony J. "The One God Topos in *Spec. Leg.* 1.52." In *1990 Seminar Papers: One Hundred Twenty-sixth Annual Meeting, November 17–20, 1990, New Orleans, LA*, edited by D. Lull, 148–57. SBLSPS 29. Atlanta: Scholars, 1990.

Hammer, Reuven. *Sifre: A Tannaitic Commentary on the Book of Deuteronomy.* New Haven: Yale University Press, 1986.

Heschel, Abraham Joshua. *Between God and Man: An Interpretation of Judaism from the Writings of Abraham J. Heschel.* New York: Harper & Row, 1959.

Hoffman, Lawrence A., ed. *My People's Prayer Book: Traditional Prayers, Modern Commentaries 1: The Sh'ma and Its Blessings.* Woodstock, VT: Jewish Lights, 1997.

Hogg, Michael A., and Dominic Abrams. *Social Identifications: A Social Psychology of Intergroup Relations and Group Processes.* London: Routledge, 1988.

Lamberz, Erich, ed. *Concilium Universale Nicaenum Secundum: Concilii Actiones I–III.* Acta Conciliorum Oecumenicorum Vol. 2.3.1. Berlin: de Gruyter, 2008.

Lamm, Norman. *The Shema: Spirituality and Law in Judaism as Exemplified in the Shema, the Most Important Passage in the Torah.* Philadelphia: Jewish Publication Society, 2000.

Moberly, R. W. L. "Toward an Interpretation of the Shema." In *Theological Exegesis: Essays in Honor of Brevard S. Childs*, edited by C. Seitz and K. Green-McGreight, 124–44. Grand Rapids: Eerdmans, 1999.

Nanos, Mark D. "'Broken Branches': A Pauline Metaphor Gone Awry? (Romans 11:11–36)." In *Between Gospel and Election: Explorations in the Interpretation of Romans 9–11*, edited by F. Wilk and J. R. Wagner, 339–76. Tübingen: Mohr Siebeck, 2010. (See volume 2 in this series of collected essays.)

———. *The Irony of Galatians: Paul's Letter in First-century Context.* Minneapolis, MN: Fortress, 2002.

———. *The Mystery of Romans: The Jewish Context of Paul's Letter.* Minneapolis, MN: Fortress, 1996.

———. "The Myth of the 'Law-Free' Paul Standing between Christians and Jews." *Studies in Christian-Jewish Relations* 4.1 (2009) 1–21. (https://ejournals.bc.edu/ojs/index.php/scjr/article/view/1511/1364). (See chapter 4 in this volume of collected essays.)

———. "Paul and Judaism: Why Not Paul's Judaism?" In *Paul Unbound: Other Perspectives on the Apostle*, edited by M. D. Given, 117–60. Peabody, MA: Hendrickson, 2010. (See chapter 1 in this volume of collected essays.)

———. "Paul's Relationship to Torah in Light of His Strategy 'to Become Everything to Everyone' (1 Corinthians 9:19–23)." In *Paul and Judaism: Crosscurrents in Pauline Exegesis and the Study of Jewish-Christian Relations*, edited by R. Bieringer and D. Pollefeyt, 106–40. London: T. & T. Clark, 2011. (See volume 4 of this series of collected essays.)

———. "The Polytheist Identity of the 'Weak' and Paul's Strategy to 'Gain' Them: A New Reading of 1 Corinthians 8:1—11:1." In *Paul: Jew, Greek and Roman*, edited by S. E. Porter, 179–21. Pauline Studies 5. Leiden: Brill, 2008. (See volume 4 of this series of collected essays.)

———. "What Was at Stake in Peter's 'Eating with Gentiles' at Antioch?" In *The Galatians Debate*, edited by M. D. Nanos, 283–318. Peabody, MA: Hendrickson, 2002. (See volume 3 in this series of collected essays.)

Parkes, James. *The Conflict of the Church and the Synagogue: A Study in the Origins of Antisemitism*. New York: Atheneum, 1979.

Trigg, Joseph W. *Biblical Interpretation*. Message of the Fathers of the Church 9. Wilmington, DE: Glazier, 1988.

Wright, N. T. *The Climax of the Covenant: Christ and the Law in Pauline Theology*. Edinburgh: T. & T. Clark, 1991.

———. "One God, One Lord, One People." *Ex Auditu* 7 (1991) 45–58.

Wyschogrod, Michael. *Abraham's Promise: Judaism and Jewish-Christian Relations*. Radical Traditions. Grand Rapids: Eerdmans, 2004.

5

Paul's Non-Jews Do Not Become "Jews," But Do They Become "Jewish"?

Reading Romans 2:25–29 within Judaism, alongside Josephus

[26] PAUL'S "*JEWISH* ASSEMBLIES" rather than "Paul's *gentile* churches"? "Paul's *Jewish* non-Jews" instead of "Paul's *Christian* gentiles"? Paul bringing non-Jews into "Judaism" rather than into "Christianity"? Am I really going to argue that these are more accurate labels for discussing the non-Jews whom Paul brought to faith in Jesus Christ and the gatherings of them with Jews sharing that conviction, as well as the communal ways of life into which Paul sought to enculturate them? Yes—and no.

BEING AND BECOMING JEWS AND/OR JEWISH

It is generally agreed that the term "Jew" is a noun that refers to people who claim to be such according to the norms for defining identity as a "Jew," although the parameters have been and continue to be a moving target among and between different groups of Jews, and even from the perspectives of different groups of non-Jews.[1] From Paul's perspective, which

---

1. Defining who is a Jew and who is not is both simple and complex, just as it was during the first century CE. There are countless studies of the topic. Likewise, defining what is Jewish and what is not is also both simple and complex. Here we are concerned specifically with these issues as they relate to Paul and his influence—not that this is without complexity, but it does provide some limits.

parallels the views of most Jews of Paul's time of whom we have evidence, being a Jew involved being born to parents who are Jews, being circumcised if a male (on the eighth day of life),[2] and, ideally, behaving according to the standards that define that identity (Rom 2; 9–11; 2 Cor 11:22; Gal 1:13–14; 2:15–16; Phil 3:4–6).[3]

[27] Being identified as a Jew and behaving like a Jew are readily recognized as two related yet not identical matters. The adjective "Jewish" is used both to refer to those who are Jews ethnically and to the cultural behavior generally associated with the way that Jews live, albeit variously defined, such as by different interpretations of Scripture and related traditions, different views of who represents legitimate authority, and different conclusions about what is appropriate for any specific time and place. This behavior can be referred to by the adverb "jewishly," and as the expression of "jewishness." In colloquial terms, [28] one who practices a Jewish way of life according to the ancestral customs of the Jews, which is also referred to as practicing "Judaism," might be called a "good" Jew. But a Jew can also behave in ways that are not considered to be Jewish—un-jewishly or gentilely, goyish or goyishly, or even to practice cult to other gods like a Greek—and thus perhaps be regarded as an "apostate" Jew, or worse, a Jew who destroys other Jews (such as Antiochus, who did these un-Jewish, even anti-Jewish

---

2. Phil 3:5; cf. Gen 17:9–14; Lev 12:3; Bernat, *Sign of the Covenant*; Thiessen, *Contesting Conversion*.

3. For the appropriateness of the choice of "Jew/Judaism" and cognates over "Judean/Judeanism" and similar cognates when discussing Paul and the texts from Josephus referred to herein (Rom 2:17–29; Josephus, *Ant.* 20.17–96; *War* 2.463; 7.45; and see 2 Macc 6:1–11; 9:13–17; cf. Philo, *Spec. Laws* 1.186); see Schwartz, "'Judaean' or 'Jew'?"; Nanos, "Paul and Judaism: Why Not Paul's Judaism?," 117 n. 2; Cohen, *The Beginnings of Jewishness*, 69–106. Related to this matter is how to identify those who are not Jews; the terms "non-Jew/s" rather than "gentile/s" are used herein to correspond to the way that Paul and Jews of his day generally used the terms, which involved seeing them as "*ethnē*," literally, "nations" or "peoples," and an individual *ethnos* would be "a member of the peoples other than Israel/people who are not Jews" (Paul uses Israel/Jews interchangeably; see e.g., Romans 9–11). See Donaldson, "'Gentile Christianity' as a Category in the Study of Christian Origins," although he concludes to use the term gentile/s with qualification; in this essay and generally I conclude from the same evidence that it is better to use "non-Jew/s" (for problems Paul was encountering with this category as well as terminology, see Johnson Hodge, *If Sons, Then Heirs*, 55; Johnson Hodge, "The Question of Social Interaction." "Christian" and "church" are also avoided herein as anachronistic, and, perhaps more importantly, as misrepresentative of the context for conceptualizing the concerns and viewpoints of Paul and his communities; see e.g., Runesson, "Inventing Christian Identity"; Eisenbaum, *Paul Was Not a Christian*.

things; Josephus, *War* 7.46–53), without thereby becoming something other than a Jew in the genealogical ethnic sense of the term.[4]

Circumcision raises an interesting element for defining identity as well as behavior. It is an identity marker for males that does not signify precisely the same thing as do other elements of Jewish behavior, such as observing days and diets, which, while ethnic, do not determine whether one is a Jew or not.[5] Jewish males are circumcised as eight-day-old infants to mark them as Jews;[6] whether [29] they will later decide to behave jewishly, including having their own sons circumcised, remains to be seen.[7] We thus can distinguish, albeit not without overlap, between the genealogical ethnic identity of Jews as Jewish people and behavior that characterizes Jews (and is thus culturally ethnic), ideally at least, which is also referred to as behavior that is "Jewish," i.e., behaving "jewishly," in a way characteristic of "jewishness," or as practicing "Judaism."

Could non-Jews become Jews? According to some Jews, including Paul (Gal 2:11-14; 5:2-3, 11-12; 6:12-13), they could.[8] There were also

---

4. Cf. *Sanhedrin* 44a for the later rabbinic view to this effect; Stern, *Jewish Identity in Early Rabbinic Writings*. See Goodblatt, *Elements of Ancient Jewish Nationalism*, esp. 11–27. Jews who willfully renounce their identity and apostatize completely are rarely referred to in the texts from Paul's time, at most representing exceptions that prove the rule; see Feldman, *Jew and Gentile in the Ancient World*, 79–83.

5. This is a distinction within Judaism between a rite marking identification (of males) and the behavioral practices incumbent upon those so marked that Pauline interpreters, and New Testament interpreters in general, do not seem to grasp, lumping them together. They thus fail to see that, e.g., in Galatians, Paul is opposing the transformation of non-Jews into Jews, signified by circumcision, but that is not the same thing as opposing the adoption of Jewish behavior by these non-Jews, which Paul's letter assumes that they have begun to do and promotes that they should do, while adamantly upholding that they must nevertheless remain non-Jews (i.e., not be circumcised). In Galatians, Paul does not oppose Torah or Torah-defined behavior (i.e., Judaism) for Jews—or for non-Jews(!)—but only circumcision for (Christ-following) non-Jews. In other words, opposing the transformation of non-Jews into Jews does not equate to opposing the adopting of Jewish norms, thoughts, and behavior—it is not the same as opposing the observance of Judaism! See Nanos, *The Irony of Galatians*; Nanos, "Paul and the Jewish Tradition: The Ideology of the *Shema*."

6. However, a Jew does not (normally) decide to be circumcised; it is decided by his parents, thus it signifies that his parents practiced Jewish behavior.

7. If one born to Jewish parents (in rabbinic terms, to a Jewish mother) is not circumcised but decides later in life to undertake the rite, that is closer to the question of choice discussed below for non-Jews.

8. In addition to the brief discussion of Izates below, for more detail see Nanos, "The Question of Conceptualization: Qualifying Paul's Position on Circumcision in Dialogue with Josephus's Advisors to King Izates." For why *ioudaïzein* in Galatians 2:11–14 indicates becoming a Jew, see Nanos, "What Was at Stake in Peter's 'Eating with Gentiles' at Antioch?" 306–12. For somewhat different conclusions, see Cohen, *Beginnings*

Jews who did not approve of or promote such policies and would not accept the identity transformation claimed, or at least that it was as complete as others supposed it to be.[9] Some informed non-Jews also recognized that non-Jews could become Jews.[10] In the texts from Paul's time it is generally clear that circumcision [30] represents a decisive rite for a (male) non-Jew to undertake to become a proselyte, a Jew by choice rather than from their family of origin. Otherwise, a (male) non-Jew remains merely a non-Jew who is in some way affiliated with or attracted to Jews or Jewish beliefs and practices, such as those recognized as "fearers of God [*theosebeis*]."[11] They may behave jewishly and even be considered "jewish," but they are generally recognized as non-Jews, certainly if known to have been born non-Jews and not undertaken the transformative rites (circumcision usually most explicitly) involved in becoming Jews. The matter is far more ambiguous where non-Jewish women becoming Jews or not is concerned, but it does not seem to have been a topic of argument among Jews whether a woman born to Jewish parents was a Jew.[12]

In other words, "Jewish" is an adjective used sometimes to refer to a Jew or group of Jews: he or she is Jewish, they are the Jewish people. But "Jewish" can also modify references to the thoughts, behavior, gatherings, and institutions of those who are "Jews," a complex known as the practice of "Judaism," and, as the texts discussed below indicate, it can also refer—on grammatical and logical grounds—to the thoughts, behavior, gatherings, and institutions of those who are "not Jews" when they think, behave, gather, or in other ways reflect norms and values that are generally associated with the thoughts, behavior, gatherings, and norms and values of Jews. In short, non-Jews can think and behave in cultural ways described as "jewish" (for

---

of Jewishness, 146–62, 175–97. For a later rabbinic statement affirming the change of ethnic identity, see b. Yeb. 47b; Cohen, *Beginnings of Jewishness*, 198–238, 342.

9. E.g., Jub. 15:26 indicates that only those circumcised on the eighth day qualified as "the sons of the covenant which the Lord made with Abraham," by definition ruling out the transformation of non-Jews into Jews as adults; see Thiessen, *Contesting Conversion*, 67–86. E.g., there were mixed opinions about whether those who were constrained to be circumcised and observe Jewish customs under Hasmonean rule (like Idumeans, and thus Herod's lineage), even if called thereafter *Ioudaioi*, were in fact fully or only partially *Ioudaioi*, or *Ioudaioi* of a different kind (Josephus, *Ant.* 13.257–58; 14.403); see Cohen, *Beginnings of Jewishness*, 109–39; Thiessen, *Contesting Conversion*, 87–110. For later rabbinic controversies, see Porton, *The Stranger Within Your Gates*; Hoffman, *Covenant of Blood*.

10. Horace, *Sat.* 1.9.68–70; Petronius, *Sat.* 102.14; Josephus, *Ag. Ap.* 2.137; Epictetus, *Discourses* 2.9.19–21; Juvenal, *Sat.* 14.96–106; Tacitus, *Hist.* 5.5.1–2; Seutonius, *Domitian* 12.2; see Cohen, *Beginnings of Jewishness*, 29–49.

11. King Izates discussed below; cf. Cohen, *Beginnings of Jewishness*, 156–74.

12. Cf. Cohen, *Why Aren't Jewish Women Circumcised?*

which I will use the lower-case form to distinguish this from Jewish when describing those who are ethnically Jews); non-Jews can practice many of the cultural elements of Judaism, the Jewish way of life developed by and for Jews; and they can do so without being or becoming Jews, just as Jews can choose not to think or behave in Jewish ways.

Because ethnic identity (Jew/s) and ethnic cultural thinking and behavior (Jewish/jewishly/jewishness/Judaism) are clearly related, but not synonymous, interchangeable terms, an interesting phenomenon arises when seeking to describe groups as Jewish. Although "Jewish" can be and is most often used to refer to Jews specifically, and thus gatherings of Jews—they are Jewish, the Jewish people, a Jewish service, and so on—as we will see, "Jewish" can also refer to groups or activities that include non-Jews among Jews: that group is Jewish, although it includes non-Jews who appear to think and behave like Jews. What if a group mostly made up of non-Jews with some Jews in leadership behaves jewishly? What if it is made up exclusively of non-Jews yet founded or advised [31] by Jews? What if it consists of only non-Jews and functions independent of any Jews yet bases its thinking and behavior on Jewish Scriptures, traditions, and ways of life? Would any of these cases fall within the adjectival descriptive "Jewish," or, as suggested above to distinguish this from ethnic Jews, "jewish"?

At this point there is an issue that arises especially for discussing Paul. It is widely recognized that Paul opposed non-Jews becoming Jews after they became followers of Christ. He often referred to this as "circumcision," the rite that signified completion of the process for males (Rom 4:9–12; 1 Cor 7:17–20; Gal 2:3; 3:3; 5:2–3, 11–12; 6:12–13). When writing to non-Jews to dissuade them from becoming Jews or to combat the otherwise obvious advantage of being a Jew when entering this movement within Judaism, Paul argued that these uncircumcised non-Jews were full and equal members of the family of God alongside of the Jewish members, indeed, equally children of Abraham and co-heirs of the promises made to him and his seed, and not simply welcome guests. This was based upon the chronometrical claim of the gospel that the day when all of the nations will join the Israelites to worship the One God of all humankind had dawned with the resurrection of Jesus as Messiah (Rom 3:29—4:25; Gal 3:6—4:7, 28).[13] When calling both Jews and non-Jews who believed in Jesus as Christ to respect each other as equals, he stated that "being circumcised or foreskinned" is not to serve as the basis for discrimination among themselves any more than should differences that remain in terms of gender and status as slave or free (Rom 3:29—4:12; 1 Cor 7:17-20; Gal 3:26-29; 5:2-6; 6:15). These highly

---

13. Nanos, "Paul and the Jewish Tradition."

contextualized arguments have often been interpreted to mean that Paul no longer regarded circumcision, and thus covenantal identity for Jews, to hold any significance, that he regarded these as *adiaphora* (indifferent things) for Christ-followers, including himself.

This deduction has led some Pauline scholars to conclude that he also abandoned even the identity of being a Jew, although most believe that Paul remained a Jew ethnically even if he no longer ascribed value to that identity.[14] Few, however, uphold that Paul is best described within Judaism.[15] It is instead widely held that Paul left behind the practice of Judaism, that he no longer [32] behaved jewishly or intentionally expressed Jewishness—he remained Jewish ethnically, but not religiously, if you will. Obviously, it follows that such a Paul would not promote Judaism or form Jewish communities, and one does not read Pauline scholars referring to Paul bringing non-Jews into a Jewish way of life, into Judaism, into Jewish synagogues or communities or even into Jewish subgroups. In fact, one often encounters descriptions of Paul opposing the conversion of non-Jews "into Judaism."

The discourse generally proceeds as if the terms "becoming a Jew" (being circumcised) and "becoming Jewish" or "practicing Judaism" are completely interchangeable—which, as just discussed, is not actually the case. The texts to which they refer seek to dissuade Christ-following non-Jews "from becoming Jews" (i.e., undertaking the rite of circumcision), which is *not* the same thing as opposing non-Jews thinking or behaving in Jewish ways, jewishly, or practicing Judaism. An ironic twist is revealed when many of these same interpreters (joined by some of those who deny Paul remained a Jew, or at least that it no longer held value for him) maintain that he viewed non-Jews who believed in Jesus to have become "spiritual" or "true" Jews, usually by appealing to Romans 2:25–29,[16] to which we will turn after a survey of a few texts from Josephus. These will help us discuss the ways to conceptualize and describe similar dynamics from the viewpoint of another first-century Jewish author who primarily addressed non-Jewish readers. We will look at several texts that describe the phenomenon of non-Jews who practice Jewish ways of life while remaining non-Jews, or who even became Jews, various levels of interaction these non-Jews had with Jews and Jewish

---

14. This is ubiquitous in traditional treatments of Paul, recently Sechrest, *A Former Jew*; it is regularly expressed by New Perspective interpreters, albeit inconsistently; see Dunn, "Who Did Paul Think He Was?" 179 vs. 192.

15. Nanos and Zetterholm, eds., *Paul within Judaism,* challenges this legacy.

16. Wright, *Paul and the Faithfulness of God*, on 1436 writes, "*Being a 'Jew' was no longer Paul's basic identity*" (emphasis his), just pages after writing, "Paul can refer to spirit-led, Messiah-believing Gentiles and Jews together as 'the Jew'; 'the circumcised'; and even on occasion as 'Israel' . . ." (1432).

Paul's Non-Jews Do Not Become "Jews," But Do They Become "Jewish"? 133

communities in the Diaspora, and different reactions to these decisions by both the Jews and the non-Jews who constitute their non-Jewish family, neighbors, and civic authorities.

"JEWISH NON-JEWS" IN THE WORKS OF JOSEPHUS

Josephus's Report of "Judaizing" Syrian Non-Jews Viewed with Ambivalence and Suspicion by Their Syrian Neighbors

Josephus chronicles a series of events in Syria that took place in approximately 66 CE. Groups of Syrian non-Jews attacked and massacred Syrian Jews, who retaliated similarly in partnership with certain Judean Jews. What is of interest [33] here is the way that Josephus refers to a group of Syrian non-Jews spared during these attacks as "judaized":[17]

> They [the majority population Syrian non-Jews] passed their days in blood, their nights, yet more dreadful, in terror. For though believing that they had rid themselves of the Jews, still each city had its Judaizers, who aroused suspicion [ἕκαστοι τοὺς Ἰουδαΐζοντας εἶχον ἐν ὑποψίᾳ]; and while they shrunk from killing offhand each ambiguous one [ἑκάστοις ἀμφίβολον] in their midst, they feared those being mixed together as if really of another tribe [μεμιγμένον ὡς βεβαίως ἀλλόφυλον; or: aliens/ foreigners]. (*War* 2:463; Loeb, trans. Thackeray, with alterations where the Greek is provided)[18]

The identity—and thus loyalty—of these Syrian non-Jews is captured by referring to them as "each ambiguous one in their [the majority Syrian non-Jews'] midst." They were spared, yet suspect.

Josephus's description of these Syrian non-Jews is far from clear. He does not identify them as having become circumcised or (proselyte) Jews

---

17. This term was used to refer to the actions of non-Jews when they adopt Jewish behavior or become Jews; it is not used to describe Jews who seek to persuade non-Jews. See Cohen, *Beginnings of Jewishness*, 175–97; Nanos, *Irony of Galatians*, 115–19.

18. It is unclear to what the participle "being mixed" refers, but it seems here to connote the mixing of the non-Jewish identity of these Syrians with their practices of Judaism among Jews, who are of another tribe, i.e., with ancestry not from Syria but Judea and thus different ancestral customs and cult practices that Syrian non-Jews would not normally be expected to observe; hence, their ambiguous identity and uncertain loyalties arise because of religious practices and associations that are not natural or traditional for them from birth. Cf. Donaldson, *Judaism and the Gentiles*, 294–96. Cohen, *Beginnings of Jewishness*, 184, suggests the last clause read: "and it was feared as if it were truly foreign, although it was mixed."

"really/certainly [βεβαίως]," such as he does identify some elsewhere (2.454; *Ant.* 3.318; 14.403; 20.38–43 [Izates]; *Ag. Ap.* 2.210; cf. Tob 1:8). The level of distrust and concern about them could suggest that they were regarded as proselytes, or on the path to becoming such. It was as if they were not fully Syrians but "really of another tribe"; that is, they feared that the loyalties of these non-Jews were with the Syrian Jews (perhaps Syrian Judeans is helpful here) more so than would be expected of Syrians who were merely practicing some ways of life characteristic of Jews, including assembling with them to do so. Are they [34] regarded as close friends of the Jews, or as if they are now family members? Given the way that these violent riots and massacres by the mob were proceeding, the nuanced, reasoned restraint towards them makes it unlikely that they had become proselyte Jews and were no longer in any way celebrating family and civic cult. More likely, these Syrians were in some ways still identifiably observing normal Syrian practices in addition to mixing with Jews and observing certain Jewish customs, at least when among the Jewish communities, if not also in certain ways when among their non-Jewish families and neighbors. If they were suspected of having become Jews, it seems to follow that the same level of hostility and concomitant actions taken against Jews would have been taken against them—perhaps even more so, since they would be regarded as traitors by choice rather than birth.

The questions I want to pose are these:

1. Are they not "jewish non-Jews," who are spared, but nevertheless suspect, their ultimate loyalties "mixed" in such a way that they cannot be completely trusted? Is not their own level of Jewish behavior or jewishness a salient issue, as well as their close affiliation with Jews?

2. Would we expect Josephus to refer to the gatherings of these ambiguous ones with Jews as "gentile assemblies" or as "Jewish assemblies" that included "judaizing non-Jews"? Does not their identification as "judaizers" suspected of being loyal to "another tribe" more than their own from birth indicate that they assembled with groups under the authority of Jewish leaders and conducted according to Jewish norms, thus that these were "Jewish" groups and that they participated in the practice of Judaism?

Another Account of Syrian Non-Jews Participating in Jewish Ceremonies and Jewish Communal Life by Josephus

In *War* 7.41-62, when relating events shortly after the fall of Jerusalem in 70 CE, Josephus refers back to earlier developments in Syria similar to those he related in the text just discussed (2.462-63; cf. 559-61). While engaged in explaining the good relations between and the mixing (ἀναμείγνῦμι) of Judeans among Syrians for many years following the hostile events that took place under Antiochus Epiphanes (7.73-74),[19] Josephus presents a number of Syrian non-Jews (which [35] he calls "a great multitude of Greeks [πολὺ πλῆθος Ἑλλήνων]") in a way that suggests that they remained recognizably non-Jews who have been socialized into the religious life of the communities of Syrian Jews:[20]

> Moreover, they [the Jews of Syria] were constantly attracting to their religious ceremonies [προσαγόμενοι ταῖς θρησκείαις: or: cult practices][21] multitudes of Greeks, and these they had in some measure incorporated with themselves [κἀκείνους τρόπῳ τινὶ μοῖραν αὐτῶν πεποίηντο: or: and also they had made them, in a way, a part of themselves]. (*War* 7.45, Loeb; trans. Thackeray)

Some interpreters have understood this to indicate active recruiting of non-Jews, yet Josephus's language need not indicate more than that Jewish communities were welcomingly leading (προσαγόμενοι) interested non-Jews, whom they generously also "incorporated" with themselves, to participate in their communal life.[22] The ambiguity in Josephus's description allows for various levels of involvement, from attraction to Jewish customs and the ideals and actions attributed to their God and ancestors, to

---

19. In this case, Josephus refers to the geographical proximity of Judea and Syria and to the Judean nation (Ἰουδαίων γένος) being dispersed among the inhabitants of the earth, thus highlighting the judeanness of these Jews, which remains salient throughout this account of the hostilities that includes the dynamics resulting from the high level of integration as well as the incorporation of Syrians among the Jews/Judeans.

20. Goodman, *Mission and Conversion*, 87, refers to them as God-fearers, which seems warranted here; so too Donaldson, *Judaism and the Gentiles*, 294-96, 305-7. However, Cohen, *Beginnings of Jewishness*, 159, interprets them to be proselytes.

21. The Greek word *thrēskeia* can refer to religious worship, rituals, and cult. Josephus uses *thrēskeia* to refer to general religious observance (*War* 2.198, 391; 7.45), general temple worship (*War* 4.324; 5.198, 199; 6.100, 442), and particular observances (Sabbath in 1.146; 2.456; Passover in 2.10; Pentecost in 2.42; temple sacrifice in 1.148, 150; 4.275; 5.229; 6.427); from Donaldson, *Judaism and the Gentiles*, 298 n. 33; and see also 307 n. 46.

22. Cf. Donaldson, *Judaism and the Gentiles*, 306-7.

affiliation resulting from employment or marriage. Some may have become proselytes, but his language does not require this. Whatever the precise details, Josephus's description suggests that the identity of more than a few Syrian non-Jews was intimately linked with that of the Jewish people, but they still remained distinguishable from Syrian Jews and Judeans.

It is unclear how many non-Jews he had in view, but even if many, the questions it poses for us remain similar to those of the text discussed above, although they might arise in the opposite order:

1. [36] How likely is it that Josephus, or his readers, including us, would refer to these communities or their *gatherings* by the adjectives "gentile" or "non-Jewish" rather than "Jewish"? Once again, would not what he describes almost certainly be better categorized as "Jewish groups" with non-Jews integrated to various degrees among them?

2. Does not the description of these non-Jews as "in some manner/measure/way" participating in Jewish communal life betray the fact that they remain distinguishable from Jews/Judeans in Syria? At the same time, they are distinguishable from other Syrian non-Jews by their *jewishness*, by their participation in Jewish communal religious activities; i.e., by behaving *jewishly*, practicing Judaism. Are they not *jewish* non-Jews?

Josephus's Narrative of King Izates of Adiabene and His Mother Helena: Jewish Non-Jews Who Become Jews?

There are many striking elements in Josephus's account about Izates, the king of the Parthian client territory of Adiabene, and his mother, Helena, who were not born Jews and ruled a non-Jewish/non-Judean people (*Ant.* 20.17–96). The events overlap with Paul's ministry in the 40s and 50s CE (20.15–17), and include interesting parallels to elements of Paul's approach to and instructions for non-Jews in the Roman Empire. Several scenes warrant discussion.

Before Izates was crowned king, his parents sent him to live in Charax Spasini for protection (20.22). While there, according to Josephus, a Jewish merchant, Ananias, taught several women of the royal family with whom Izates was staying "to worship God [the Deity] according to the Jewish ancestral traditions [ὡς Ἰουδαίοις πάτριον]" (20.34). When Izates learned of this, he too was successfully "persuaded/urged [συνανέπεισεν]" to do the same (20.35). Josephus specifically identifies them as women, and makes no mention of any other Jewish figures present, or of a Jewish community there. These non-Jews seem to have taken up several ideas and behaviors recognizably Jewish, presumably adding these to the practices of their other native customs. It seems *unlikely* that their gatherings represent Jews' gatherings or would be properly called synagogues or Jewish assemblies; rather, they apparently represent the assembling of non-Jews to observe certain Jewish customs. It does seem likely that others in their family and from their people, as well as they themselves, would recognize that these meetings involve non-Jews behaving jewishly/practicing Judaism *in some ways/at some times*.

When Izates returned to the kingdom of Adiabene to assume the crown following the death of his father, he learned that his mother had simultaneously [37] begun to observe certain Jewish customs under the direction of a different Jew, who remains unnamed (20.35–38). Izates is described as becoming aware of Helena's "rejoicing in the Jews' customs [τοῖς Ἰουδαίων ἔθεσιν]" (20.38), referred to also as "their laws/conventions [νόμους]" (20.35). Izates thus resolved to go beyond merely adopting the ancestral traditions observed in Charax while remaining a non-Jew; instead, he "hastened to also change/crossover/convert [μεταθέσθαι] into them [ἐκεῖνα] himself" (20.38). Izates is presented to reason that he would not be "definitively/genuinely a Jew [βεβαίως Ἰουδαῖος] if he has not been circumcised, which he was ready to do" (20.38).

It remains unclear whether Izates supposed heretofore that he had become a Jew, or if he was simply unaware of the distinction between adopting (some) Jewish behavior, most likely adding such behavior to the rest of the customs and cult practices of his people as well as those of the people among whom he was residing, and becoming a Jew. Since the matter of circumcision with its signification of identity transformation does not pertain to Helena, it is also unclear if she is still a non-Jew or is recognized to have become a Jew. Izates's sudden interest in undertaking to be circumcised at this point might suggest that Helena's teacher has raised this matter directly, or perhaps Izates just inferred it, maybe from the way that she articulated her commitment or experience.

Upon learning of Izates's plan to become circumcised, Ananias, who has accompanied him to Adiabene, and his mother both vehemently oppose this step for him (20.39–42). They argue that his subjects, who are not Jews, will rebel against such a change of identity for their king. They did not, however, oppose him observing certain Jewish beliefs and behavior! But becoming a Jew by way of undertaking circumcision would send a very different message, one involving rejection of their native gods and customs, which they (correctly) anticipate will lead to rebellion against his rule.

Before we get to the introduction of the next Jewish figure, it is worth pausing to ask whether Helena and Izates at this point represent *jewish* non-Jews. They are in some ways behaving jewishly, and their jewishness is observably different from that of other nobles and their subjects, except some other female members of the royal household of Helena. There is still no mention of any Jewish community in Adiabene,[23] or of them participating in [38] meetings with Jews other than the two Jews who have been instructing them in Jewish customs, which they have done independently of each other.

1. Thus, unless Helena is regarded to be a Jew, are not their gatherings to practice Jewish customs (whatever they were, and however often observed) still best described as *gatherings of non-Jews/gentiles*?

2. Although they behave in and thus think in some ways associated with Jews, i.e., *jewishly*, practicing Judaism, do they not do so as *non-Jews*; hence, are they not *jewish non-Jews*?

The next development in Josephus's story is of interest in many ways. Here we will focus on the change of identity for Izates that the new Jewish person on the scene in Adiabene, Eleazar, explicitly promotes (20.43–45). In contrast to the opposition to circumcision upheld by Helena and Ananias, Eleazar argues that to piously conform to the teachings of Torah that Izates has been reading for guidance he must become circumcised; otherwise, he is guilty of impiety for failure to act according to what he has learned! Hearing this logic, Izates calls for the physician in order to be circumcised and "complete what was commanded [τὸ προσταχθὲν ἐτέλει]," thereby accomplishing "the act/rite" that will render him genuinely a Jew. The rest of the story develops around how God comes to Izates's rescue, because of his "faithfulness alone" to do that which God instructed in Torah (20.48, 89–91) in the face of the negative reactions from his fellow nobles and the people of his kingdom, who seek to overthrow Izates's rule because he rejected their gods and customs for those of a foreign people, just as Helena and Ananias anticipated (20.75–91). As you can see, there are many interesting dynamics to explore, not least for those interested in understanding Paul.[24]

Remaining on topic, and recognizing that there are no larger or even other Jewish communities explicitly mentioned, or any involvement in them by Izates and his mother (or after his death, by his brother, who

---

23. Elsewhere Josephus mentions many Jews in Babylon and in the major cities of Parthia, and their collection, treasury, and transportation of the tax for the Jerusalem temple (*Ant.* 18.310–13, 314–79).

24. See Nanos, "The Question of Conceptualization."

follows his example and wants to practice Judaism),[25] the taxonomical issues nevertheless become more taxing. They seem to be Jews behaving jewishly, known by others for their jewishness, for their Jewish beliefs and behavior, even at the cost of significant social pressure, rather than to have remained non-Jews who simply added Jewish customs and beliefs to those they already upheld according to Adiabene traditions. After Izates has undertaken circumcision in order to be completely faithful to what Torah prescribes according to Eleazar, is he not a Jew? In the case of Helena, there is no such marker to identify her transformation, yet she [39] may well be regarded to have become a Jew also. In either case, based on Izates's change of identity, is he not a Jew after choosing to adopt the identity, beliefs, and practices of the Jews, i.e., Judaism? The salience of judeanness is also raised: Helena goes to Judea with alms (probably during the same famine that Paul reportedly responded to with alms), and she wants to be and is buried there (as also is Izates); moreover, several of Izates's sons go to school in Jerusalem (*Ant.* 20.49–53, 71, 95).[26]

1. Rather than a "jewish" *non-Jew*, is Izates (if not also Helena) now not a *Jew*, indeed, a *Jewish Jew*? Is he not a Jew practicing Judaism?

2. Once they are recognized as Jews, when they meet together, are their gatherings not *Jewish assemblies* or *synagogues*?[27]

PAUL'S NON-JEWS, WITH SPECIAL ATTENTION TO ROMANS 2:25-29

Paul prohibited non-Jews who turned to God in Christ from becoming Jews, yet at the same time he also instructed them not to practice one of the most basic ways of being non-Jews in the Roman world of Paul's time, namely, family and civic cult (Rom 3:29–4:25; 6; 1 Cor 7:17–22; Gal 4:8–10; 1 Thess 1:9–10).[28] Their turning to the worship of Israel's God under the influence

---

25. The decision of his brother(s) and a few stories of their rule are related in 20.75–76, 92–96.

26. Additional stories, including in the rabbinic material, are discussed in Rajak, "The Parthians in Josephus"; Schiffman, "The Conversion of the Royal House of Abiabene [*sp*] in Josephus and Rabbinic Sources"; Feldman, *Jew and Gentile in the Ancient World*, 328–31.

27. *Synagōgē* was used during Paul's period not only to refer to the space where assemblies took place, which included homes and other spaces adopted for certain activities, but also to the assembly or gathering itself, being in each of these uses synonymous with usage of the term *ekklēsia*; see Runesson, *The Origins of the Synagogue*.

28. Cf. Fredriksen, "Judaizing the Nations"; Fredriksen, "The Question of Worship."

of a Jewish teacher of non-Jews would almost certainly suggest to many of their family members and neighbors that they were acting jewishly, practicing Judaism, the way of life developed by Jews—and that is indeed what Paul promoted that these non-Jews should do, although insisting they do so while remaining non-Jews. If they were attending subgroup meetings of local Jewish groups defined around allegiance to [40] Jesus as Christ/Messiah, even if small and marginalized by some other Jews, that inner-group dynamic would probably be unrecognized among non-Jewish observers of this phenomenon: they would most likely (and correctly) perceive that these fellow non-Jews gathered within Jewish groups and practiced Jewish ways of life and cult. When they began to substantiate their ways of thinking and living by appeal to Jewish Scriptures and traditions—as does Paul, whom presumably they would imitate—they would almost certainly (and rightly) be considered to be behaving like Jews.[29]

Instead of a survey of the many ways that Paul instructed Christ-following non-Jews to behave jewishly,[30] I want to briefly look at a text that seems to most Pauline scholars to close the door to a Paul who continued to value his Jewish covenantal identity by behaving according to Torah-defined ways of life, and all the more to one promoting Judaism in the way he proclaimed the gospel and instructed the non-Jews attracted to his message. That text is Romans 2:25–29.

Paul's Message in Romans 2:25–29

The chapter within which this text appears begins with a challenge to anyone judging others, based on the argument that the very act of knowing there is a standard to which the other is held logically involves knowing that one has also failed to achieve it. Realizing that God is the judge who is fully aware of both one's own intentions and actions as well as those of one's neighbors, the message Paul drives home is to focus on one's own responsibilities to do what is required of one, to judge oneself and leave the judging of others to the Judge, rejoicing in the knowledge that God is kind and forgiving toward those who err along the way when they make proper amends. Paul completes the argument of verses 1–11 by asserting that God is impartial, both kind and just with the Jew first, and also with the non-Jew.[31]

In the next argument (vv. 12–16), Paul makes it plain that God judges according to faithful behavior, which is not expected to represent precisely

---

29. Cf. Ehrensperger, *Paul at the Crossroads of Cultures*.
30. Covered in many of the chapters throughout this series of volumes.
31. Additional details of this reading are provided in Nanos, "Romans," 257–61.

the same standards for Jews and non-Jews; instead, each is held to the standard of what they know to be proper behavior. God knows both what they do and what [41] they intended for that action to achieve, including when they have exploited the very laws and principles that were designed to guide them to do right rather than to justify the doing of wrong by, for example, legal loopholes. The real intentions behind one's actions do not escape God's notice any more than actions that run contrary to the behavior publicly known. Each is judged by what they know to be right—a just God would have it no other way. That means Jews are judged first just as they are forgiven first, because they have been given the gift of God's "Guidance" (Torah), but non-Jews will also be judged and can be forgiven according to that which the created order revealed and society's *nomos* (laws/conventions) recognized to be proper and improper, which is not always the same as that of which one's peers approve (a point that reaches back to the argument in 1:18–32, that there are conventions developed around improper behavior too).

This leads to the argument in verses 17–24, which introduce a fictive character: "But if you name yourself [or: are being named] a Jew, and . . ." (v. 17).[32] The continuation of the sentence following "and" is paramount to following the critique Paul mounts to this one, but it is often not sufficiently appreciated by commentators. Paul's critique is "if" he would announce his identity publicly [or is announced publicly to be such] "*and* rely on *nomos* [law/convention/Torah] and glory in God, and know the will and approve the things that matter, instructing (or: being instructed) from the *nomos* [Torah], so [that] you persuaded yourself to be a guide to the blind, a light to those in darkness, an instructor of foolish ones, a teacher of children, having the shape of the knowledge and the truth in the *nomos* [Torah]: You, therefore, teaching others, will you not teach yourself?" (vv. 17–21a).[33]

---

32. The verb can be passive. On the diatribal features throughout this section, see Stowers, *A Rereading of Romans*; Elliott, *The Rhetoric of Romans*. On 2:17ff. in particular, see Stowers, *Rereading of Romans*, 143–58; Thorsteinsson, *Paul's Interlocutor in Romans 2*.

33. Cf. m. 'Abot 1:12–17 (Neusner trans.): "Hillel says, 'Be disciples of Aaron, loving peace and pursuing peace, loving people and drawing them near to Torah.' He would say, 'A name made great is a name destroyed. . . . If I am not for myself, who is for me? And when I am for myself, what am I? And if not now, when?' Shammai says, 'Make your learning of Torah a fixed obligation. Say little and do much. . . .' Simeon his [Rabban Gamaliel's] son says, 'All my life I grew up among the sages, and I found nothing better for a person than silence. And not the learning is the main thing but the doing. And whoever talks too much causes sin.'" Also consider: "Abba Saul b. Nanos said: There are four types of scholars: . . . 'He who taught others but did not teach himself'—how is this? A man learnt an Order or two or three [of the Mishnah] several times and taught them to others, but he did not occupy himself with them so that he

[42] Paul proceeds to indict the one presuming to teach, but it is not for any of the motives listed, which are all praiseworthy, including the impulse to teach the nations, which Paul makes central to what it means to be a Jew and to be circumcised in 3:2—for the Jew is the one entrusted with the oracles of God! Moreover, the teaching of the nations as a spokesperson from Israel is precisely Paul's own purpose, which he makes plain throughout the letter, and in several cases Paul specifically invokes his own credentials as a Jew, and related claims to authority with respect to those to whom he writes (Rom 11:1–14; 15:15–32; 2 Cor 11:21—12:21; Gal 3:14–16; Phil 3:3–6). The critique is for such a fictive teacher "if" he does not *also* first of all hold himself to the very standards that he promotes to others. The specific elements, including stealing, adultery, and robbing temples, represent behavior that any teacher of reputable laws, and all the more Torah, would agree are egregious sins; but for a teacher of the values they transgress, these are hypocritical. Verse 24 wraps up the accusation with a citation from Isaiah 52:5 (LXX; bearing witness to an ancient Israelite tradition concerned with this matter), that such failure to live according to the values that one proclaims others should adopt would give the nations cause to blaspheme the God to which such a teacher called attention![34]

The criticism is not of boasting, as so often stated, or of bigotry;[35] what is circumscribed is *hypocrisy*, claiming to represent norms that others should embrace that one has not internalized to guide one's own aims and behavior. There is nothing wrong with boasting (glorying) in God—Paul appeals to it later [43] in this letter and he boasts/glories in Christ![36] There is something terribly wrong, however, "if" one would glory in God "and" then proceed to make himself God's spokesperson without *also* making it his first order of business to behave in accordance with what he teaches. Instead of bringing glory to God, it creates disgust—for a God presumed to endorse such behavior is hardly to be praised.

Note, too, that it is not a list of the fictive teacher's motives that are exposed as hypocrisy, but, importantly, it is his activities that are listed as

---

forgot them—he is one who taught others but did not teach himself."; 'Abot de-Rabbi Nathan (A) 29.3; Cohen and Brodie, *The Minor Tractates*, 1.140.

34. Although the original context for Isaiah concerned the state of Israel in captivity, the idea is similar in that instead of bearing witness to being indeed God's chosen instrument, such a state of hypocrisy betrays that witness from the perspective of the outside observer.

35. Jewett, *Romans*, 222–37; if presuming it is Israel's role to declare these things to the nations constitutes "cultural exceptionalism" and "bigotry," then Paul is equally guilty of these by his own argument here and throughout his letters—indeed, by the presumption of his ministry as a representative of God and Israel by definition.

36. Rom 5:2, 3, 11; Phil 3:3.

self-condemning. The way that he (hypothetically) behaves undermines the values that he should stand for based on what he teaches, and supposedly, the reasons that he teaches these values—specifically, if known to be a Jew. Paul's appeal to the title of "Jew" is apparently based upon assuming awareness among his readers of a widely held stereotype that Jews by definition served as the model for practicing what one preaches.[37] Paul thus develops a rhetorical gambit to illustrate a principle that he wants his readers as non-Jews to grasp for themselves by employing a fictive Jew, much like the prophet Nathan employed the example of a rich man exploiting the poor man to teach David what his own actions would look like if he could rightly see himself from a distance (2 Samuel 12). Paul wants to censure hypocrisy among the non-Jews to whom he writes, not among Jews, in this case, the fictive Jew whom he constructs toward that end.[38] (Unfortunately, after followers of Christ were no longer part of Judaism and the movement had no Jews, Paul's original rhetorical character was subverted and served as a foil for negative Christian portrayals of and policies toward Jews and Judaism, seemingly in concert with Jesus's critique of Pharisees as self-righteous hypocrites.[39]) This argument leads us up to verses 25–29, on which I wish to focus. But before we turn to that, it is also worthwhile to briefly mention the way that Paul's argument continues thereafter, in chapter 3.

Following the argument at 2:29, the diatribe question raised in 3:1 is whether there is thus any value—in the literal sense—in being a Jew or [44] circumcised. The reply in verse 2 is an emphatic, "Much, in every way!" Why? Because "they have been entrusted with the oracles of God." It is thus apparent that Paul means to undermine neither the value of literal circumcision nor genealogical descent for Jews, nor the impulse to teach those from the nations the words of God, yet he recognizes that these could be inferred from his argument, so he directly denies that they should be. That the question is raised about "them" (not "us" non-Jews) indicates that Paul did not anticipate the later interpretive tradition's deduction that his argument in 2:29 meant that these non-Jews had become in fact Jews in some way, often labeled "spiritual" or "true" or "real" or "reconfigured Jews," or that they had replaced

---

37. Epictetus, *Discourses* 2.9.19–22; 2.19.19–28, provides an example from a non-Jew philosopher; Stowers, *Rereading of Romans*, 144–48, lists several others.

38. Cf. Elliott, *The Arrogance of Nations*, 103–5.

39. The Gospels's Jesus is critical, but it is in terms of intra-Jewish group hyperbole with a close and feared rival, and its impact would only be successful if Pharisees actually decried hypocrisy also, and would, for example, agree with Jesus that doing things that are public if not also done for the right reasons are empty, although this contextual qualification has been largely overlooked in the history of interpretation. Cf. Stowers, *Rereading of Romans*, 143–44.

ethnic Jews and the rite of circumcision in the flesh, rendering the literal Jews and circumcision superfluous. The way that the argument proceeds demonstrates that being a Jew and being circumcised remain literally of value for Jews, which sets them apart, as Jews, to be especially entrusted with God's words among the nations. What Paul has found fault with is the failure, "if" one identified in this way is inclined to speak to the nations, and yet not concomitantly dedicated to living according to the ideals to which that person's teaching points, but instead behaves contrary to that teaching.

Within this contextual frame, we can return to examine Paul's argument in 2:25–29. The translation I suggest, including the explanatory phrases inserted, assumes that Paul is still addressing the hypothetical one who would publicly declare himself (or: be declared) to be a Jew who teaches non-Jews without first of all intentionally observing that which he teaches them.

In verse 25, Paul writes: "For indeed circumcision is valuable (or: helpful) if you would be observing Torah, but if you would be one who [is circumcised yet intentionally] sidesteps Torah, then your circumcision has become [of no more value than if you still had] foreskin."[40] The translation proposed does not differ much from that offered in the NRSV. The changes bring out the conditional element present in the verbs, in keeping with the hypothetical person constructed for the diatribe to do its inductive teaching. The phrases inserted seek to capture the thoughts between the lines. It is one who is circumcised that is in view if they would not live according to Torah, to which circumcised identity sets them apart from those of the other nations, who are not under Torah. Paul is playing circumcised and foreskinned identities against each other here; circumcised identity is only of value if the one so marked as set [45] apart to God actually seeks to behave accordingly; otherwise, such a one is no different from the rest of humankind.[41] The implied value is that by definition those who are circumcised should be different, set apart to behave according to the Guidelines (Torah) God has given to the people of the covenant God made with Israel that circumcision signifies. The value of circumcising flesh is not intrinsic but imputed, it is the value of setting apart one's (usually, one's male

40. Περιτομὴ μὲν γὰρ ὠφελεῖ ἐὰν νόμον πράσσῃς· ἐὰν δὲ παραβάτης νόμου ᾖς, ἡ περιτομή σου ἀκροβυστία γέγονεν; NRSV: "Circumcision indeed is of value if you obey the law; but if you break the law, your circumcision has become uncircumcision."

41. Paul's argument is not against this hypothetical Jew supposing that being circumcised "saves" him, as commentators regularly assert (e.g., Cranfield, *Romans*, 1.172), and moreover, the supposed error of "*complacent* reliance upon circumcision" hardly makes sense of the effort attributed to this hypothetical teacher; it is not an issue for the fictive Jew, or for Jews and Judaism generally, unlike it has been supposed by later Christian interpreters.

child's) body, and thus whole being, to God, thereafter procreating within the family that God has chosen to bring blessing to all humankind. This is an argument with which any circumcised Jew, certainly one proposing to enlighten non-Jews to the ideals of Jewish identity and Torah-defined behavior, would be expected to agree.[42] The one Paul describes here could be labeled "an un-Jewish-like Jew."

In verse 26, Paul turns the point around: "Therefore, if the foreskinned one protects the righteous requirements of Torah, will his foreskin not be valued as [equivalent to] circumcision?"[43] Paul works from the propositional premise that the requirements/claims/judgments of Torah are righteous/just (δικαιώματα: a detail that the NRSV translation "requirements" fails to communicate). Thus, one who would seek to "watch out" that these are kept (hence: protect/guard/keep) would in effect be behaving as the circumcised should by definition behave. Circumcision sets the covenant people apart to God's Guidance; it is thereafter their covenant obligation to protect it by living [46] accordingly. Within the contrast being developed, as well as the rest of the letter and Paul's arguments against Christ-following non-Jews undertaking literal circumcision, it is illogical to suppose that Paul means that the non-Jew actually becomes circumcised. He has in view how his body is "valued/regarded [λογισθήσεται]" similarly, that it is dedicated to doing God's will in the way that the person with a circumcised body should be.[44] When such righteous concern to live in genuine faithfulness to God rather than hypocrisy is demonstrated by a non-Jew it represents the equivalent of acting like a Jew should—protecting the righteous ideal of Torah-defined behavior for the circumcised—and, indeed, it represents how all humans should behave. Paul appeals to the theoretical "jewish-like non-Jew" in contrast to the theoretical "un-Jewish-like Jew" of the previous verse.[45]

42. Boyarin, *A Radical Jew*, 86–95, makes the same point—that Jews would have generally agreed with these values—although he follows Dunn in supposing that Paul is actually seeking to attack Jews who rely upon being Jews apart from proper actions, rather than that this is a fictive example Paul creates in order to show non-Jews what it would be like *if* they would not turn their focus to doing what is now right and leave justice up to God. Like most Pauline scholars, Boyarin understands Paul to be universalizing Jewish identity in verse 29, applying it to non-Jews as well.

43. ἐὰν οὖν ἡ ἀκροβυστία τὰ δικαιώματα τοῦ νόμου φυλάσσῃ, οὐχ ἡ ἀκροβυστία αὐτοῦ εἰς περιτομὴν λογισθήσεται; NRSV: "So, if those who are uncircumcised keep the requirements of the law, will not their uncircumcision be regarded as circumcision?"

44. This is a scriptural value among the literally circumcised Israelites and later Jews to which Paul's argument appeals (Deut 10:16; 30:6; Jer 4:4; 9:25–26; 38:33; Ezek 44:7; 1QS 5.5; Philo, *Spec. Laws* 1.6; QG 3.46–52).

45. Cf. *Sifra* 86b: "Also a gentile, if he practices the Torah, is equal to the High Priest"; such rhetoric, like Paul's, is not proposing that he becomes the High Priest, but is reckoned/valued as if equivalent in standing. Consider too that one might refer to

Verse 27 draws out an inference from the previous two verses: "And the one foreskinned from birth [i.e., the non-Jew] yet fulfilling Torah will judge you who through [or: notwithstanding (having)] letter and circumcision [or: literal circumcision] sidestep Torah."[46] It is unclear if Paul meant to appeal to the attendant circumstances of having these gifts yet disregarding the help or value they offered ("notwithstanding/in spite of [having]"),[47] and also whether he meant to indicate the hendiadys, "literal circumcision,"[48] or two different elements, "letter" and "circumcision." By adding letter to circumcision he might be simply indicating the additional possession of Scripture or Torah. Paul could be implying the exploitation of these gifts (if διά is understood as causative: "by means of"), but the fictive Jew has been theoretically guilty of failing to act in keeping with what their knowledge of Scripture and marking as one set apart to God should guard above all, whereas if one not circumcised and without Torah [47] to guide them actually behaved in a manner that did protect the righteous aims of Torah, that one would naturally stand in judgment of such a Jew.

The entire chapter has censured judging of others, so it seems that Paul means here that their behavior will naturally stand as a witness against the behavior of the other, rather than that he is endorsing judging them, or even the impulse to want to judge them at some future time. Paul's approach veers close to playing on the temptation to envy (begrudge); in this case, to enjoy the fall of one's social superiors, giving one the sense of increased self-worth at the expense of the other's experience of being brought down (leveled). It is obvious from the way that criticisms of Jews and Judaism are indulged in the commentary tradition on this passage—often building implicitly when not explicitly on the trope of the self-righteous Pharisee, although apparently without recognizing that commentators themselves are probably "guilty" of seeking to practice the right way to please God—that Paul's approach is a dangerous one. In spite of the impulse to judge that Paul's argument has fueled for many commentators, it seems more likely that his conscious goal for this rhetorical gambit was not to encourage his audience to embrace the role of judging (which is so contrary to the message of 2:1 and the chapter

---

someone exemplifying American values as more American than (some) Americans, without thereby inferring that they have thus actually thereby become Americans (as if now having U.S. citizenship).

46. καὶ κρινεῖ ἡ ἐκ φύσεως ἀκροβυστία τὸν νόμον τελοῦσα σὲ τὸν διὰ γράμματος καὶ περιτομῆς παραβάτην νόμου; NRSV: "Then those who are physically uncircumcised but keep the law will condemn you that have the written code and circumcision but break the law."

47. Jewett, *Romans*, 234, approvingly notes commentators who choose this option.

48. Cranfield, *Romans*, 1.174, recognizes this option.

overall), but to convince them to recoil from behaving in a similar way themselves (i.e., to judge *themselves*). Whatever the case might be, Paul argues that a non-Jew behaving jewishly ("a jewish non-Jew") would logically represent the righteous judgment (by God) of a Jew who did not behave jewishly ("a non-Jewish Jew") in spite of the Jew having the help of Scripture and circumcision (or: in spite of being literally circumcised).

In verses 28–29 Paul completes this thought in the argument: "For the Jew is not [seeking validation] in the public acknowledgement[49] [i.e., calling himself or being called the Jew], nor is [the validation by] circumcision in the visible display in the flesh,[50] but the Jew [is validated] in that which is concealed,[51] even as circumcision of heart is in spirit not letter [or: literal (in [48] flesh)]; the praise [valued] is not from humans, but from God."[52] The prevailing translations and interpretations of this passage proceed from the conviction that Paul devalues Jewish ethnic identity and the ritual of circumcision (as well as Jewish ritual identity and behavior overall, and Judaism). They give the reader the impression that Paul is here calling for inward spirituality and attributing both the identity "Jew" and the mark of circumcision, when idealized in spiritual terms, to Christ-followers in general, and non-Jews who follow Christ in particular (i.e., to "Christians" as the "real" or "true" or "spiritual Jews"), while also denying that they any longer belong to Jews (since they are deemed to be like the fictive Jewish hypocrite by definition if they have not become Christ-followers, and thus without circumcised hearts, faith, or spirituality, etc.). It is obviously possible to translate and interpret the passage in these ways, but that does not sit well with the message of the passages within which it is embedded. Moreover, if Paul continued to value his Jewish identity and Jewish behavior, and if he presumed his audiences to know that, then such choices are unwarranted.

---

49. Cf. Bultmann/Lürhmann, "φανερος," *TDNT* 9.2.

50. οὐ γὰρ ὁ ἐν τῷ φανερῷ Ἰουδαῖός ἐστιν οὐδὲ ἡ ἐν τῷ φανερῷ ἐν σαρκὶ περιτομή; NRSV: "For a person is not a Jew who is one outwardly, nor is true circumcision something external and physical." Note that "true" is not in the manuscripts.

51. Paul uses κρυπτός, an adjective usually referring to something "concealed," hidden behind that which is seen (such as results when a rock is rolled over a cave opening), that which is behind the façade. Paul is probably seeking to contrast the public/visible credentials (of the Jew who teaches non-Jews) and that which remains impossible to see even in visible behavior (whether that Jew seeks to exemplify the values to which those credentials point).

52. ἀλλ᾽ ὁ ἐν τῷ κρυπτῷ Ἰουδαῖος, καὶ περιτομὴ καρδίας ἐν πνεύματι οὐ γράμματι, οὗ ὁ ἔπαινος οὐκ ἐξ ἀνθρώπων ἀλλ᾽ ἐκ τοῦ θεοῦ; NRSV: "Rather, a person is a Jew who is one inwardly, and real circumcision is a matter of the heart—it is spiritual and not literal. Such a person receives praise not from others but from God." Note that "real" is not in the manuscripts.

I have made several suggestions for the literal components here to try to capture what seems to be the spirit of the message. Based upon the preceding concern with what is valued, which is precisely what the question following in 3:1 poses as well, it seems appropriate to read this terse summary statement as an affirmation of what the one who is *in fact* a Jew ethnically by descent and circumcised in the flesh—which are indicated by reference to "letter/literal"—should be expected to value. He wants to be recognized by the conduct of his life, "of heart in/by spirit," that is, motivated by faithful service to God and neighbor, per Torah, with God's assistance. The jewishness a Jew values is the praise of God for a job faithfully performed rather than the accolades of fellow humans, particularly if gained, as Paul qualifies the alternatives here (although, obviously, they do not need to be bifurcated into contrary indicators), by gaming the system. The argument has not been to strip the literal (identity/behavior/teaching) of Jews of their value, but to affirm that their value for a Jew is in that which they signify, a heart and thus actions set apart to God and the best interests of one's neighbors, just as Torah describes what ought to occupy those in the covenants made with the fathers; these are the ideals of jewishness. This is the ideal Jew who is teaching those from the nations because of his [49] dedication to God's words, which have been entrusted to him; he first of all seeks to obey them faithfully, in contrast to the atypical hypothetical Jew who theoretically would teach those from the nations but not practice what he preaches. Verses 25-29 champion the ideal of faithful service for empirical Jews in contrast to the fictive, uncharacteristic hypocritical Jew portrayed in verses 17-24. It makes little sense to suppose that Paul is thus seeking to inform non-Jews that *they* are instead the ideal Jews, or circumcised in heart in contrast to Jews who are circumcised in flesh. One must be circumcised in flesh to be a Jew, and circumcised also in heart to represent the jewishness that being a Jew signifies, or should.[53]

Paul is appealing to a well-known trope in Greek and Roman as well as Jewish cultures, the difference between legal credentials and the spirit of the ideals to which those credentials should point. What I have tried to bring out is how this passage can be read to affirm the value of jewishness being raised for the audience of non-Jews, to whom Paul writes a letter to encourage dedication to "obedience of faithfulness." The entire argument is about this Jewish ideal versus the example of a theoretically hypocritical (non-stereotypical!) Jewish teacher. Thus, it makes sense for Paul to conclude that the ideal Jew is the ethnic Jew who understands the real purpose of the visible signs of being the historical people of God and teacher among the nations.

---

53. Cf. Fitzmyer, *Romans*, 323: "the real Jew is an Israelite with a circumcised heart."

The contrast is not between the outward and inward per se, but about the motive for undertaking the outward behavior, based upon the conviction that the one who undertakes to teach others these actions should conduct himself according to that which is taught as a matter of dedication to God, not simply the fulfilling of an office without the spirit of seeking to do so in order to serve the neighbor sincerely. One behaving from such motivation wins approval from God even if the neighbor might remain unaware of the level of dedication such service requires.[54] The argument can be read as an expression of Judaism's concern with faithful action rather than as a call to faith or an inner life or spirituality in contrast to action or service, with the latter negatively valued as representing merely the outward, [50] ritualistic, carnal, and so on. Paul is thus trying to portray the jewishness of the Jew so that the non-Jews will internalize this ideal for themselves, becoming non-Jews who exemplify jewishness although remaining non-Jews.

Paul's argument is constructed to encourage non-Jews to avoid making the same mistake they are quick to recognize in this diatribal caricature. Paul calls them to concentrate on being faithful to what they are responsible to do in service of (instead of judgment toward) the other, including toward the one who may be judging them to be making inappropriate claims to have joined the righteous ones of God apart from becoming Jews, and if males, apart from completing the rite of circumcision. That is a marker for Jews, not for non-Jews. But the ideals for which it stands—belonging to God and serving the other, leaving judgment of others to the God to which one belongs—should inspire and restrain everyone equally, whether Jew or non-Jew. Paul's next point arises from making just that case about equal responsibility: this does not abrogate difference and therefore nullify that there are some different advantages and responsibilities for Jews than there are for non-Jews, even those who belong to God through Christ. But the general principle remains nevertheless true, that each is fully responsible to be completely devoted to that to which each is called, to behave "genuinely," intentionally (from the heart) with their whole being (with their bodily behavior) both toward God and all others, at all times, convinced that God is aware, just, and merciful toward all, just as one hopes God is toward oneself.

---

54. This is attested among non-Jew philosophers too: e.g., Epictetus, *Diss.* 4.8.17–20: "... whatever I did well, I did so, not on account of the spectators, but on my own account ... it was for myself and for God.... And what harm was there in having the philosopher that I was, recognized by what I did, rather than by outward signs?" Note that here too the outward actions express the unseen intentions, but are distinguished from outward credentials per se. See Stowers, *Rereading of Romans*, 146–49, for additional examples.

Read this way, Romans 2 helps us to see that Paul wrote this letter to call Christ-following non-Jews to behave jewishly, to strive for the ideals of jewishness, to faithfully practice Judaism (as Christ-following non-Jews). They were, from Paul's perspective, *jewish* non-Jews. Likewise, their groups were most likely seen by their peers as Jewish, at least Jewish-like, as behaving jewishly in ways associated with Jews and Judaism and jewishness. In fact, Paul's arguments assume that they were non-Jews who gathered with Jews who shared their convictions about Jesus within the larger Jewish community and gatherings, where many Jews and guests who were non-Jews did not understand or share those convictions.[55] They assembled in what might best be referred to as Jesus- or Christ-following *Jewish* subgroups rather than *gentile* churches. Hence, we would be closer to the historical context to refer to Paul's *Jewish* subgroups or [51] Paul's *Jewish* assemblies. When seeking to refer specifically to the non-Jews therein, who were the target of Paul's extant rhetorical addresses, it would be useful to refer to the non-Jews of the Christ-following *Jewish* gatherings or subgroups.

CONCLUSION

What some Christians today refer to as "the *Christian* thing to do," we see Paul in Romans 2 instead still calling "the *Jewish* thing to do." In contrast to Käsemann's negative valuation of Christians discovering "the hidden Jew" within themselves, which for him represents the temptation "to validate rights and demands over against God,"[56] Paul was exhorting non-Jews turning to God in Christ to seek to discover within themselves the noble values of jewishness, what being a Jew ideally signifies. They should learn to internalize jewishness as the highest value for themselves, albeit remaining non-Jews because of the propositional claims of the gospel that members from the nations, which they represent, are now turning to the One God of the Jews, as expected at the arrival of the age to come. Just as a Jew knows (or should know) that the highest value of the circumcised body is that it signifies being set apart to God, who by spirit circumcises the heart of the faithful, so too these non-Jews should dedicate their bodies and hearts to faithful service to God, even though the circumcision of body—and thus the circumcision of heart[57]—does not apply (literally, and thus figuratively) to them.

---

55. Nanos, "The Jewish Context of the Gentile Audience"; Nanos, "To the Churches within the Synagogues of Rome."

56. Käsemann, "Paul and Israel," 186; see Boyarin, *A Radical Jew*, 209–14.

57. The idea of cutting off part of the heart is itself strange if taken literally, and

Paul's opposition to these non-Jews undertaking proselyte conversion *to become Jews* ethnically (circumcision signifying the completion of that ethnic "conversion" rite) should not be mistaken as opposition to these non-Jews beginning to observe *Judaism*, which *he actually promotes*. His letters consist precisely of instruction in the Jewish way of life for non-Jews who turn to Israel's God as the One God of all the nations; he enculturates them into God's Guidance (Torah) without bringing them under Torah technically, since they do not become Jews/Israel. They are non-Jews who are learning, by way of Paul's instructions, to practice Judaism!

[52] I have argued that it is logical and relevant to speak of Paul's *jewish* non-Jews, just as it seemed appropriate to describe some of the non-Jews about whom Josephus wrote as jewish non-Jews in distinction from other non-Jews, such as Izates. He was a non-Jew who adopted some Jewish practices in the earliest part of the narrative but eventually undertook circumcision in obedience to Torah's commandment for those who seek to be faithful to Israel's God (as interpreted by Eleazar), which changed him into a Jew. Moreover, Josephus represents this step approvingly as an expression of faithfulness alone, at the same time acknowledging that there are other interpretations of what represents faithfulness for a non-Jew, given certain particular considerations. Developing this kind of specificity for discussing Paul and his communities is important if we are to avoid the long-standing tradition of referring to Paul's audiences and others within these movements as Christians and Christian gentiles or gentile Christians, among other advantages, such as advancing the discussion of the different views on virtually any topic that arose between Jews and Jewish groups (including Paul and his groups) without supposing that any group was seeking to express something other than faithfulness to God within Judaism and thus according to Torah, variously interpreted. Nevertheless, applying the terms "Jewish" and "Judaism" and various other cognates to non-Jews can create a new set of problems, since these are generally reserved for describing Jews and the behavior of Jews. This strategy, therefore, could create confusion instead of introducing defamiliarization that informs, helping us to think, ask questions, and pursue historical accuracy in new ways. The use of the lowercase "j" is thus suggested, for example, to help raise awareness that the phenomenon is not best imagined as "Christian" in contrast to "Jewish," and also to reflect that these non-Jews have not become Jews.

I do not have similar reservations about referring to "*Jewish* communities/assemblies," "subgroups within the *Jewish* communities," or "subgroup

---

apart from the literal act of circumcision continuing to be practiced, does not seem to be a useful way to conceptualize the dedication of those who are not circumcised in body (which women have no doubt long recognized).

assemblies of the *synagogues*" to describe the groups to which Paul wrote, and, beside the Roman assemblies, for the groups that he founded. Again, just as was the case for discussing the groups of non-Jews about whom Josephus wrote, these descriptive phrases represent the communal situations of the non-Jews Paul addressed better than the anachronistic paradigm perpetuated in phrases like "Paul's *Christian* churches" or even "Paul's *gentile* churches/assemblies," and so on, which continue to characterize discussions even when it is explicitly recognized that this was not yet Christianity but a nascent movement *within Judaism*. This change in terminology can help facilitate the development of new approaches to familiar texts in ways more likely to discover and represent their [53] original meaning, for the author and his audiences, within Greco-Roman Judaism.

From Paul's perspective, Christ-following non-Jews were not to become Jews, and Romans 2:25–29 does not indicate that Paul wanted them to believe that they became Jews in some alternative sense because of their faith in Jesus. Yet they had been brought into the practice of Judaism, the way of life developed by and for Jews, which was taking place within Jewish subgroups formed around the conviction that Jesus was the awaited Messiah, just as was the case in the groups that Paul founded. It was precisely as non-Jews that they were to learn to live in the ways that being a Jew exemplified—or should exemplify, because God established this special identity in the service of reconciling all humankind to the Creator. In order to demonstrate the chronometrical-based propositional truth claims of these groups—that the awaited age had dawned within the midst of the present age through the resurrection of Christ—these non-Jews were to be "jewish" ("jewish-like" or "jewish*ish*") non-Jews; they were to behave "jewishly," to exemplify "jewishness," to practice "Judaism." Paul's bold reminder and intended trip to Rome were designed to "establish" their understanding of "obedient faithfulness" within this cultural milieu (Rom 1:5, 11–12).

BIBLIOGRAPHY

Bernat, David A. *Sign of the Covenant: Circumcision in the Priestly Tradition*. Ancient Israel and Its Literature 3. Atlanta: Society of Biblical Literature, 2009.

Boyarin, Daniel. *A Radical Jew: Paul and the Politics of Identity*. Contraversions 1. Berkeley: University of California Press, 1994.

Cohen, A., and Israel Brodie. *The Minor Tractates of the Talmud: Massektoth Ketannoth*, Vol. 1. London: Soncino, 1966.

Cohen, Shaye J. D. *The Beginnings of Jewishness: Boundaries, Varieties, Uncertainties*. HCS 31. Berkeley: University of California Press, 1999.

———. *Why Aren't Jewish Women Circumcised? Gender and Covenant in Judaism*. Berkeley: University of California Press, 2005.

Cranfield, C. E. B. *A Critical and Exegetical Commentary on the Epistle to the Romans.* ICC. Edinburgh: T. & T. Clark, 1975.
Donaldson, Terence L. "'Gentile Christianity' as a Category in the Study of Christian Origins." *Harvard Theological Review* 106.4 (2013) 433–58.
Dunn, James D. G. "Who Did Paul Think He Was? A Study of Jewish-Christian Identity" *New Testament Studies* 45 (1999) 174–93.
Ehrensperger, Kathy. *Paul at the Crossroads of Cultures: Theologizing in the Space-between.* London: Bloomsbury, 2013.
Eisenbaum, Pamela Michelle. *Paul Was Not a Christian: The Real Message of a Misunderstood Apostle.* New York: HarperOne, 2009.
Elliott, Neil. *The Arrogance of Nations: Reading Romans in the Shadow of Empire.* Paul in Critical Contexts. Minneapolis: Fortress, 2008.
———. *The Rhetoric of Romans: Argumentative Constraint and Strategy and Paul's Dialogue with Judaism.* JSNTSup 45. Sheffield, UK: Sheffield Academic Press, 1990.
Feldman, Louis H. *Jew and Gentile in the Ancient World: Attitudes and Interactions from Alexander to Justinian.* Princeton: Princeton University Press, 1993.
Fitzmyer, Joseph A. *Romans: A New Translation with Introduction and Commentary.* New York: Doubleday, 1993.
Fredriksen, Paula. "Judaizing the Nations: The Ritual Demands of Paul's Gospel." *New Testament Studies* 56 (2010) 232–52.
———. "The Question of Worship: Gods, Pagans, and the Redemption of Israel." In *Paul within Judaism: Restoring the First-century Context to the Apostle*, edited by Mark D. Nanos and Magnus Zetterholm, 175–202. Minneapolis: Fortress, 2015.
Goodblatt, David. *Elements of Ancient Jewish Nationalism.* Cambridge: Cambridge University Press, 2006.
Goodman, Martin. *Mission and Conversion: Proselytizing in the Religious History of the Roman Empire.* Oxford: Clarendon, 1994.
Hoffman, Lawrence A. *Covenant of Blood: Circumcision and Gender in Rabbinic Judaism.* CSJH. Chicago: University of Chicago Press, 1996.
Jewett, Robert. *Romans.* Hermeneia. Minneapolis: Fortress, 2006.
Johnson Hodge, Caroline. *If Sons, Then Heirs: A Study of Kinship and Ethnicity in the Letters of Paul.* New York: Oxford University Press, 2007.
———. "The Question of Social Interaction: Gentiles as Gentiles—But Also Not—in Pauline Communities." In *Paul within Judaism: Restoring the First-century Context to the Apostle*, edited by Mark D. Nanos and Magnus Zetterholm, 153–74. Minneapolis: Fortress, 2015.
Käsemann, Ernst. "Paul and Israel." In *New Testament Questions of Today*, translated by W. J. Montague, 183–87. The New Testament Library. Philadelphia: Fortress, 1969.
Nanos, Mark D. *The Irony of Galatians: Paul's Letter in First-century Context.* Minneapolis: Fortress, 2002.
———. "The Jewish Context of the Gentile Audience Addressed in Paul's Letter to the Romans." *Catholic Biblical Quarterly* 61 (1999) 283–304. (See volume 2 of this series of collected essays.)
———. "Paul and the Jewish Tradition: The Ideology of the *Shema*." In *Celebrating Paul: Festschrift in Honor of Jerome Murphy-O'Connor, O.P., and Joseph A. Fitzmyer, S.J.*, edited by Peter Spitaler, 62–80. CBQMS 48. Washington, DC: Catholic Biblical Association of America, 2012. (See chapter 4 in this volume of collected essays.)

———. "Paul and Judaism: Why Not Paul's Judaism?" In *Paul Unbound: Other Perspectives on the Apostle*, edited by Mark Douglas Given, 117-60. Peabody, MA: Hendrickson, 2010. (See chapter 1 in this volume of collected essays.)

———. "The Question of Conceptualization: Qualifying Paul's Position on Circumcision in Dialogue with Josephus's Advisors to King Izates." In *Paul within Judaism: Restoring the First-century Context to the Apostle*, edited by Mark D. Nanos and Magnus Zetterholm, 105-52. Minneapolis: Fortress, 2015.

———. "Romans." In *The Jewish Annotated New Testament*, edited by Amy-Jill Levine and Marc Zvi Brettler, 253-86. New York: Oxford University Press, 2011.

———. "To the Churches within the Synagogues of Rome." In *Reading Paul's Letter to the Romans*, edited by Jerry L. Sumney, 11-28. Atlanta: Society of Biblical Literature, 2012. (See volume 2 of this series of collected essays.)

———. "What Was at Stake in Peter's 'Eating with Gentiles' at Antioch?" In *The Galatians Debate: Contemporary Issues in Rhetorical and Historical Interpretation*, edited by Mark D. Nanos, 282-318. Peabody, MA: Hendrickson, 2002. (See volume 3 of this series of collected essays.)

Nanos, Mark D., and Magnus Zetterholm, eds. *Paul within Judaism: Restoring the First-century Context to the Apostle*. Minneapolis: Fortress, 2015.

Porton, Gary G. *The Stranger within Your Gates: Converts and Conversion in Rabbinic Literature*. CSHJ. Chicago: University of Chicago Press, 1994.

Rajak, Tessa. "The Parthians in Josephus." In *Das Partherreich un seine Zeugnisse: Beiträge des internationalen Colloquiums, Eutin (27- 30 Juni 1996)*, edited by J. Wiesehöfer, 309-24. Stuttgart: Steiner, 1998.

Runesson, Anders. "Inventing Christian Identity: Paul, Ignatius, and Theodosius I." In *Exploring Early Christian Identity*, edited by Bengt Holmberg, 59-92. Tübingen: Mohr Siebeck, 2008.

———. *The Origins of the Synagogue: A Socio-historical Study*. CBNTS 37. Stockholm: Almqvist & Wiksell, 2001.

Schiffman, Lawrence H. "The Conversion of the Royal House of Abiabene in Josephus and Rabbinic Sources." In *Josephus, Judaism, and Christianity*, edited by Louis H. Feldman and Gohei Hata, 293-312. Detroit: Wayne State University Press, 1987.

Schwartz, Daniel R. "'Judaean' or 'Jew'? How Should We Translate *ioudaios* in Josephus?" In *Jewish Identity in the Greco-Roman World: Jüdische Identität in der griechisch-römischen Welt*, edited by Jörg Frey, Daniel R. Schwartz, and Stephanie Gripentrog, 3- 27. Leiden: Brill, 2007.

Sechrest, Love L. *A Former Jew: Paul and the Dialectics of Race*. LNTS. London: T. & T. Clark, 2009.

Stern, Sacha. *Jewish Identity in Early Rabbinic Writings*. AGJU 23. Leiden: Brill, 1994.

Stowers, Stanley Kent. *A Rereading of Romans: Justice, Jews, and Gentiles*. New Haven: Yale University Press, 1994.

Thiessen, Matthew. *Contesting Conversion: Genealogy, Circumcision, and Identity in Ancient Judaism and Christianity*. Oxford: Oxford University Press, 2011.

Thorsteinsson, Runar M. *Paul's Interlocutor in Romans 2: Function and Identity in the Context of Ancient Epistolography*. CBNTS 40. Stockholm: Almqvist & Wiksell, 2003.

Wright, N. T. *Paul and the Faithfulness of God*. COQG 4. London: SPCK, 2013.

6

Reading Paul in a Jewish Way
"Oh be joyful all you peoples, with God's People" (Rom 15:10): Who Are the people?[1]

[436] To SPEAK OF reading Paul *in a Jewish way* can allude to the fact that I am a Jewish person engaged in historical research on Paul and his communities, factors that shaped the origins of what became Christianity. As a historian, I believe the perspective I bring to the research can be useful to others who are interested in reassessing Paul's original voice and the influence its interpretive trajectory continues to have on Christians, and as a result, on Jews. The more important allusion, however, is to the idea that *Paul* wrote to his assemblies in a Jewish way. I do not mean simply to signify that Paul was *from* a Jewish ethnic and religious *background*, as commonly held. I mean that Paul continued to *practice* Judaism—and, moreover, that he continued to *promote* it to those who became followers of Jesus Christ, non-Jews as well as Jews.

Yes, you read me correctly: my view of what it means to read Paul as a Jewish figure is very different from the traditional and still prevailing perspectives on the apostle, which approach him—variously phrased—as one who converted from Judaism to join a new religion, Christianity, and become its most famous missionary. I maintain instead that Paul remained *within*

---

1. This chapter includes a few elements in the paper presented that were omitted in the conference volume. See the Preface for details.

Judaism, called to declare Israel's message of the dawning of the awaited time of restoration through Jesus to the rest of the nations *also*.[2]

When approached in this way, it becomes possible to understand the communities that Paul founded and to which he wrote these letters as practicing Judaism, functioning as subgroups of the larger Jewish communities in each of these locations. Upholding this perspective in no way involves questioning [437] that he believed Jesus was the Messiah. In his time, the very idea of a *Mashiach*—a Hebrew term for one whom God "anointed" as king—would have been an inscrutable concept outside of Jewish communities and their hope for God's eventual rule over all humankind. Later, it meant believing in "Christ," the Hellenized and Latinized ways of designating the Hebrew word *Mashiach*, and it eventually was regarded to be a part of Jesus's proper name instead of an honorific title. When the designations "Christian" and "Christianity" arose late in the first or early second century, these were ways to refer to a particular Jewish subgroup identity, and that sub-identification remained salient for decades;[3] it highlighted the focus, however strange or questionable, of a *messianic*-centered branch of Judaism (and one probably recognized by Jews as a branch of Pharisaic Judaism).[4]

---

2. See my "Paul and Judaism: Why Not Paul's Judaism?"; and the essays in the volume I co-edited with Magnus Zetterholm, *Paul within Judaism*.

3. Even the reference to Nero's persecution of *christiani* is from the early second century looking backward and giving it a name that is not otherwise attested at that time, and arguably referring to a particular Jewish group (Suetonius, *Nero* 16.2; Tacitus, *Ann.* 15.44.2–8); likewise Acts 11:26 is looking back and saying *where* it first was used for a particular Jewish group, not *when* (Acts is arguably from the end of the first century and some now date it to the middle of the second).

4. Paul not only continued to appeal to his identity as a Pharisee in his letters (Gal 1:14; Phil 3:5), the later author of Acts still portrayed Paul that way (Acts 23:6; 26:5). Paul's arguments and use of Scripture appear to represent first-century Pharisaism, and his democratizing theological principles also betray Pharisaic orientation. The traditional anti-Pharisaic reading of the Gospels and Paul is based on failure to distinguish the use of prescriptive inter-group rhetorical polemic from ostensibly descriptive accounts. How likely was it that Pharisees would not have responded to the accusations of self-righteousness or subverting Torah with denial and counter-accusations? Or that the reason that Jesus was represented in such hostile rivalry with them was because they did not represent real threats to the movement, upholding the same or very similar ideals? Or that the movement was other than a branch of Pharisaism from which it sought to distinguish itself as superior? That interpretive tradition also ironically fails to consider that Jesus is represented in the Gospels to be guilty of the same kinds of behavior of which he accuses "the Pharisees," but which, in the case of Jesus, are celebrated as demonstrating God's enabling and valued as noble acts; e.g., praying and doing his good deeds and miracles in public! Shocking as it may seem, Jesus and the early Jesus movements, including the community-founding efforts of Paul, probably represented Pharisaism (more than any other branches of Judaism of which we are aware). See esp. Runesson, "From Where? To What? Common Judaism, Pharisees, and the Changing

Reading Paul in a Jewish Way   157

In time, however, Christian identity and behavior were understood to be very different from that of Judaism, from what Jews believed and practiced. Christianity and Judaism became two very different religions over the centuries, so much so that it became, and for many people still is, inconceivable that Paul practiced and promoted Judaism. Yet it is widely recognized by New Testament scholars that there was no such thing as Christianity during Paul's time, so he could not have converted from Judaism to join something called that. This logically points—as ironic as it may be—to Paul remaining within and thus representing Judaism, even if a small sect thereof, one that in time became estranged from other sects of Judaism and eventually turned into something different from and opposed to Judaism per se.

The present conundrum is readily witnessed in scholarship on Paul. Specialists regularly observe that Paul never addressed anyone as a Christian or referred to himself as one in his extant letters. However, the implications of this insight are mitigated almost immediately. How? By the decision to continue to describe Paul as a Christian and those to whom he wrote as Christians, whose religion is referred to as "Christianity." Yet Paul wrote to people he called non-Jews, and he discussed non-Jews, those from the (rest of the) nations (the *ethnē*), and Jews, those from *the* nation *Israel*—and he included himself among the latter. He further distinguished between those who followed Jesus and those who did not. His interpreters have not adopted this constraint. When practiced, however, it highlights a cross-cultural separation between the reader and the subject, arguably a very helpful step towards reading Paul in a more historically accurate way even if accentuating a seam between his intended audience and the modern reader. But should not even the devotional reader want to hear Paul first (what "exegesis" should represent), and then seek to interpret (hence, this practice is called "hermeneutics") what that means thousands of years later in the different cultures and languages of him or herself?

The same lack of historical clarity, with significant implications today, results from referring to the communities to which Paul wrote as "churches." [438] In later centuries, this became a term of reference for gatherings of Christians and for their institutions and structures. You are, for instance, celebrating "Church Council" (*Kirchentag*), which could hardly be confused with the practice or celebration of Judaism. In Paul's time, however, the word "*ekklēsia*" simply meant "assemblies" or "gatherings," and it was used for both Jewish and non-Jewish gatherings and associations. It is thus historically more helpful to speak of Paul's *assemblies*. Likewise, the use of "gentile" and "gentiles" in English is misleading, especially when coupled

---

Socioreligious Location of the Matthean Community."

with "churches" in the common refrain, Paul's "gentile churches." At dispute is not whether there were non-Jews in the assemblies that Paul founded and to which he wrote letters; indeed, I am among those convinced that these non-Jews were the target (or: encoded, implied) audiences of his letters. It is historically most probable that these non-Jews joined Jewish communities and learned to practice righteousness according to Jewish cultural norms that were derived from the interpretation of Torah over the centuries. To help us think with Paul in his context, I recommend that we instead refer to "Paul's Christ-following Jewish subgroup communities," "gatherings," and "assemblies."[5]

If you try to talk about Paul and the people of his assemblies in these terms, you will immediately become aware of the kinds of shifts in thinking that are provoked: for example, substitute Jews and non-Jews for Jews and Christians, Christ-following for Christian, and Jewish subgroup assemblies for gentile churches (ironic reversals of the familiar tropes). These defamiliarizing shifts help us recognize, for example, that it was the identity issues of belongingness and the associated behavioral norms *for non-Jews* within the Christ-following *Jewish* subgroups that provoked Paul's letter writing! The problems arose for these non-Jews, and thus for Paul and the other Jews involved in these groups, precisely because they remained non-Jews yet at the same time had begun to re-identify their loyalties from the gods of their own people to the God of the Jews, of Israel. Such a radical change for them naturally involved many adjustments to their habits and behavioral norms: they began to stand out as abnormal on usual Jewish guest terms for non-Jews among themselves, and all the more on usual Greek or Roman and other local ethno-religious cultural terms among their families and neighbors and civic leaders. We might regard the issues the leaders such as Paul sought to solve by appealing to Jewish Scriptures and traditions, mirroring later Christian rhetorical invective, as "the *gentile* problem" of the early Jewish followers of Jesus—such as Paul.

Since other Jewish groups and assemblies included non-Jews, what made this movement so distinctive among other Jewish movements of the time, and [439] especially where the non-Jews who joined it were concerned? Although it is clear from literary and material evidence that many Jewish groups welcomed interest in Judaism by non-Jews, including various levels of communal integration, nevertheless most of these would have apparently expected those interested in being guests to continue to practice family and civic cult when not among the Jewish communities—after all, they were not Jews and thus not permitted by Roman law to refrain

---

5. See my "Paul's Non-Jews Do Not Become 'Jews,' But Do They Become 'Jewish'?"

from cult to the gods, unlike Jews, and any such confusing of identity and concomitant expectations would have posed a threat to the continuation of their special Jewish communal exemption.[6] Alternatively, at least in the groups whose influence Paul sought to counter, when non-Jews expressed interest in full membership they would have been steered toward undertaking the rites involved in proselyte conversion (*erga nomou*), by which they could become Jews, members of Israel.[7] But this option was not to be advocated in the Jesus-following groups, according to Paul: they were to proclaim instead the arrival of the end of the ages, a time when the rest of the nations would turn back to the One Creator God of all humankind, of all the nations, who until then had been recognized only by the people of Israel. Because of this "chronometrical" claim,[8] the non-Jews joining these Jewish subgroups had to abandon other gods and associated "sinful" behavior and turn to the One God and righteousness as outlined in Jewish communal terms, based upon interpretations of Jewish communal texts and traditions, not least the Tanakh, or Old Testament.

You could say that Paul and his fellow Jesus-following Jews maintained a kind of exclusivistic position that it was no longer appropriate for these non-Jews to become Jews. They must remain non-Jews, members of the other nations turning to the God of Israel as their own God. Isaiah 11:6-10 provides metaphorical terms that are particularly relevant, not least because in a text we will explore, Romans 15:12, Paul cites verse 10! These non-Jews must remain the wolves eating alongside the Jewish lambs, to stay with Isaiah's metaphorical terms, exemplifying the hoped-for utopian *shalom* among those [440] who remain different yet no longer defined as enemies, instead now regarded as equals among the people of God (cf. Isa 65:17-25). These Jewish groups were to demonstrate the gospel's

---

6. Cf. Josephus, *Ant.* 14.185-267; 19.299-306; *J.W.* 2.285-308; Philo, *Embassy* 132-34. The fact that these rights, granted since Julius Caesar, were sometimes contested locally, bears witness to the importance of internal policing of the conditions upon which the exemptions turned, namely identification as Jews (not merely non-Jew guests, however welcome) and thus with a long-standing tradition of avoiding cult to other gods and human leaders such as was Caesar.

7. I have argued that this is the situational context that Paul confronted in Galatians, in *The Irony of Galatians*.

8. The term "chronometrical" is intended to offer a shorthand way to repeat the point that it is the time-oriented claims and policies of this group that are so central to its purpose and the conflicts that it experienced initially with other Jews and Jewish groups. The issue was not so much the ideas that they upheld, which other groups might also subscribe to when the proper time has arrived, but the claim that now the "time" of the arrival of the awaited age had been initiated with the age-to-come event of the resurrection of Jesus, and thus that today was the proper time for those ideas to be implemented in the Jewish communities.

propositional claim that the awaited time had begun among themselves. No, it had not arrived in full; but with the resurrection of Jesus, of which they were persuaded, it had dawned.

One can argue whether the sun has risen during the first light of the morning, and so too about this claim. It did not seem to many others that the awaited time had arrived. It still looked like night, and still does to many, who still await the time when God will reign, when injustice will end, when all will be healthy and well fed, when there will be war no more. But for Paul and his fellow followers, that time had begun, and it was paramount that these assemblies exemplified this reality as a witness to Israel of the beginning of her awaited liberation from the oppression of other nations and powers with the full restoration to God's rule, which would involve the reconciliation of the rest of the nations too. This propositional policy to remain different yet to regard each other as equal was confusing for the non-Jews who now joined Jewish communal subgroups, not least when they found that their new self-identifying claim to be part of the people of God—the result of trusting Paul's message—was not always welcomed on the terms that they believed applied to themselves as non-Jews entitled to expect this because of the resurrection of Jesus. It was all the more confusing to anyone—Jew or non-Jew—who was not persuaded of those claims.

Paul wrote the letters that we study to this day, including the language we are to consider from Romans 15, to address the confusion such propositional claims created for these non-Jews, and the associated judgments, resentment, and reactions. When looked at from this perspective, one can understand why Paul wrote, and what he hoped to communicate, in very different ways than traditionally conceptualized. This is nowhere more evident than in how to approach the question of why Paul forbade these non-Jews to become circumcised, and thus to remain non-Jews even though they had begun to practice Judaism, a Jewishly defined way of life.

The traditional reasons given for Paul's opposition to these non-Jews becoming Jews depend upon universalizing Paul's arguments as if they applied equally to *everyone*. But it makes little sense to suppose that what he expressed to Christ following *non-Jews* about themselves would be the same as what he would express if writing to Jews. This (mis)take, however, is fundamental to the widely-held view that Paul was against Jewish identity and behavior per se, that is, for Jews as well as non-Jews who turned to Jesus; thus, for *everyone*. Good historical practice requires scholars to interpret rhetoric contextually, and, in this case, Paul signals that he is discussing the topic of adult male Jesus-following non-Jews becoming circumcised to become Jews and thus under Torah, not Jewish parents already under Torah obeying the commandment with respect to their infant sons. The traditional views are also based upon later Christian assumptions that Paul considered Jewish practices like circumcision and Torah-observance inferior, wrong, or passé, whether because of supposed pride, ethnocentrism, or [441] even the practical limitations that continuing these practices would have created for bringing the nations into the people of God.

These conclusions are of critical importance: the answers are an integral part of traditionally negative Christian characterizations of Jews and Judaism, including so-called Jewish Christianity as distinguished from Pauline or gentile Christianity;[9] they represent implicit, when not explicit, denigrations of the Jewish other from which many Christians of good will would like to find better alternatives. I submit that he upheld it to be just as important that Jews remain Jews, and thus observe Torah, the "Guidance" God had given to Jews for how to live rightly, which is why it logically follows that Paul remained a Torah-observing Jew.[10] The traditional conclusions also exemplify the problem of zero-sum thinking, of proceeding as if one's own success depends upon the failure of the other, of requiring a negative binary comparison to the other's ostensible inferiority to highlight one's own supposed superiority.

The alternative that I propose is to learn to read Paul *within Judaism*. This cross-cultural exercise offers Christians positive ways to conceptualize and discuss Jewish identity and behavior as a part of their own historical origins, and not simply as the *background of* or the *context of* Jesus or *of* Paul or *of* the origins of Christianity, as if related but essentially different. The various differences that emerged and later led to defining them as different religions need not be qualified in contrastive value-laden terms to make sense of them, including how and why they came about as each group sought to establish self-esteem and access to limited goods, entirely normal social processes by which differences are often turned into warrants for discrimination.[11] There are many other benefits too, including the ideal of allowing Paul to be Paul, as far as we are able, and the ideal of working from the notion of God's unlimited resources, so that, going forward with full awareness of what we have learned from the tragic past, which all too often reflects the privileging of the interests of "our group" against those of "their group," we can work toward a future not dictated by the zero-sum thinking that "they" need to lose for "us" to win.

---

9. E.g., see the insightful work of Gerdmar, *Roots of Theological Anti-Semitism*.
10. See my "The Myth of the 'Law-Free' Paul Standing between Christians and Jews."
11. Cf. Hogg and Abrams, *Social Identifications*.

WHY NON-JEWS REMAIN NON-JEWS YET FELLOW MEMBERS OF THE PEOPLE OF GOD

[442] In Romans 3:29–31, Paul raises the question of whether God is *only* the God of the Jews. This formulation is based upon the assumption that Paul's audience shares with him the conviction that God is obviously still the God of Jews; the question is whether non-Jews must become Jews to share in this standing as the people of God. Paul argues in "a very Jewish way" that this God is *also* the God of the nations. He reasons that this is because God is *one*. One could instead reason that it is because everyone is human, so from the oneness of humanity, which would be a very Greek way to proceed. But Paul argues in reductive, binary terms that everyone fits into in one of two categories: either one is a Jew, a descendent of the ancient tribes of Israel, or one is from the nations other than Israel, a non-Jew. He makes his case by turning to the logic of the Jewish prayer, the *Shema Israel*: "*Sh'ma Yisrael, Adonai Eloheinu, Adonai echad*"; in English, "Hear, O Israel, the LORD is our God, the LORD is one [or: the LORD alone]"; in German, "Höre, Israel, der HERR ist unser Gott, der HERR allein" (Luther transl.).

This ideologically charged prayer is repeated twice a day, and it was developed in a direction similar to the one Paul argues here by later Jewish scholars who did not share Paul's convictions that this time had arrived, even partially. For example, roughly halfway between Paul's time and our own, the famous Jewish scholar known as Rashi explained the repetition of "The Name" (*Haššēm*, a rabbinic circumlocution for the tetragramaton, the four-letter Hebrew word translated as LORD or HERR) in the Shema as follows:

> The LORD who is our God now, but not (yet) the God of the (other) nations, is destined to be the One LORD, as it is said, "For then will I give to the peoples a pure language, that they may all call upon the name of the LORD, to serve Him with one consent" (Zeph 3:9). And (likewise) it is said, "And the LORD shall be king over all the earth; on that day shall the LORD be One and His name One" (Zech 14:9).

When the awaited day arrived it would be a time when people from all of the other nations would join alongside of Israelites declaring praise for the One God, similar to Paul's own language in Romans 15, and this expectation is tied to the prophecy of Zechariah.[12]

---

12. For fuller discussions of this dynamic for Paul, see my *Mystery of Romans*, 179–201; and "Paul and the Jewish Tradition: The Ideology of the Shema."

Rashi, like Paul, did not see the collapse of the distinction between Jews and non-Jews with the arrival of that awaited time, but their joining together as with one voice to the One God. The difference between Rashi (along with many other Jews) and Paul (with his fellow Christ-followers) was not one of principle, of theology related to the awaited reign of God on earth or the joining of those from the nations alongside of Israel to honor God, so that all are on the same winning team so to speak, but to the *timing* of that eventuality. Most would agree that such a day *will* come; that is a Jewish expectation. Paul upheld the chronometrical claim that this day *had* come, dawned at least with [443] the resurrection of Jesus, and thus that this utopian way of life was now to be embodied by the assemblies of followers of Jesus.

Paul's logic is this: If, following the resurrection of Jesus, all who worship the One God are Israelites or become Israelites, then God is still only the God of one nation, not of all the nations, just as has been the case in the so-called present age. But if the non-Jews who turn to Israel's God do so while remaining non-Jews, not as members of the nation Israel, then they worship the God of Israel as the One God of all the nations *also*, just as is expected upon the arrival of the awaited age. Thus, he wrote to non-Jews to join as one *alongside* of Jews (whether followers of Jesus or not) in the praise of God as One, as foretold. They were to practice Judaism, that is, to behave in ways designed by and for Jewish communities to live, but they were not allowed to become Jews, the adult males were not to be circumcised to represent the completion of the rite of passage to Jewish identity. By retaining their identity as non-Jews but behaving as if no longer non-Jews, they would exemplify the arrival of the day that they proclaimed in their assemblies.

Paul's letters are full of instruction about how to live on behalf of the other, without discrimination among themselves or toward those who were not part of their subgroups, all the while retaining many distinctions among themselves, including gender differences, occupational differences, and ethnicity in terms of being a member of Israel or from the other nations; that is, whether Jew or non-Jew, which he often called simply Greek. As Paul put the matter in Romans 13:8–10, to live according to Torah, to God's *Guidance*, is to live according to Love. In God's design, contributing to the success of the other person or group is integral to experiencing the success of one's own, as counterintuitive as it may be. And, especially relevant for this session, he draws on this unlimited sum logic explicitly throughout Romans to instruct Jesus-following non-Jews in the positive ways that they are to think about and behave toward non-Jesus-following Jews.

TOWARD READING ROMANS 15:10 WITH PAUL'S AUDIENCE IN ROME

As we turn now to our text in Romans 15, I trust you will see that what I have been setting out shapes what we should expect Paul to be explaining in very different terms than those created by the traditional presuppositions. The text is a citation among several others Paul selects to support his argument in Romans 15:7–13 (NRSV):

> ⁷Welcome one another, therefore, just as Christ has welcomed you, for the glory of God. ⁸For I tell you that Christ has become a servant of the circumcised on behalf of [444] the truth of God in order that he might confirm the promises given to the patriarchs, ⁹and in order that the Gentiles might glorify God for his mercy. As it is written,
>
> "Therefore I will confess you among the Gentiles, and sing praises to your name"; [2 Sam 22:50]
>
> ¹⁰and again he says, **"Rejoice, O *Gentiles*, with his *people*"**; [Deut 32:43]
>
> ¹¹and again, "Praise the Lord, all you Gentiles, and let all the peoples praise him"; [Ps 116:1]
>
> ¹²and again Isaiah says, "The root of Jesse shall come, the one who rises to rule the Gentiles; in him the Gentiles shall hope." [Isa 11:10]
>
> ¹³May the God of hope fill you with all joy and peace in believing, so that you may abound in hope by the power of the Holy Spirit.

For verse 10, the Kirchentag program uses a German translation: "Freut euch, ihr Völker, mit Gottes Volk"; and an English translation: "Oh be joyful all you people, with God's people." Luther translated it slightly differently: "Freut euch, ihr Heiden, mit seinem Volk!" The Greek reads: *euphránthēte*, ***ethnē***, *metá toú **laoú** autoú*.

Notice the distinction that arises from the Greek alternating between two words here, which I have highlighted in bold: first, the *ethnē*, and second, the *laos*. Luther also brought out a distinction between them, but his choice for *ethnē*, "heathen," which was a later Christian moniker used to refer to non-Christians, can be misleading, not least because this connotation turned Paul's original contextual meaning on its head. Although Luther distinguished Jews from heathens, it is likely that for many of his readers since, Jews who did not become Christians and turn from Judaism might be imagined when encountering the epithet "heathens." The German and English translations used in the Kirchentag program avoid this connotation, but they unfortunately blur the distinction retained in the original languages, and thus risk undermining the contextual distinctions to which Paul was pointing with these citations when read in "a Jewish way." I suggest the translation: **"Be joyful, *nations*, with God's *people*."**

Paul did not invent this statement: he was citing an ancient text from the Torah portion of the Bible! This fact alone brings into question the logic inherent in the frequent refrain that for Paul the role of Torah, of Law, had ended in Christ. Rather, for Paul Torah anticipates and instructs the followers of Christ to whom he wrote, or it should. The text cited in verse 10 is Deuteronomy 32:43, which is from the so-called "*Song* of Moses"; that itself could be relevant to why Paul chose it. The Septuagint Greek version of Deut. 32:43 (LXX) that we have is slightly different from Paul's citation: εὐφράνθητε οὐρανοί ἅμα αὐτῷ: "Be joyful, o heavens, together for them" (NRSV), and the Hebrew Masoretic text is also different: *harnînû gôyim 'ammô*; "O nations, [445] acclaim his people" (JPS).[13] We can see that the general theme is that the people other than Israelites are enjoined to rejoice "with" or "for" or possibly "to" the Israelites.

Paul joined this citation together with three other texts. The closest link is in the preceding verse 9, which cites from 2 Samuel 22:50 (cf. Ps 17:50 LXX, or 18:49 MT). Note that David is represented to declare that he will acknowledge the God who has delivered him from his enemies while *amongst* them.[14] Paul draws on this text from the Prophets (where Samuel is located in the Hebrew Bible/Tanak) to interpret the text from Torah (where Deuteronomy is located in the Hebrew Bible/Tanak) in support of the instruction he seeks to communicate. It is not without interest that Paul's linkage represents the same linkage that the later rabbis make in the homiletical tradition known as the Haftarah, from which sermons proceed on a set day within the annual liturgical cycle. These two verses remain linked together in the Haftarah readings to this day. Although it is not a topic we can take up here, this does raise some interesting questions: Was this proto-tradition already in place among the Pharisaic groups in which Paul operated, for synagogues in which he was active, for the Christ-following (Jewish subgroup) assemblies he established, so that he designed his argument this way because he could expect it to resonate with his addressees on this additional level of communal in-group awareness?

Paul is using the verse in tandem with the citation from Deuteronomy 32:43 in the following verse to highlight that these Christ-following

---

13. The manuscript traditions were fluid in Paul's time; the canons as we know them had not been fixed.

14. There are several interesting translation issues in this citation, but we will not take them up here.

non-Jews are to celebrate the One God of all humankind *within the midst of Jews* celebrating this same One God. The non-Jews proclaim the *mercy* shown to them as former enemies of God by joining in joyful recitation of psalms *together with Jews*, who are doing so because of God's *truthfulness* to fulfill the promises made to them. The groups remain recognizably *different*, yet, in terms of expressing gratitude to God, they do so together in *unison*. That Jews are portrayed to be giving thanks for promises fulfilled does not exclude in any way that they celebrate the mercy God has demonstrated toward themselves as well, which is certainly recognized, for Israelites were quite aware that they had not lived up to the ideals to which they agreed.[15] At the same time, Paul's use of these texts logically suggests these non-Jews rejoice in God's steadfast faithfulness to fulfill promises made to Israelites. After all, if God was not faithful to those to whom earlier promises were made, by definition how can one expect God always to be faithful to their own group?

The same message is highlighted in the third text that Paul cites next in verse 11, which is Psalm 116:1 (LXX; or 117:1 MT), the Writings section of the Hebrew Bible/Tanak that is also used to link with Torah passages in the Haftarah tradition: "Praise the Lord, all the nations [*ethnē*] and extol God all the peoples [*laoi*]. Again, there is a shift from *ethnē*, "people of the nations" to the plural of *laos*, "peoples" or "tribes." The first case seems to refer to those who are not Israelites, and the second to Israelites, perhaps including other tribes of Abraham's descendants who dwell among the Israelites. The point is that everyone from every nation is called to join together in praise to the One God and Lord of Israel as the One God and Lord of all humankind.

The fourth and final citation in verse 12 is from the major prophet, Isaiah 11:10 (LXX), which has a distinctive messianic message: "The root of Jesse will be [*i.e., alive*], even the one arising to be ruler of nations [*ethnōn*], unto him nations [*ethnē*] will [*look in*] hope." Jesse was the father of David, who was promised [446] that a descendant would always reign as king. By the time of Paul, however, that had not been the case for many centuries, and thus this promise had been construed by some Jews to refer to a future descendent from the family of David who would reestablish that rule, one some called the Messiah, and one Paul understood to be Jesus. Now, as Paul

---

15. It should also be noted that in the next sentence, 2 Samuel 22:51 (Ps 17:51 LXX or 18:50 MT), which Paul does not cite, is about God showing "mercy" to Israel through David and his seed: "Magnifying the saving deeds of his king/ And performing mercy for his Messiah,/ For David and his seed forever." Hence, the idea of Israel *and* the nations joining together to sing in praise of God's mercy is salient, and if read in liturgical or back-and-forth way, that would be enhanced.

brings that message to the nations, he calls them to submit to the rule of the Messiah, and to look to him for hope, just as should Jews.[16]

CONCLUSIONS

Let us now return to the surrounding argument for which these citations served as proof-texts, which represent conclusions to which Paul has been building in the preceding chapters. We can see that Paul is calling for the harmonious celebration of God by people and groups that are by definition in some ways different, and remain distinguishably so, whether fellow members of the assemblies of followers of Jesus, or those who are not members of them but also worship the same One God. He draws on Jewish scriptural witnesses to the celebration of the inclusion of the nations in the awaited age, rather than hope for their destruction. He does so in order to instruct the *reciprocal* concern among those from the nations for the Israelites, especially those who do not share their convictions about Jesus and thus that the time when that would be celebrated has arrived, who therefore may contest the claims of these non-Jews to full membership in the people of God and their assemblies apart from becoming Israelites too.

Paul's point is to learn to live in celebration of God's good will toward the other, to welcome and live *for* them, to live in kindness and mercy, convinced that they have received God's mercy *also*, or the hope that they will. It is normal to celebrate the receipt of God's good will toward one's self or group, and to hope to receive the same from others, but not to want to be judged, or for others to wish that one would be condemned so that they can be vindicated by God.

How that is to be lived out in real terms, when facing the struggles of life and family and neighborhood and national interests, in conflict situations all the more, is obviously not a simple matter. But Paul offers a kind of mantra, a way to think about living *for* the success of others, here represented in singing psalms of rejoicing for the success of the other in every thought and word and action—values enjoined in the Scriptures and thus central to the self-identity of the Jews who celebrate them. These non-Jews are to see themselves in the midst of Jews, celebrated and celebrating together.

---

16. Paul does not include the phrase "in that day" found in extant Septuagint manuscripts, which might suggest alternative traditions of which we do not have evidence, or perhaps, because Paul believes that day is precisely what has now arrived, at least in part, he thus adjusts the text to reflect his conviction that it is being enacted presently, or that it should be.

Paul's instructions here, I believe, offer Christians a wonderful call to leave the judging of the eventual outcome for the other to God alone. Paul appeals to them to look to the God of *hope*, the central topic in verse 13 that follows immediately after the citations in verses 9–12. Such hope and the [447] good will toward others that it engenders is possible for those who believe that God is always faithful and always merciful as well as just, that God's gifts are not in limited supply, even when it may seem to be so from human perspective in the present age, which seems to be a time where taking the most generous course is undermined by the ostensible reality of limited-good or zero-sum calculations.

The major theme of all of the chapters up through our texts in chapter 15, since it was introduced in the transition of 12:1, has been how to live respectful of one's fellow human beings, to seek peace with everyone in view of the times in which one who follows Jesus claims to have arrived, which is possible for those who live in the *hope* that God will provide. The "therefore" of 12:1 follows Paul's passion-filled explanation in chapters 9–11 of the intertwined destinies of the non-Jews turning to God through Jesus, and Jews. This includes Jews who believe in Jesus as Messiah who are thus engaged as ambassadors in declaring the reconciliation to the nations, such as is Paul, and the rest of the Jewish people, whom Paul is convinced will join him eventually in that conviction and the undertaking of that task. But he seeks to explain that this will not happen before he has succeeded to reach and persuade members from the other nations to demonstrate by their righteous and gracious behavior the truth of the gospel's claim to many of his so-far-unpersuaded fellow countrymen: then, the promise that "all Israel will be protected" through this difficult time of transition will be fully realized.[17] Also then, and only then, will the full benefits of God's bounty be realized by the nations.

Paul seems to recognize the problem of zero-sum thinking that can emerge when celebrating the receipt of God's mercy for one's self or group, thinking that can lead, ironically enough, to arrogant superiority, envy, judgmentalism, dismissal of the interests of the other, replacement theology, and so on. He thus instructs how to live on behalf of the other, rather than against them, and warns them of the risk to their own self-interest that will result from failure to uphold the responsibilities that their confession of faith in the one God of all humankind by definition entails: love of one's neighbor. That way of life includes hope for as well as undertaking to help the other to achieve *success*, a central connotation in the term "blessing."

---

17. The various translation and interpretive decisions are explained in the essays collected in volume 2 of this series on Romans, and one can also consult the annotations I did for "Romans" in *The Jewish Annotated New Testament* (*JANT*).

At the heart of Paul's message leading up to our passage, at the opening of chapter 15, Paul makes the point in verses 1–9 that he hopes his readers will embrace to guide their own life as they interact with the other: "For Christ did not please himself" (v. 3). Here is the full passage leading up to the texts we have discussed:

> ¹We who are strong ought to put up with the failings of the weak, and not to please ourselves. ²Each of us must please our neighbor for the good purpose of building up the neighbor. ³For Christ did not please himself; but, as it is written,
> "The insults of those who insult you have fallen on me."
> ⁴For whatever was written in former days was written for our instruction, so that by steadfastness and by the encouragement of the scriptures we might have hope. ⁵May the God of steadfastness and encouragement grant you to live in harmony with one another, in accordance with Christ Jesus, ⁶so that together you may with one voice glorify the God and Father of our Lord Jesus Christ.
> ⁷Welcome one another, therefore, just as Christ has welcomed you, for the glory of God. ⁸For I tell you that Christ has become a servant of the circumcised on behalf of the truth of God in order that he might confirm the promises given to the patriarchs, ⁹and in order that the Gentiles might glorify God for his mercy. (NRSV)

May we all experience and contribute to the experience of peace, of *shalom*, regardless of whether we share Paul's precise reasoning for doing so, including with respect to where we are on God's timeline. The ideal of living graciously towards those who are different from ourselves, of extending "welcome," of living *for* instead of *against* them, are principles central to Judaism, witnessed by the texts that Paul cites in support of his vision for the Jewish movement that eventually became Christianity. When Paul is read in a Jewish way: are these not programmatic principles from which we can all learn, that we should all embrace?

BIBLIOGRAPHY

Gerdmar, Anders. *Roots of Theological Anti-Semitism: German Biblical Interpretation and the Jews, from Herder and Semler to Kittel and Bultmann*. Studies in Jewish History and Culture 20. Leiden: Brill, 2009.

Hogg, Michael A., and Dominic Abrams. *Social Identifications: A Social Psychology of Intergroup Relations and Group Processes*. London: Routledge, 1988.

Nanos, Mark D. *The Irony of Galatians: Paul's Letter in First-Century Context*. Minneapolis: Fortress, 2002.

———. "The Myth of the 'Law-Free' Paul Standing between Christians and Jews." *Studies in Christian-Jewish Relations* 4 (2009) 1–21. https://ejournals.bc.edu/ojs/index.php/scjr/article/view/1511/1364 (See chapter 3 in this volume of collected essays.)

———. "Paul and the Jewish Tradition: The Ideology of the Shema." In *Celebrating Paul. Festschrift in Honor of Jerome Murphy-O'Connor, O.P., and Joseph A. Fitzmyer, S.J.*, edited by Peter Spitaler, 62–80. CBQMS 48. Washington DC: Catholic Biblical Association of America, 2012. (See chapter 4 in this volume of collected essays.)

———. "Paul and Judaism: Why Not Paul's Judaism?" In *Paul Unbound: Other Perspectives on the Apostle*, edited by Mark D. Given, 117–60. Peabody, MA: Hendrickson, 2010. (See chapter 1 in this volume of collected essays.)

———. "Paul's Non-Jews Do Not Become 'Jews,' But Do They Become 'Jewish'?: Reading Romans 2:25–29 within Judaism, alongside Josephus." *Journal of the Jesus Movement in Its Jewish Setting* 1.1 (2014) 26–53. http://www.jjmjs.org/uploads/1/1/9/0/11908749/nanos_pauls_non-jews.pdf. (See chapter 5 in this volume of collected essays.)

———. "Romans." In *The Jewish Annotated New Testament*, edited by Amy-Jill Levine and Marc Zvi Brettler, 253–86. New York: Oxford University Press, 2011.

Nanos, Mark D., and Magnus Zetterholm, eds. *Paul within Judaism: Restoring the First-century Context to the Apostle*. Minneapolis: Fortress, 2015.

Runesson, Anders. "From Where? To What? Common Judaism, Pharisees, and the Changing Socioreligious Location of the Matthean Community." In *Common Judaism: Explorations in Second-Temple Judaism*, edited by Wayne O. McCready and Adele Reinhartz, 97–113. Minneapolis: Fortress, 2008.

PART III

A Jewish Contribution to Pope Benedict XVI's Celebration of the Year of St. Paul

7

Paul and Judaism (*Codex Pauli*)

[54] I AM HUMBLY grateful for the opportunity to participate in this the celebration of the Jubilee Year to the apostle Paul according to the declaration of Pope Benedict XVI.

A celebration of Paul represents an interesting challenge. Jews have not generally studied Paul. When we have, he has been predictably approached as an apostate from Judaism. We instinctively respond to the prevailing Christian portrayals of the Apostle to the Nations, but from the opposite perspective. For the victories attributed to Paul's voice have traditionally been juxtaposed with negative assessments of the Jewish people and Judaism, at times accompanied by harmful policies. The celebration of his mission has been intimately connected with the idea of converting everyone from their religion, including Jews from Judaism.

Nevertheless, I join with those who believe that, in addition to the challenge to express goodwill between our religions in new ways, there is a historical basis for the reevaluation of Paul's voice that is in keeping with the church's commitment to seeking the truth, which may challenge some traditional perspectives on Paul. This year's focus on Paul's letters provides an opportunity for Jewish scholars who study the apostle to vigorously undertake this task alongside of Christians.

In keeping with the call of Vatican II to attend to the historical context of the language of Scripture, and the many strides already taken, the sketch offered here briefly indicates some of the ways that re-reading Paul in his first-century Jewish, as well as Greco-Roman contexts, can continue to challenge previous interpretations. The implications are many, not only for the study of first-century Judaism and Christian origins, but also for improved understanding and relations between Christians and Jews in the future.

It is widely agreed that Paul was born and raised a Jew, and observed Judaism according to Pharisaic standards (Rom 9:1–5; 11:1; 2 Cor 11:22; Gal 1:13–16; Phil 3:4–6; cf. Acts 9; 21–26). The challenging question to pose is this: Following his encounter with Christ, did Paul continue to practice Judaism, albeit Christ-believing Judaism, rather than converting from Judaism to a new religion that no longer represented Jewish communal norms, including Torah? If he continued to be a part of Judaism, a reformer from within, in keeping with prophetic tradition, rather than a critic from outside, then what are the implications for interpreting Paul's letters that follow from this insight?

There are many indications that Paul's way of living continued to be highly observant of Torah, similar to the representation of James and Peter in the Acts of the Apostles. In addition to constant appeals to the authority of Torah to make and prove his positions throughout all of his letters, Paul is portrayed introducing the Apostolic Decree, with its Torah-based norms for the guidance of Christ-believing non-Jews associating with the synagogue communities (Acts 15–16), undertaking a Nazarite vow in the Jerusalem Temple to dispel rumors that he was teaching against Torah for Jews, which included a burnt offering (Acts 21), claiming to live blamelessly according to Pharisaic interpretation of Torah, by whose standards he legitimated his own belief in the resurrection of Jesus (Acts 23:6; 24:14–21; Phil 3:5–6), and planning his travel around Jewish festivals, including Shavuot/Pentecost, which celebrates Israel's receipt of Torah at Mt. Sinai as a gift from God (Acts 20:6, 16; 1 Cor 16:8). It is interesting to note that Augustine appealed to Paul's continued observance of Torah in his interpretation of the conflict between Peter and Paul at Antioch (Gal 2:11–15; Augustine, *Letter* 40.3–6, to Jerome), although Jerome took exception to the ideological risk of any Christian, much less an apostle, practicing Torah, an objection which has guided the prevailing views ever since (*Letter* 112.5–18).

PROSELYTE CONVERSION

The topic of proselyte conversion (signified by circumcision of males) highlights the issues under discussion in Paul's letters to the Romans and Galatians. The entrance of non-Jews into the family of Abraham discussed in these letters is not the same matter as whether Jews should observe Torah, which is not directly raised, but assumed. The implicit logic of Paul's position is that Jews, such as himself, are still to be faithful to their covenant obligations as Israelites, which by definition includes the faithful observance of Torah. It is because Israelites were and are entrusted with the "words of God" for the nations that Paul undertook his mission to declare the gospel to the nations, including to Rome itself (Rom 1:1-7; 3:2; 9:4-5; 10; 15:15-21). For Paul, this privilege constituted an irrevocable promise to Israel (11:28-29). He was certain that "all Israel" would be restored to exercising its special task, a mysterious twist in God's plan that he sought to reveal to the Romans (11:11-15; 25-32).

Note that in 1 Cor 7:17-24, Paul says his "rule" in all his assemblies is for everyone to remain in the state they were in when called, whether circumcised or not, nevertheless that all must "obey the commandments of God." When this rule is coupled with Paul's attestation in Gal 5:3 that anyone in a circumcised state is obliged to observe the whole Torah, it becomes evident that Paul worked from a propositional logic that required all Jewish Christ-believers to remain faithful to their Jewish covenant identity by the observance of Torah.

This brings us to the topic of non-Jewish Christ-believers. In all of Paul's extant letters he addresses non-Jews and their concerns, and his for them. Paul believed that he and his fellow Israelites had a special privilege to announce that it was time for the nations to turn to Israel's God as the One God of all humankind. The members of the nations do not become members of the nation Israel when that day arrives; rather, they must remain members of the other nations. But they do become fellow-members of the Jewish communal way of life, of Judaism. They become the rest of the children of Abraham he was led to hope for, because the promise was that he would be "the father of many nations" (Gen 12:1-3; 17; 22:15-18; Romans 4; Gal 3:6-9). As Luke explains in Acts 15, these non-Jews were not to undertake proselyte conversion (i.e., males were not to be circumcised) to become Jews, and thus they were not obligated to observe Torah on the same terms as Jews. But they were obliged to observe Jewish purity norms for righteous members of the nations, because they were entering into a religious life that takes place within the Jewish communities (cf. Romans 6; 14).

It is thus imperative when reading Paul's letters to keep the contextual distinction between instructions designed for these non-Jews, who must remain representatives of the other nations, and thus not become Israelites through proselyte conversion, and the norms upheld for Israelites, such as himself. It is useful to note that there is evidence of other Jewish teachers among Paul's contemporaries who were also against proselyte conversion of non-Jewish worshippers of the One God, albeit for different reasons, as in the example of King Izates discussed by Josephus (*Ant.* 20.38-42).

One way to help us accomplish this nuanced but historically and theologically important task when reading Paul is to add "for Christ-believing *non-Jews*" to virtually all of his statements of instruction. Otherwise, the universalizing of such comments as if inclusive of Jews, of everyone regardless of this distinction, misses the thrust of the proposition of his gospel, and leads often to the implicit, when not explicit, view that Paul was against Jewish identity and behavior for Jews.

[55] Paul's basis for his policy of maintaining ethnic (and gender and other forms of) difference in the assemblies of Christ, at the same time denouncing the discrimination generally associated with difference, is based explicitly on the *Shema Israel*, the sacred prayer of Judaism that declares the oneness of God. Roughly halfway between our time and Paul's, Rashi similarly upheld that the God whom Israelites worship in the present age will be known to be the One God of all the other nations when the age to come arrives (Rashi on Deut 6:4; cf. Sipre on Deut 6:4 [Piska 31]). In other words, it was not that other Jews and Jewish groups did not share Paul's conviction that non-Israelites will remain non-Israelite brothers and sisters who will worship together the One God in the age to come, but that other Jewish groups did not believe that the time had come to make this the communal norm in the present age. Paul believed that this age had in fact dawned, but at the same time, paradoxically, that it had not yet arrived in full—in the meantime, it was the responsibility of Christ-following groups to demonstrate the truth of that proposition by remaining different, yet equal: "since God is one" (Rom 3:29–31; 4:9–12; 15:5–12; 1 Cor 8:5–6; Gal 3:28–29). For when that day arrives, just as the wolf will lie down with the lamb, not becoming a lamb, but no longer a threat to it either, so too the members of the nations will join alongside of Israel in worship of the One God of all the *kosmos*, and practice righteousness thereafter (Isa 65:25; cf. 65–66; 2:2–4).

A SYMBIOTIC RELATIONSHIP

Much has changed since Paul's time and initial understanding of his calling within Judaism to bring about the restoration of all of humankind. Christianity emerged from this subgroup movement among Jews within Judaism, and it found its own voice as a religion that is not Judaism, and that became almost entirely comprised of non-Jews, of people from the nations other than Israel. Rabbinic Judaism has similarly developed in ways that make it quite distinct from Christianity. Nevertheless, there is a symbiotic relationship that cannot be denied in the inceptions of both of these religions during the time that Paul was traveling and writing, prior to the destruction of the temple in 70 CE.

This relationship has had many dark moments, some painfully recent, and Paul's voice has been all too often invoked by some of the perpetrators. At the same time, it is from the original vision and language of the apostle Paul that *Nostra Aetate* (no. 4) framed a new and promising outlook on Jews as brothers and sisters in the faith of the One God, and Judaism as a sibling's way of expressing that conviction in the world.

Jews and practitioners of Judaism are enormously grateful for the results of such reinterpretations of the Apostle to the Nations in the pursuit of truth as well as mutual respect. It is my hope that we can help you nurture new engagements with Paul's letters that will uphold the ideals of the age to come, while earnestly awaiting, and working together, *mutatis mutandis*—for the hope of eternal *shalom*.

Ancient Document Index

TANAKH/HEBREW BIBLE

Genesis

12:1–3	175
17	175
17:9–14	128
22:15–18	175

Exodus

15:11	96, 109
20:2–6	96
22:28	96
23:24	96
24:7	109

Leviticus

12:3	128
19:17–18	78
19:18	82
23:15–16	41
26:13	78

Numbers

15:37–41	108

Deuteronomy

4:19	96
4:39	110
5:15	78
6:4–8	108
6:4	109
7:5	96
10:16	145
11:13–21	78, 108
15:1–15	78
16:1–12	78
24:17–22	78
29:26	96
30:6	145
32:8–9	96
32:16–17	96
32:21	96
32:43	xxi, 165
32:43 LXX	165

2 Samuel

12	143
22:50	165
22:51	166

Psalms

17:50 LXX	165
17:51 LXX	166
18:49	165
18:50	166
24:1	101
37:33	23
50:12	101
82:1	96
106:36–39	96
116:1 LXX	166
117:1	166

Ecclesiastes

7:20	109

Isaiah

2:2–4	176
8:19	96
11:6–10	159
11:6	116
11:10 LXX	166
19:3	96
40	96
44	96
45:7	110
49:1	30
52:5 LXX	142
52:6–10	78
65—66	176
65:17–25	159
65:25	116, 176
66:18–20	21

Jeremiah

1:5	30
1:7	30
4:4	145
9:25–26	145
38:33	145

Ezekiel

44:7	145

Micah

4:5	96

Habakkuk

2:4	89

Zephaniah

3:9	21, 39, 115, 162

Zechariah

2:15	21
14:9	39, 115, 162

Malachi

2:10	109

APOCRYPHA

Tobit

1:8	134
13:11	21
14:5–6	21

Wisdom of Solomon

13–16	96

Sirach

24	34
39:1–8	34

1 Maccabees

7:13	3
10:21	23

2 Maccabees

6:1–11	4, 128
9:13–17	4, 128

4 Maccabees

18:5	3

PSEUDEPIGRAPHA

1 Enoch

19	96

Joseph and Aseneth

	21, 117

Jubilees

11.4–6	96
15:26	130

NEW TESTAMENT

Matthew

5:18	77
Acts	83
2:5–11	3
2:22	3
9	31, 174
9:1–2	31
11:26	156
15–16	174
15	21, 85, 91, 93
15:5	30
15:20	97
15:29	97
15:30	80
16:1–13	80
16:4	80
17:1–3	27
17:16–34	27, 99
20:6	174
20:16	174
21–26	80, 174
21	25, 41, 174
21:15–26	80
21:19–26	25
21:25	97
23	31
23:6	31, 156, 174
24:14–21	174
26	31
26:5	31–32, 156

Romans

1:1–7	175
1:1–5	123
1:5	152
1:11–12	152
1:17	89
1:18–32	141
2	128, 150
2:1–11	140
2:1	146
2:12–16	140
2:17–29	128
2:17–24	141, 148
2:17–21a	141
2:17	141
2:17ff.	141
2:24	142
2:25–29	xx, 24, 127, 132, 139–40, 143–44, 148, 152
2:25	144
2:26	145
2:27	146
2:28–29	147
2:29	143, 145
3	119, 143
3:1–2	44, 79, 89
3:1	24, 44, 143, 148
3:2	38, 55, 112, 123, 142–43, 175

Romans *(continued)*

3:11	89
3:16–21	89
3:27—4:25	89
3:28—4:25	85
3:29—4:25	139
3:29—4:12	131
3:29–31	111, 162, 176
3:29–30	18, 35, 43
3:29	119
3:31	44, 79, 123
4	175
4:9–12	131, 176
4:18–20	101
5:2	142
5:3	142
5:6–10	96
5:11	142
6–8	83
6	139, 175
7:12	44
7:14	44, 79
9–11	5, 37, 48, 128, 168
9:1–5	174
9:3–5	89, 123
9:4–5	43, 79, 101, 120, 175
9:4	3
10–11	44
10	175
10:12	35
10:14—11:12	38
10:14–17	38
10:15–18	123
10:15	78
11	36, 50
11:1–14	142
11:1	174
11:11–36	37, 50, 120
11:11–15	175
11:13–36	38
11:25–32	175
11:25–29	101
11:25–26	50
11:26–29	120
11:28–29	40, 175
11:33–36	50
12	40
12:1–2	25, 120
12:1	168
13:8–14	123
13:8–10	163
13:8	82
14–15	87
14	41, 85, 175
14:1—15:13	123
14:1—15:7	100
14:14	100
15	160, 162, 164, 168–69
15:1–9	169
15:3	169
15:5–13	35
15:5–12	89, 115, 176
15:7–13	164
15:7–12	84
15:8–12	123
15:8–9	112
15:9–12	168
15:9	165
15:10	xxi, 155, 164
15:11	166
15:12	159, 166
15:13	168
15:15–32	142
15:15–21	175
15:25–31	41
15:30–32	48

1 Corinthians

5:7–8	41
7:17–24	25, 42, 79–80, 119, 122, 131, 175
7:17–22	139
7:17–20	xix
7:19	37, 44, 78, 80
8–10	27, 83, 87, 94–95, 97, 99
8	96
8:1–6	95
8:4–6	120
8:4	96
8:5–6	176

8:5	96	2:14–16	119
8:7	95	2:14	25
8:11–12	96	2:15–21	43
9	97	2:15–16	128
9:19–23	6, 9, 26–27	2:15	18, 25, 43, 80, 89
9:19–22	95, 97–98	2:16–17	39
9:20f.	6	2:16	45, 89
10	97	2:21	74
10:19—11:1	101	3	119
10:20–21	96	3:1	36
10:26	101	3:3–6	80
11	xxii	3:3	131
12–14	40	3:5	156
15:5–8	33	3:6—4:7	131
16:8	41, 174	3:6–9	175
		3:14–16	142
		3:20	120

2 Corinthians

		3:23–25	36
11:21—12:21	142	3:26–29	131
11:22	42, 80, 128, 174	3:28–29	89, 176
11:23–33	31	3:28	35, 80, 82
		4:3–5	69

Galatians

		4:3	70
		4:5	70
1:1	33	4:8–10	82, 84
1:6–9	36	4:9	66
1:8–9	49	4:10	41
1:10–12	33	4:12	36, 69–70
1:11–17	49	4:17–18	36
1:12–16	117	4:21	17, 36
1:13–16	33, 85, 174	4:28	131
1:13–14	4, 29, 69–70, 128	5:2–6	122, 131
1:13	29, 31	5:2–3	129, 131
1:14	29, 156	5:3	25, 41, 43, 79, 81, 119, 122, 175
1:16	33		
1:17—2:10	33	5:5	36–37, 120
1:23	31, 85	5:6	43
2	39	5:7–12	36
2:1–21	37	5:11–12	129, 131
2:1–10	91–92	5:11	25, 31, 34, 36, 85, 117
2:1–2	33		
2:2	33	5:12	49
2:3	131	5:13—6:10	78
2:7–10	41	5:13–14	43, 94, 123
2:7–8	33	5:14	82
2:11–15	87, 93, 174	5:21	43
2:11–14	39, 43, 129	6:12–15	31

Galatians *(continued)*

6:12–13	36, 129, 131
6:13	25
6:14	36
6:15	131

Philippians

3	84
3:2–7	9
3:3–11	31
3:3–6	142
3:3	142
3:4–16	86
3:4–7	42
3:4–6	43, 128, 174
3:5–6	30–31, 174
3:5	128

1 Thessalonians

1:9–10	139
2	83
2:15–16	48

2 Peter

	169

James

	83
2:19	96

Revelation

2:14	97
2:19–20	97

DEAD SEA SCROLLS

1QH

7.29–39	78
8.11–18	78
15.15–25	78

1QM

XI.4	78

1QS

5	34
5.5	145
8	34
11	78

4QMMT

C 25–32	23

4QpPs[a]

1–10 iv 7–9	23

QpHab

8:10–13	23
11:2–8	23

RABBINIC LITERATURE

Mishnah

m. 'Abodah Zarah

1:12–17	141
3.14	108

Tosefta

t. 'Abodah Zarah

8.4	21

t. Sanhedrin

13.21	21, 117
44a	129

Talmuds

b. Berakot

61b	109

y. Berakot

2.1	109
9.5	78, 109

b. Baba Meşia

59b	34

b. Megillah

13a	21

b. Yebamot

46a	20
47b	130

Other

Abot de-Rabbi Nathan

(A) 29.3	142

Deuteronomy Rabbah

3.11	109

Genesis Rabbah

44.1	101

Leviticus Rabbah

13.3	101

Maimonides

Hilkhot Melakhim

12.1	116

Mekilta de R. Ishmael

[Bahodesh 1] on Exod

19:2	21

Sifra on Leviticus

18:1–5	21
86b	145
93d	101

Sifre on Deuteronomy

6:4 (Piska 31)	39, 114, 176

ANCIENT JEWISH WRITERS

Philo

Abraham

3–6	21, 117
60–61	21, 117

On the Life of Moses

2.4	21, 117

On the Special Laws

1.6	145
1.51	21, 117
1.186	4, 128
2.42–48	21, 117
2.164–66	116
4.178	21, 117

On the Virtues

102	21, 117
181–82	21, 117
212–19	21, 117

On the Embassy to Gaius

132–34	159

Questions and Answers on Genesis

2.2	21, 117
3.46–52	145

Josephus

Against Apion

2.137	130
2.210	134

Antiquities of the Jews

3.318	134
13.257–58	130
13.297	30
14.185–267	159
13.408	30
14.403	130, 134
17.41	30
18.12	33
18.310–13	138
18.314–79	138
19.299–306	159
20.15–17	136
20.17–96	19, 128, 136
20.22	136
20.34–48	4, 21, 117
20.34	136
20.35–38	137
20.35	136–37
20.38–43	134
20.38–42	20, 175
20.38	137
20.39–42	137
20.41	21, 117
20.43–45	138
20.43	32
20.48	138
20.49–53	139
20.71	138
20.75–91	139
20.75–76	139
20.89–91	138
20.92–96	139
20.95	139

Jewish War

1.146	135
1.148	135
1.150	135
2.10	135
2.42	135
2.198	135
2.285–308	159
2.391	135
2.454	134
2.456	135
2.462–63	135
2.463	128, 133
2.559–61	135
4.275	135
4.324	135
5.198	135
5.199	135
5.229	135
6.100	135
6.427	135
6.442	135
7.41–62	135
7.45	128, 135
7.46–53	129
7.73–74	135

GRECO-ROMAN WRITINGS

Epictetus

Dissertation (Diatribeai)

1.9.4–6	97
1.13.4	97
2.9.19–22	143
2.9.19–21	130
2.19.19–28	143
3.22.81–82	97

Ancient Document Index

4.8.17-20	149

Horace

Satires

1.9.68-70	130

Juvenal

Satires

14.96-106	140

Marcus Aurelius

2.1	97
7.22	97
9.22-23	97

Petronius

Satires

102.14	130

Pliny the Younger

Letters

10.96	

Seutonius

Domitian

12.2	130

Nero

16.2	156

Tacitus

Annales

15.44.2-8	156

Histories

5.5.1-2	130

EARLY CHRISTIAN WRITINGS (inc. Apostolic Fathers)

Aristides

Apology

15.4	97
15.12	97

Augustine

Letters

40.3-6	174
40.4.6	113

On Lying

	58

Chrysostom

Hom. 1 Cor.

117 [XX]	97

Clement of Alexandria

Stromateis

4.15.97.3	97

Council of Nicea II

Canon 8	114

Didache

6.3	97

Ignatius

Martyrdom of Polycarp

1.2	97

To the Ephesians

10	97

To the Magneians

10.3	123

Jerome

Letters

40.3–6	174
104.13	113
104.17	113

Justin

Dialogue with Trypho

34.8	97
35.1–2	97

Tertullian

Apology

9.13–14	97
42.1–5	97

Monogamy

5.3	97

On Fasting

2.4	97
15.5	97

The Crown

10.4–7	97
11.3	97

The Shows

13.2–4	97

8–10

www.ingramcontent.com/pod-product-compliance
Lightning Source LLC
Chambersburg PA
CBHW030109170426
43198CB00009B/551